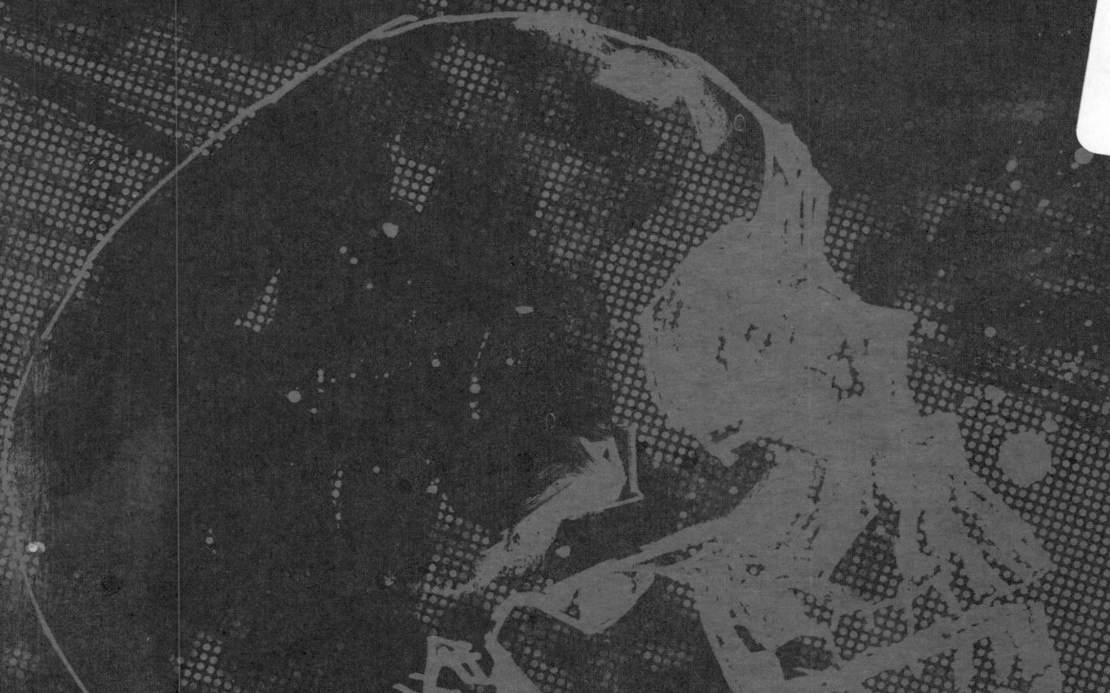

IVAN BRANDON   NIC KLEIN

VIKING™

THE LONG
COLD FIRE.

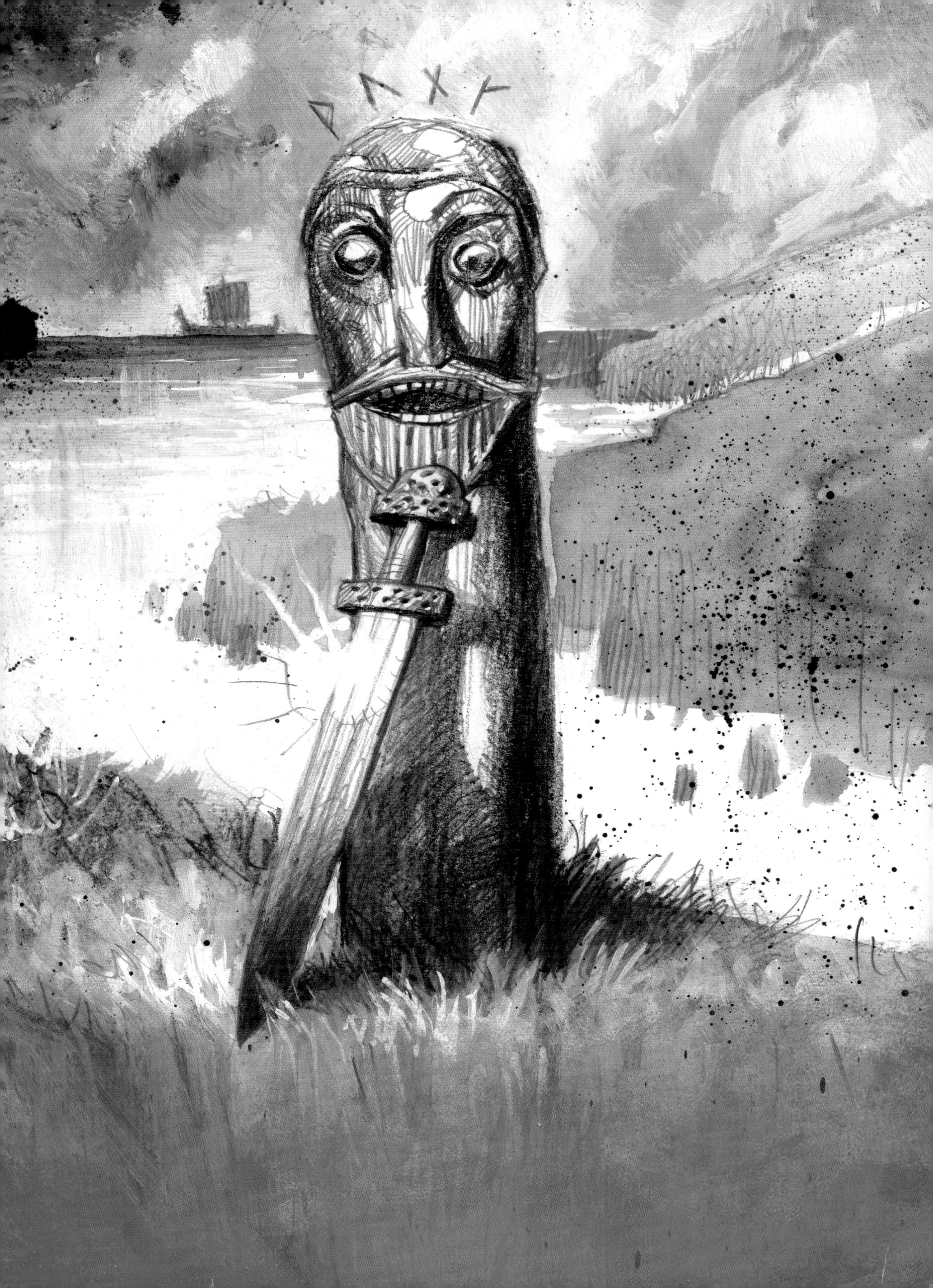

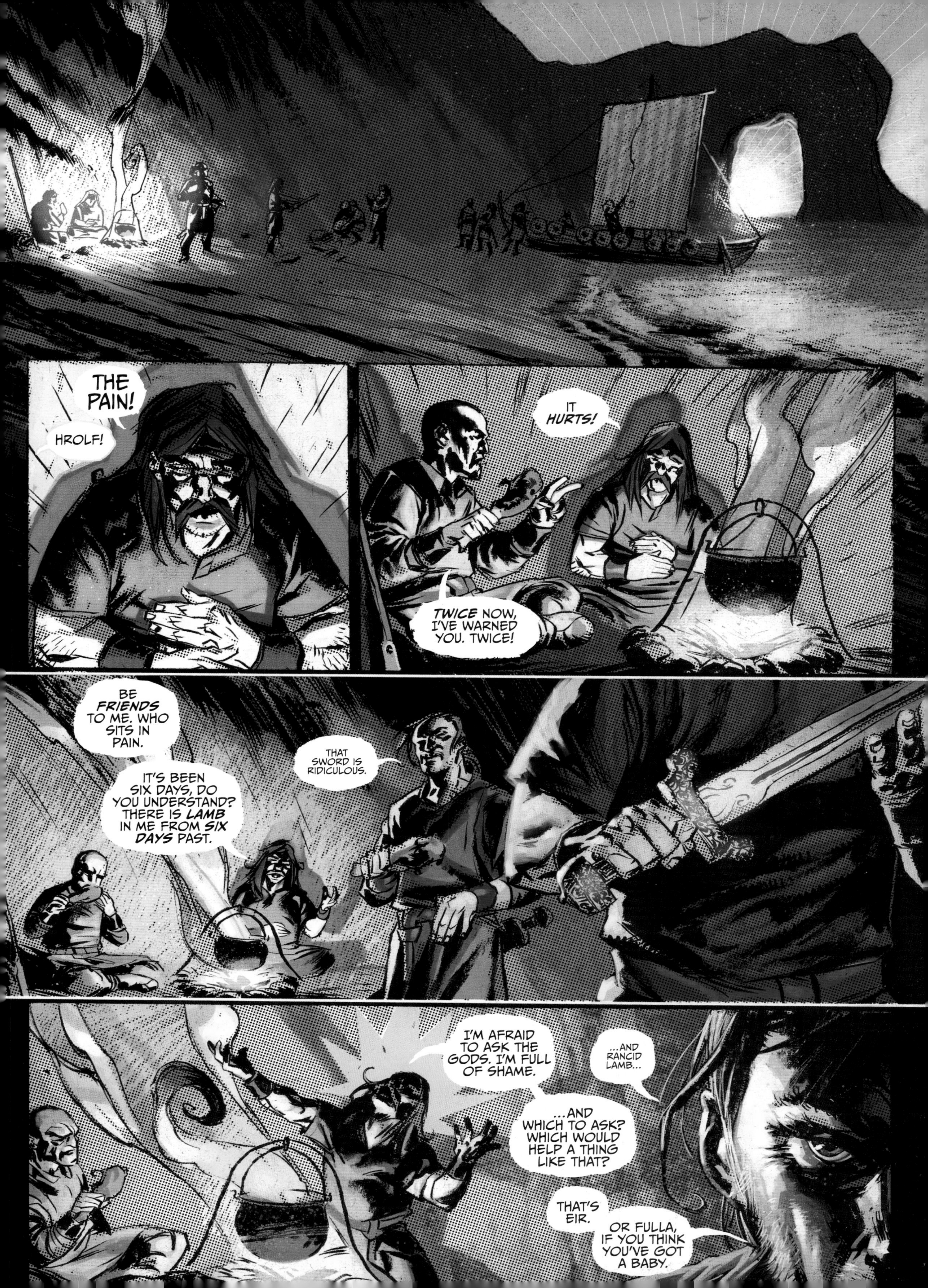
THE PAIN!
HROLF!
IT HURTS!
TWICE NOW, I'VE WARNED YOU. TWICE!
BE FRIENDS TO ME. WHO SITS IN PAIN.
IT'S BEEN SIX DAYS, DO YOU UNDERSTAND? THERE IS LAMB IN ME FROM SIX DAYS PAST.
THAT SWORD IS RIDICULOUS.
I'M AFRAID TO ASK THE GODS. I'M FULL OF SHAME.
...AND RANCID LAMB...
...AND WHICH TO ASK? WHICH WOULD HELP A THING LIKE THAT?
THAT'S EIR.
OR FULLA, IF YOU THINK YOU'VE GOT A BABY.

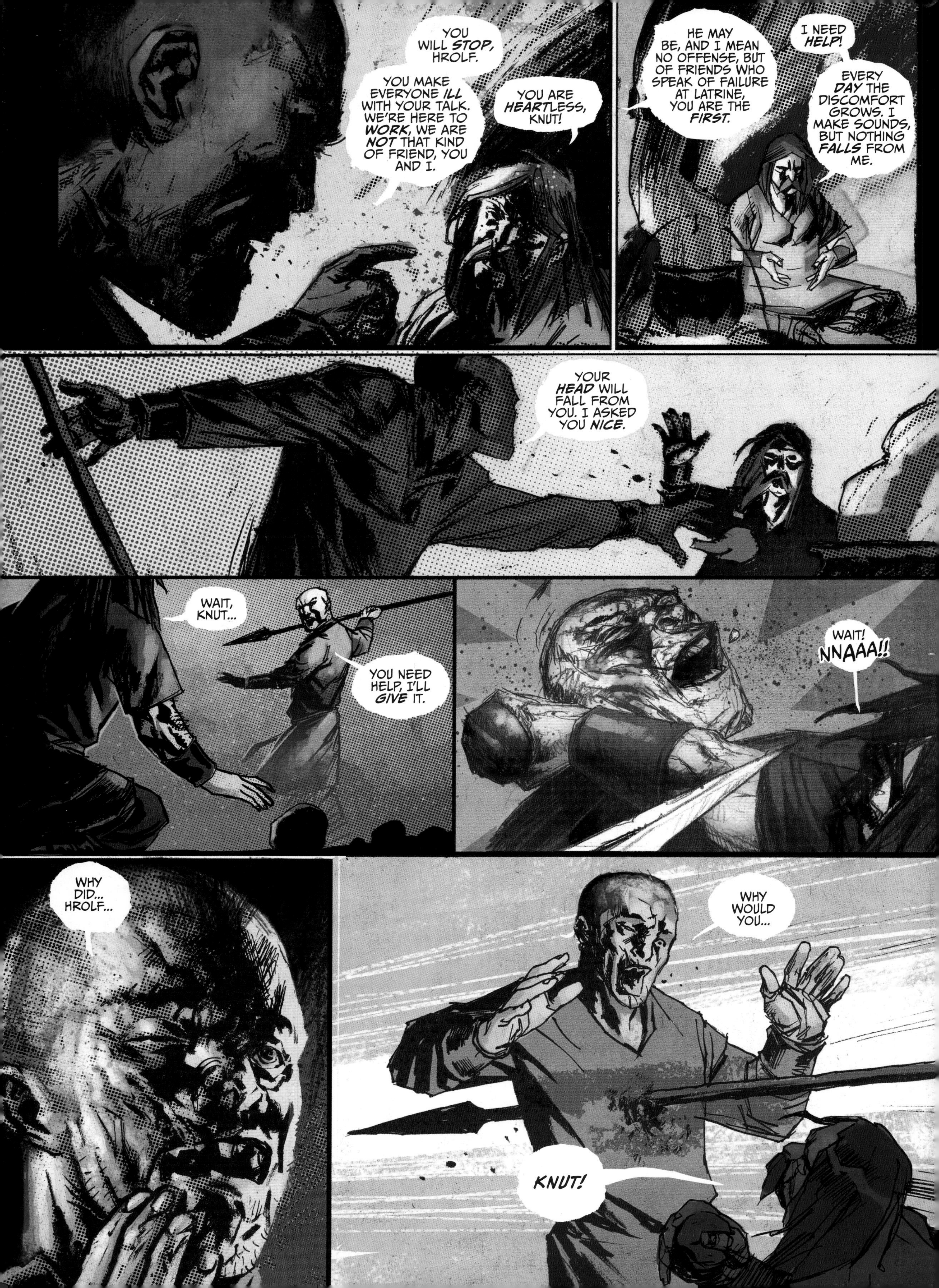
YOU WILL STOP, HROLF.
YOU MAKE EVERYONE ILL WITH YOUR TALK. WE'RE HERE TO WORK, WE ARE NOT THAT KIND OF FRIEND, YOU AND I.
YOU ARE HEARTLESS, KNUT!
HE MAY BE, AND I MEAN NO OFFENSE, BUT OF FRIENDS WHO SPEAK OF FAILURE AT LATRINE, YOU ARE THE FIRST.
I NEED HELP!
EVERY DAY THE DISCOMFORT GROWS. I MAKE SOUNDS, BUT NOTHING FALLS FROM ME.
YOUR HEAD WILL FALL FROM YOU. I ASKED YOU NICE.
WAIT, KNUT...
YOU NEED HELP, I'LL GIVE IT.
WAIT! NNAAA!!
WHY DID... HROLF...
WHY WOULD YOU...
KNUT!

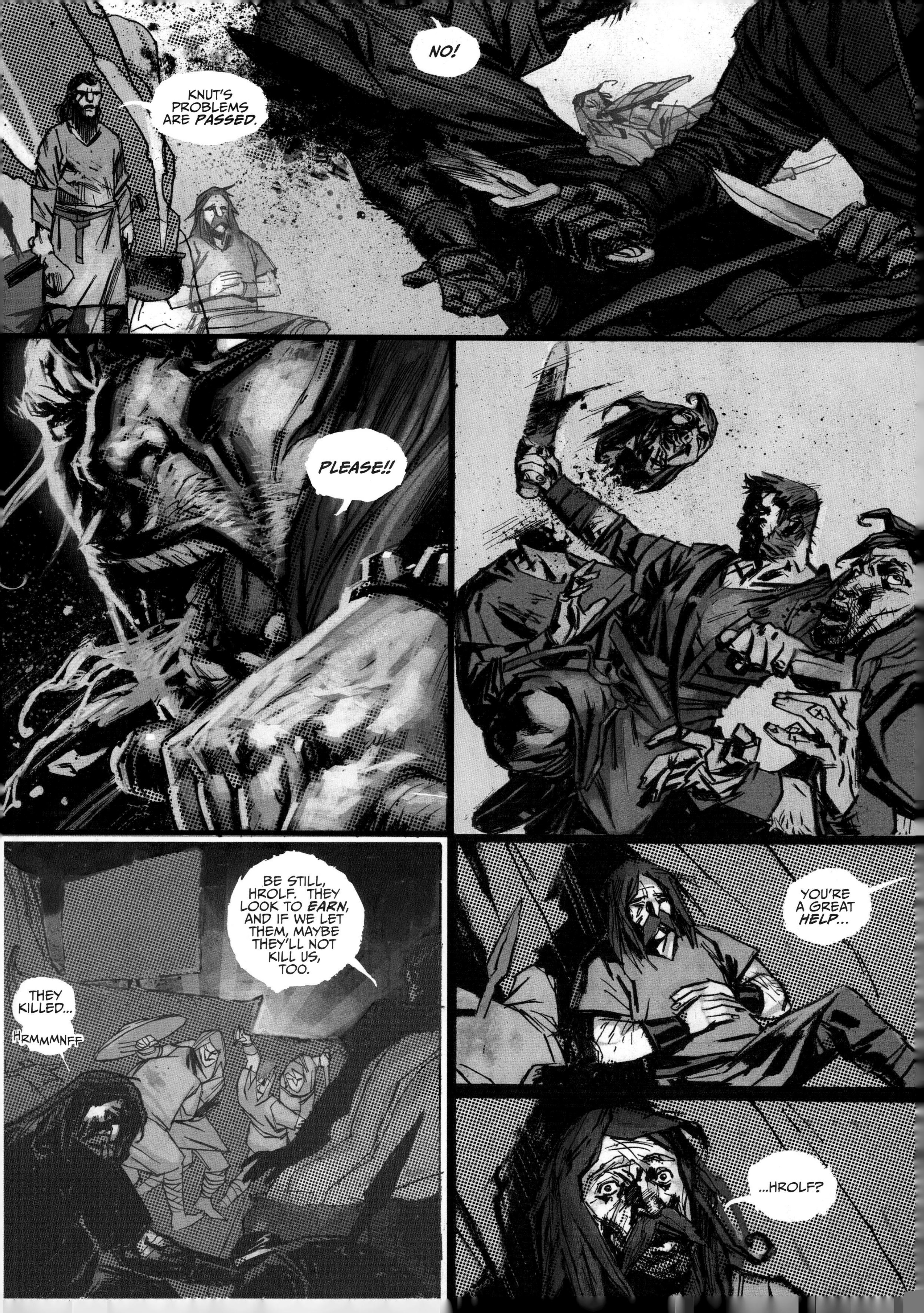
NO!
KNUT'S PROBLEMS ARE PASSED.
PLEASE!!
BE STILL, HROLF. THEY LOOK TO EARN, AND IF WE LET THEM, MAYBE THEY'LL NOT KILL US, TOO.
THEY KILLED...
HRMMMNFF
YOU'RE A GREAT HELP...
...HROLF?

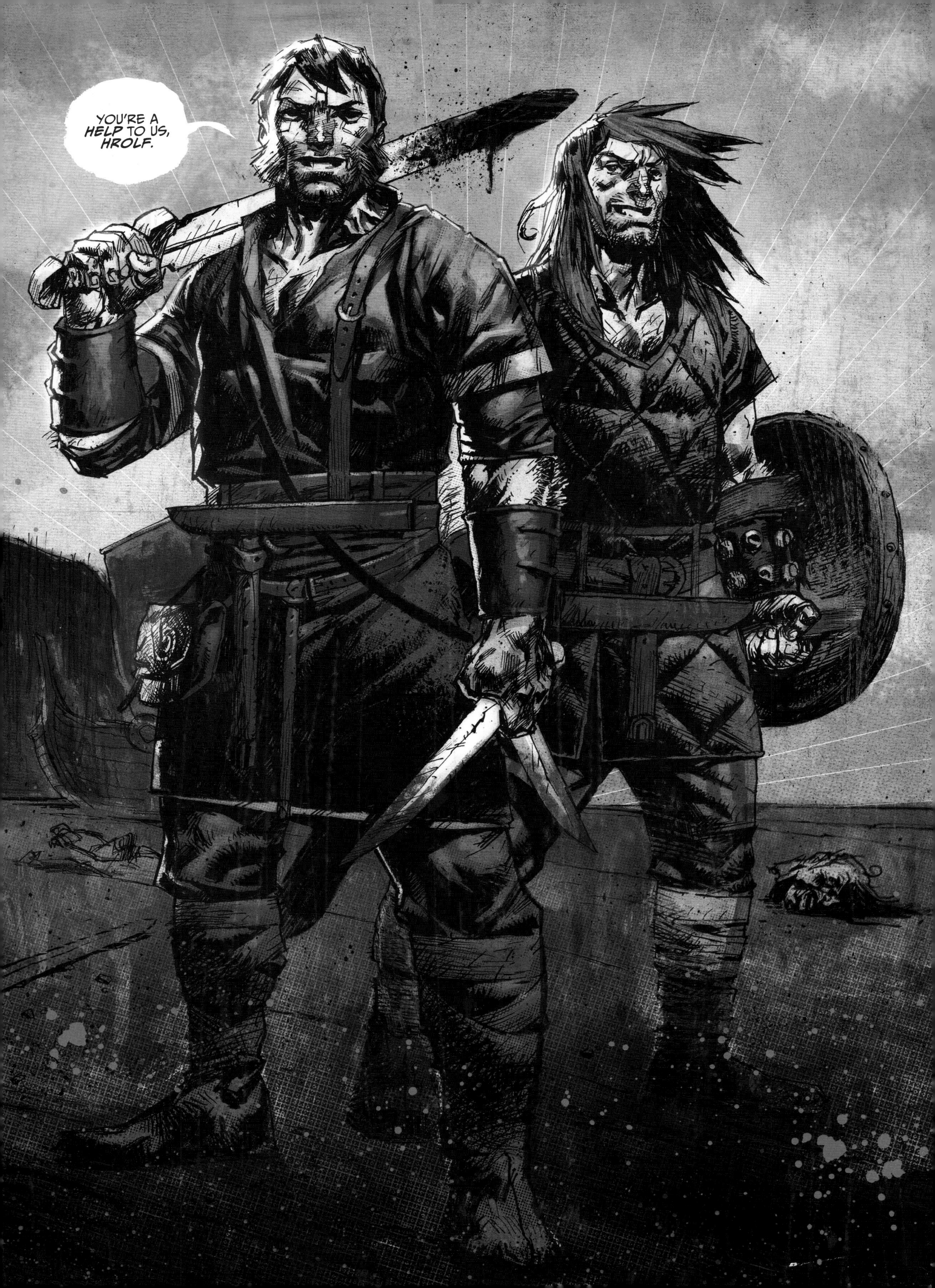
YOU'RE A HELP TO US, HROLF.

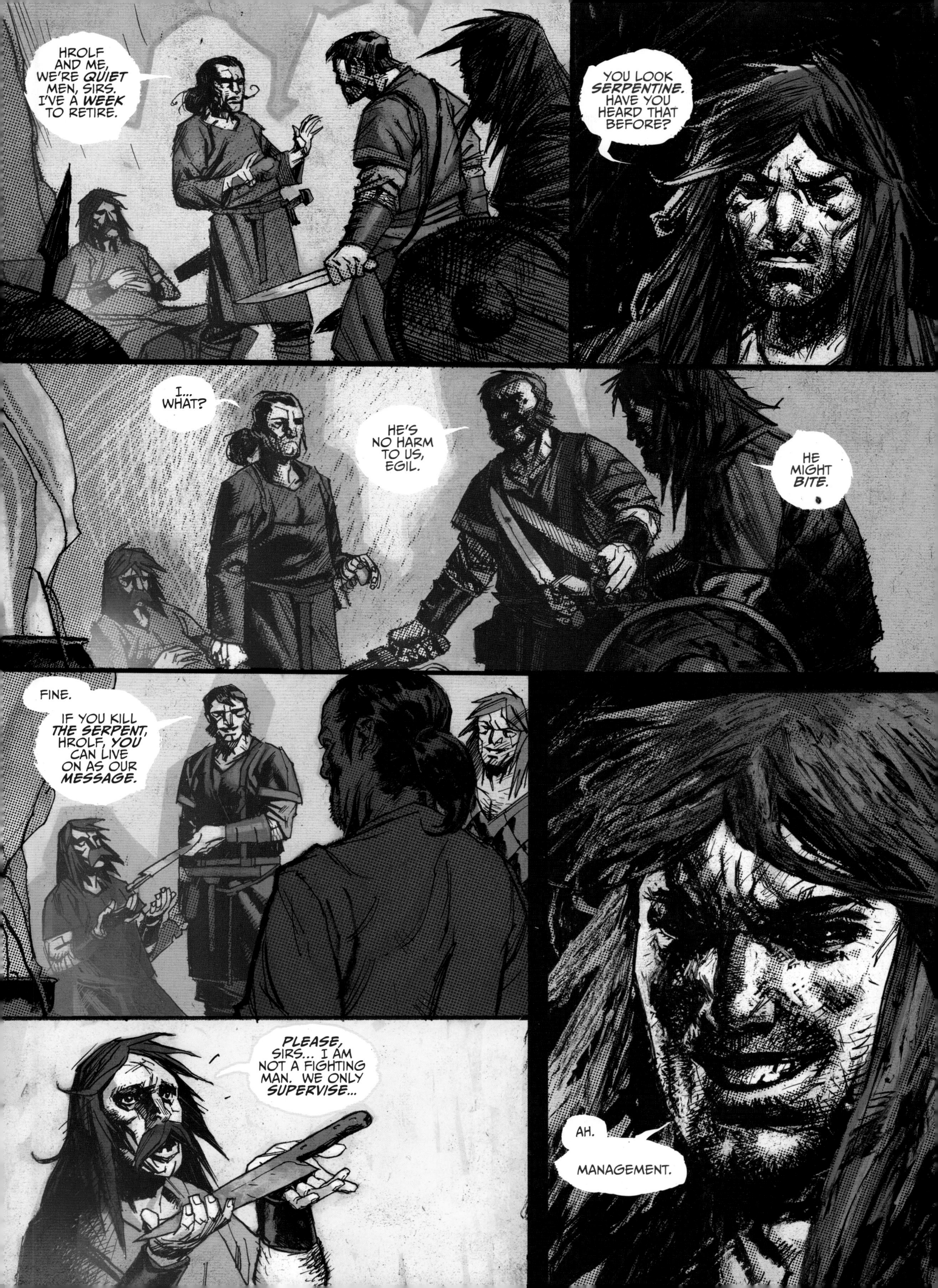

HROLF AND ME, WE'RE QUIET MEN, SIRS. I'VE A WEEK TO RETIRE.
YOU LOOK SERPENTINE. HAVE YOU HEARD THAT BEFORE?
I... WHAT?
HE'S NO HARM TO US, EGIL.
HE MIGHT BITE.
FINE.
IF YOU KILL THE SERPENT, HROLF, YOU CAN LIVE ON AS OUR MESSAGE.
PLEASE, SIRS... I AM NOT A FIGHTING MAN. WE ONLY SUPERVISE...
AH.
MANAGEMENT.

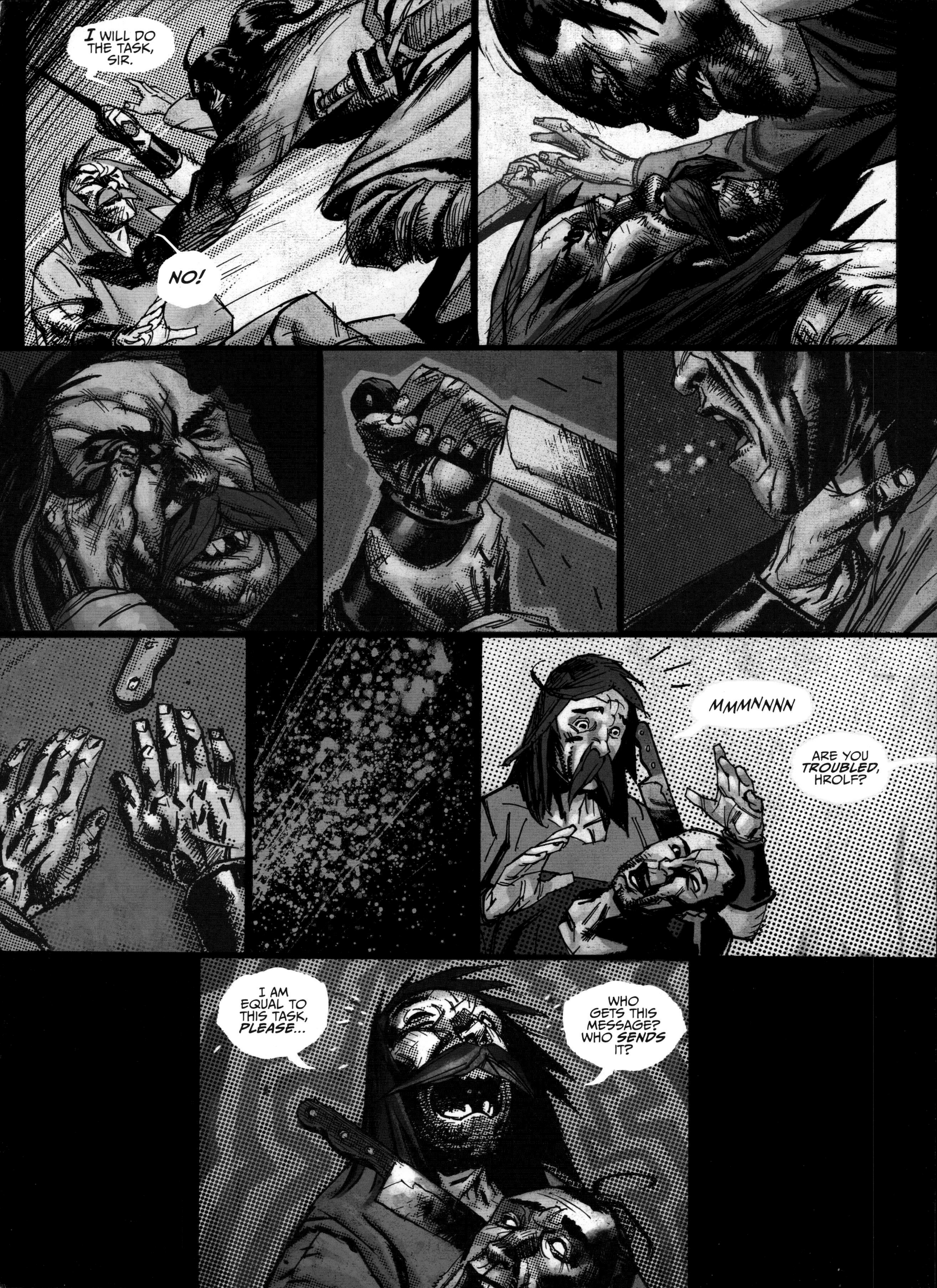
I WILL DO THE TASK, SIR.
NO!
MMMNNNN
ARE YOU TROUBLED, HROLF?
I AM EQUAL TO THIS TASK, PLEASE...
WHO GETS THIS MESSAGE? WHO SENDS IT?

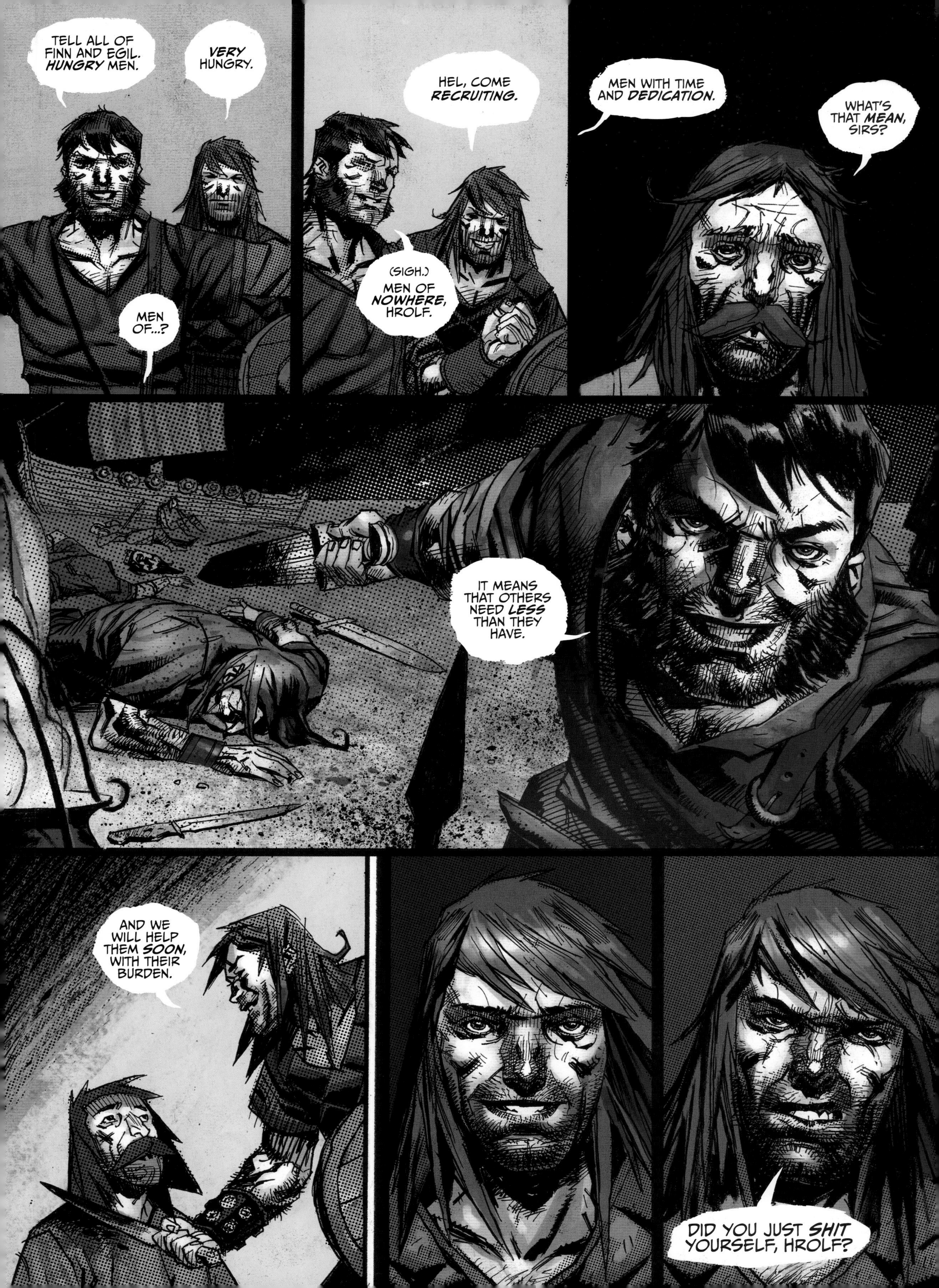

TELL ALL OF FINN AND EGIL. HUNGRY MEN.
VERY HUNGRY.
MEN OF...?
HEL, COME RECRUITING.
(SIGH.) MEN OF NOWHERE, HROLF.
MEN WITH TIME AND DEDICATION.
WHAT'S THAT MEAN, SIRS?
IT MEANS THAT OTHERS NEED LESS THAN THEY HAVE.
AND WE WILL HELP THEM SOON, WITH THEIR BURDEN.
DID YOU JUST SHIT YOURSELF, HROLF?

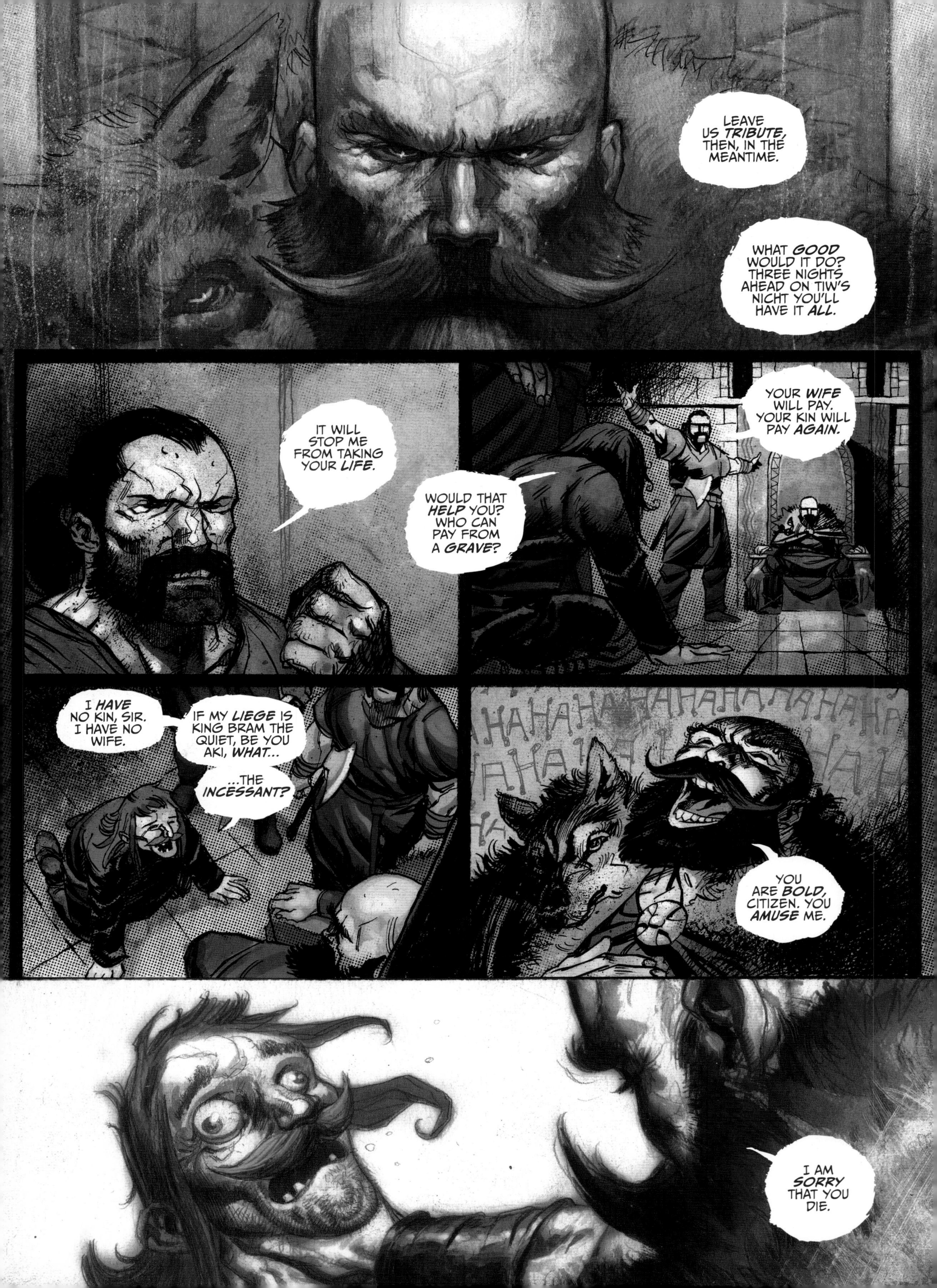

LEAVE US TRIBUTE, THEN, IN THE MEANTIME.
WHAT GOOD WOULD IT DO? THREE NIGHTS AHEAD ON TIW'S NIGHT YOU'LL HAVE IT ALL.
IT WILL STOP ME FROM TAKING YOUR LIFE.
WOULD THAT HELP YOU? WHO CAN PAY FROM A GRAVE?
YOUR WIFE WILL PAY. YOUR KIN WILL PAY AGAIN.
I HAVE NO KIN, SIR. I HAVE NO WIFE.
IF MY LIEGE IS KING BRAM THE QUIET, BE YOU AKI, WHAT...
...THE INCESSANT?
YOU ARE BOLD, CITIZEN. YOU AMUSE ME.
I AM SORRY THAT YOU DIE.

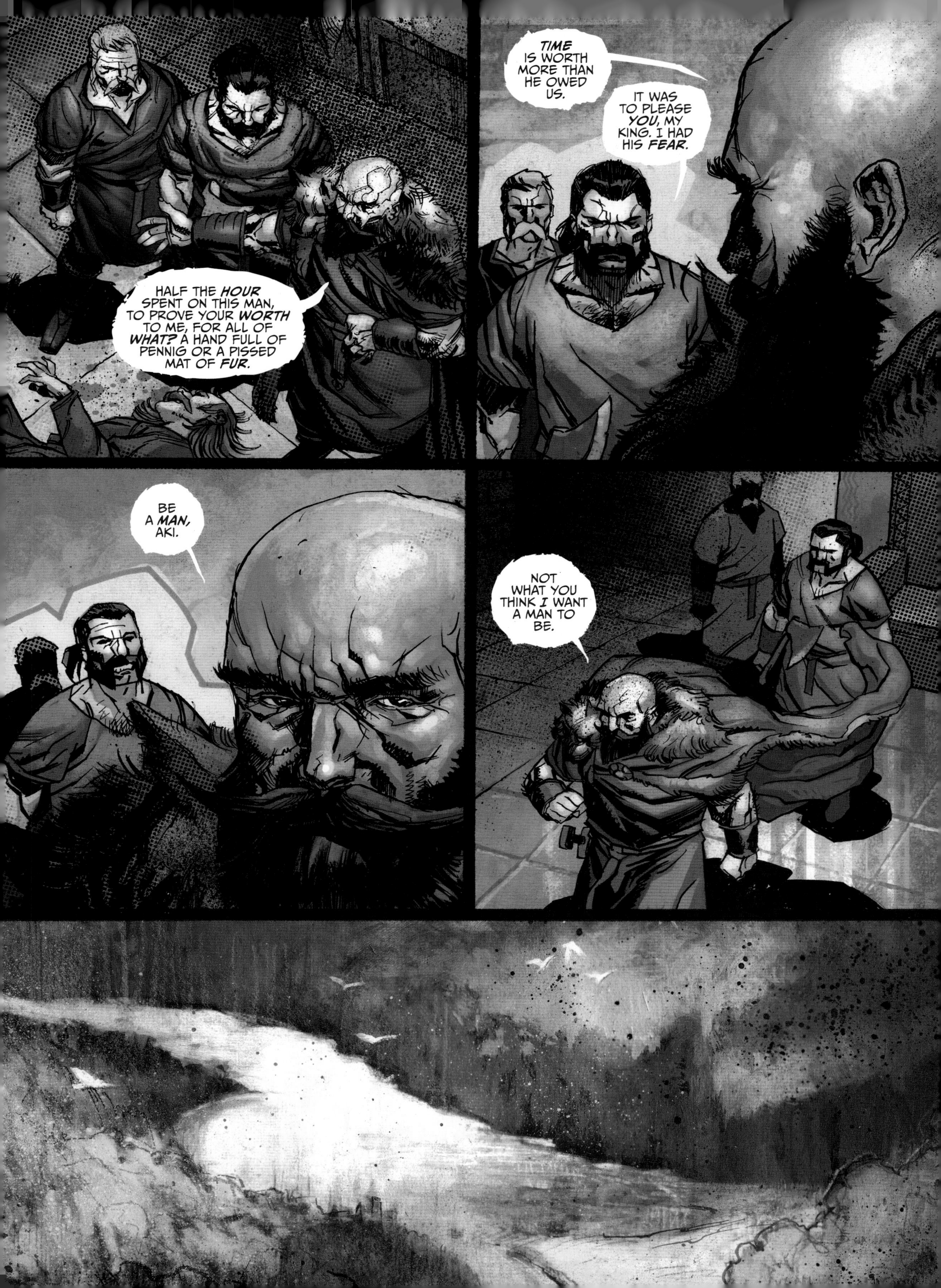
HALF THE HOUR SPENT ON THIS MAN, TO PROVE YOUR WORTH TO ME, FOR ALL OF WHAT? A HAND FULL OF PENNIG OR A PISSED MAT OF FUR.
TIME IS WORTH MORE THAN HE OWED US.
IT WAS TO PLEASE YOU, MY KING. I HAD HIS FEAR.
BE A MAN, AKI.
NOT WHAT YOU THINK I WANT A MAN TO BE.

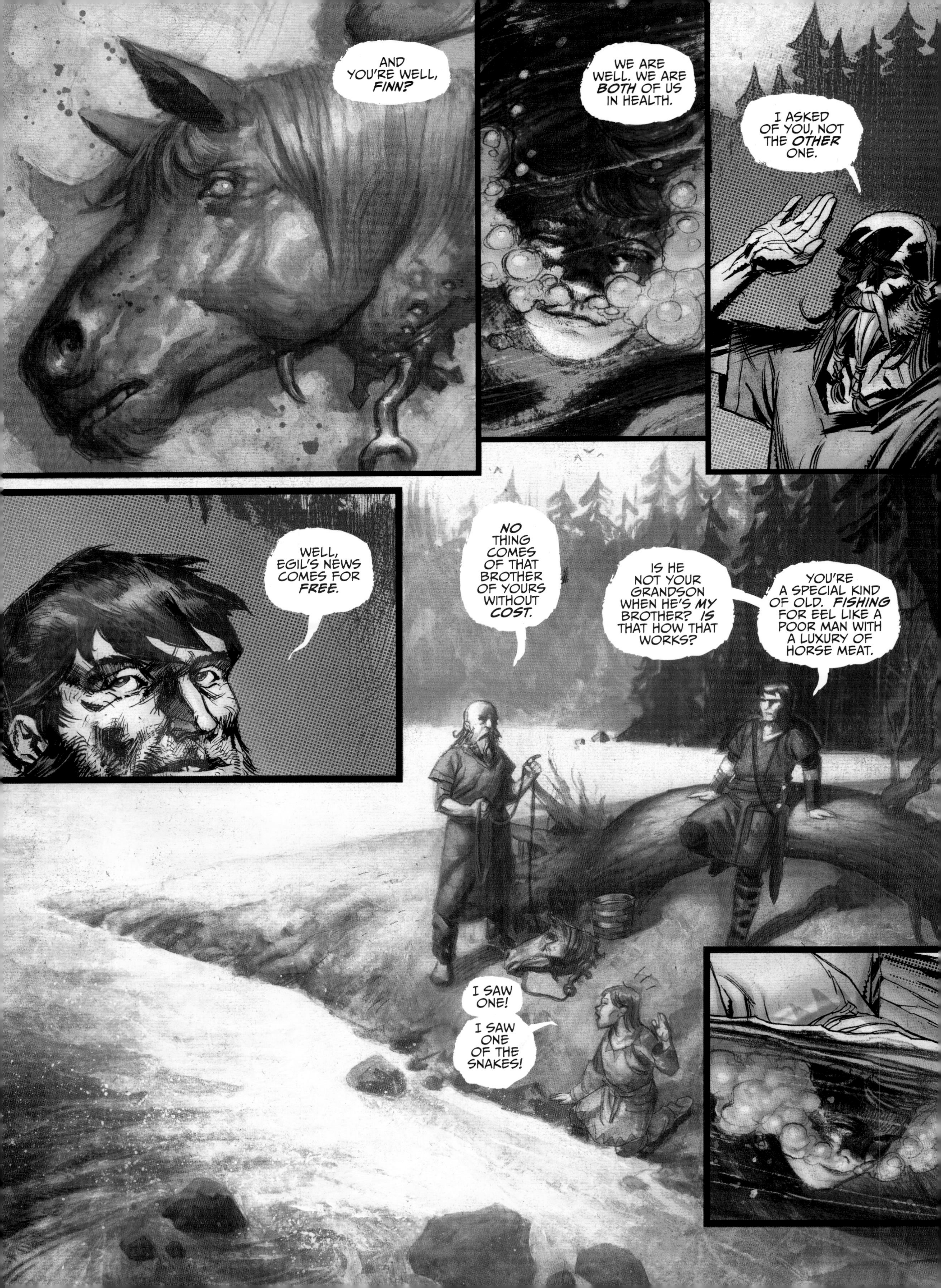

AND YOU'RE WELL, FINN?
WE ARE WELL. WE ARE BOTH OF US IN HEALTH.
I ASKED OF YOU, NOT THE OTHER ONE.
WELL, EGIL'S NEWS COMES FOR FREE.
NO THING COMES OF THAT BROTHER OF YOURS WITHOUT COST.
IS HE NOT YOUR GRANDSON WHEN HE'S MY BROTHER? IS THAT HOW THAT WORKS?
YOU'RE A SPECIAL KIND OF OLD. FISHING FOR EEL LIKE A POOR MAN WITH A LUXURY OF HORSE MEAT.
I SAW ONE!
I SAW ONE OF THE SNAKES!

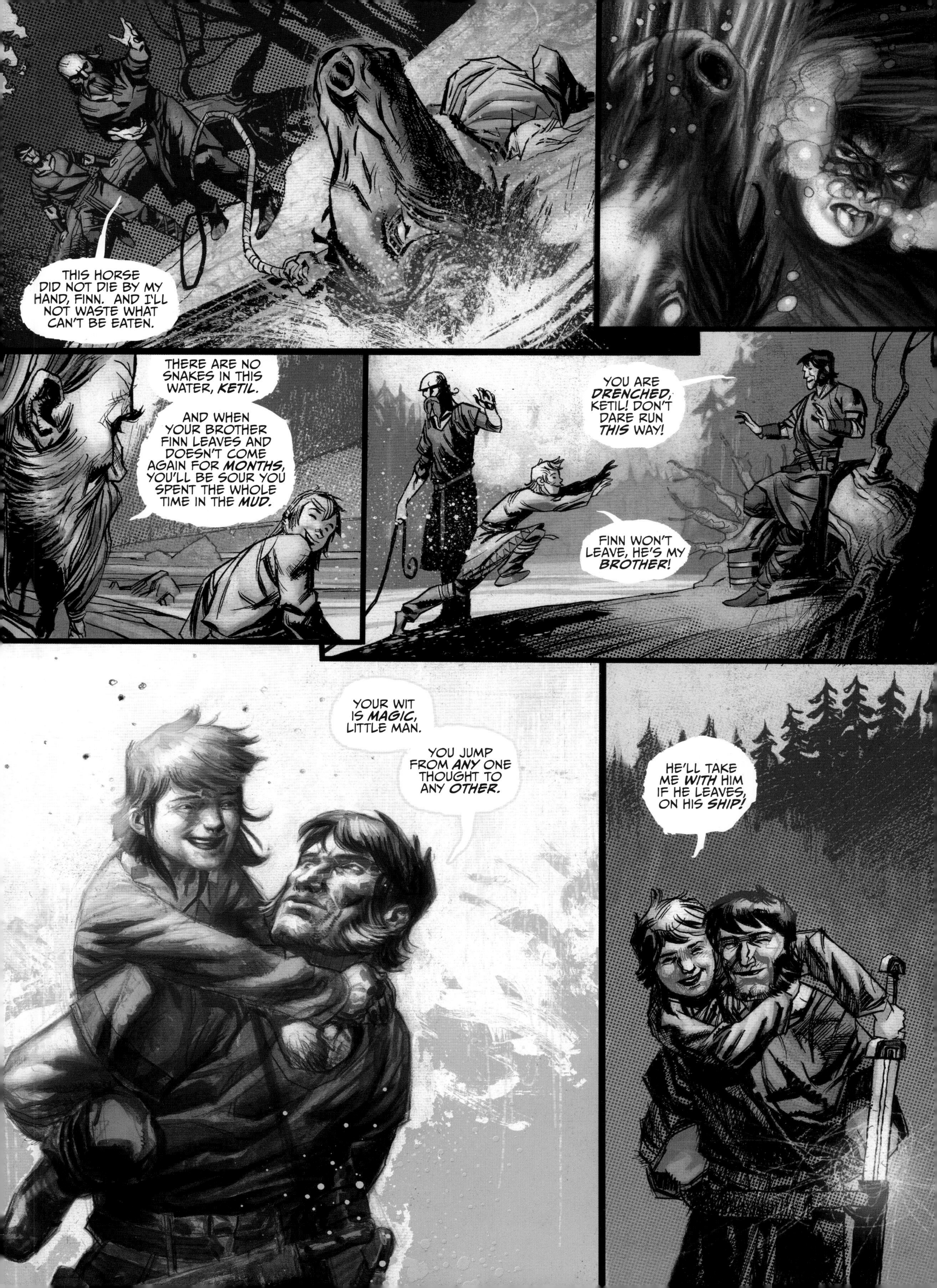
THIS HORSE DID NOT DIE BY MY HAND, FINN. AND I'LL NOT WASTE WHAT CAN'T BE EATEN.
THERE ARE NO SNAKES IN THIS WATER, KETIL.
AND WHEN YOUR BROTHER FINN LEAVES AND DOESN'T COME AGAIN FOR MONTHS, YOU'LL BE SOUR YOU SPENT THE WHOLE TIME IN THE MUD.
YOU ARE DRENCHED, KETIL! DON'T DARE RUN THIS WAY!
FINN WON'T LEAVE, HE'S MY BROTHER!
YOUR WIT IS MAGIC, LITTLE MAN.
YOU JUMP FROM ANY ONE THOUGHT TO ANY OTHER.
HE'LL TAKE ME WITH HIM IF HE LEAVES, ON HIS SHIP!

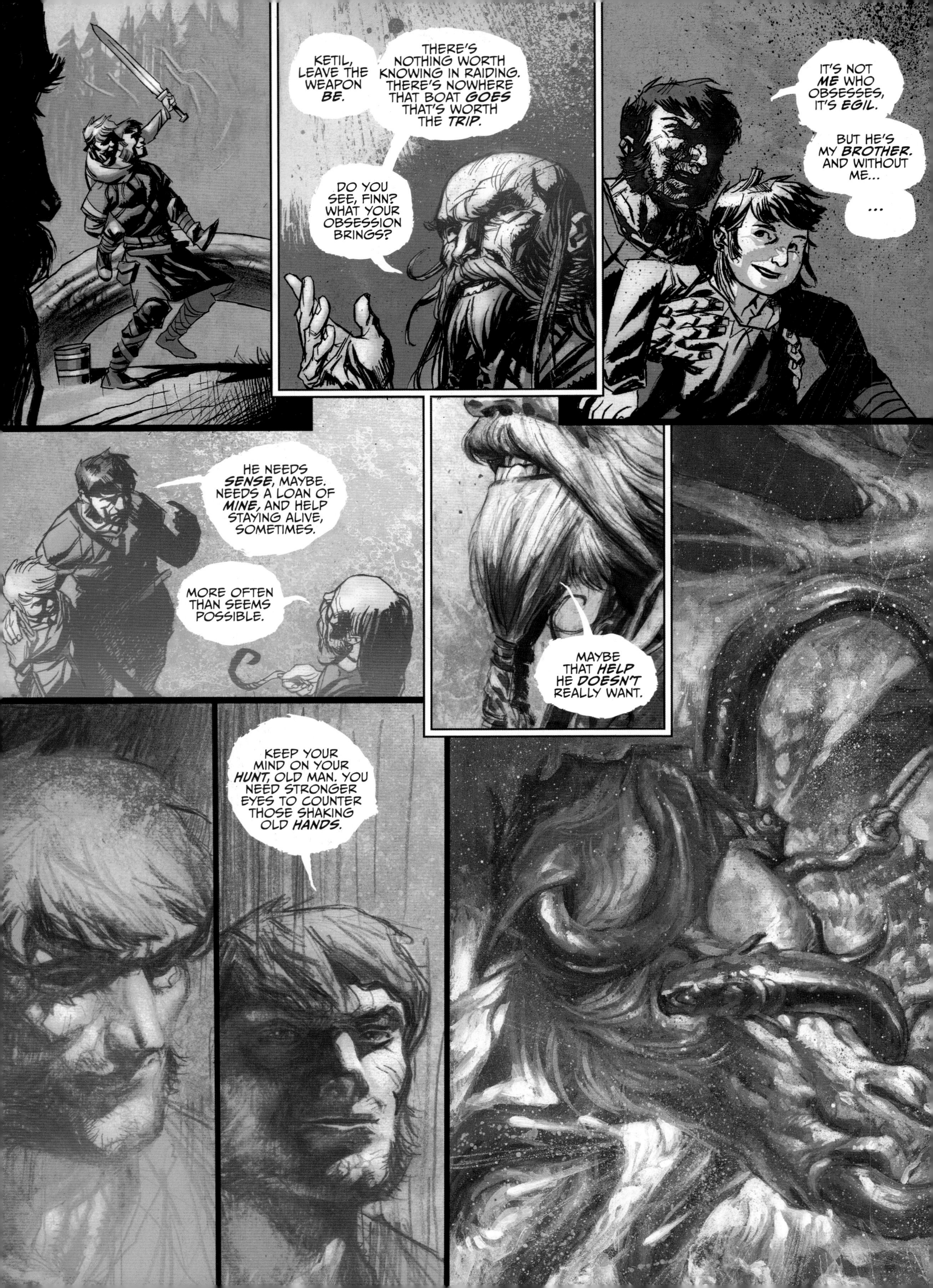
KETIL, LEAVE THE WEAPON BE.
THERE'S NOTHING WORTH KNOWING IN RAIDING. THERE'S NOWHERE THAT BOAT GOES THAT'S WORTH THE TRIP.
DO YOU SEE, FINN? WHAT YOUR OBSESSION BRINGS?
IT'S NOT ME WHO OBSESSES, IT'S EGIL.
BUT HE'S MY BROTHER. AND WITHOUT ME...
...
HE NEEDS SENSE, MAYBE. NEEDS A LOAN OF MINE, AND HELP STAYING ALIVE, SOMETIMES.
MORE OFTEN THAN SEEMS POSSIBLE.
MAYBE THAT HELP HE DOESN'T REALLY WANT.
KEEP YOUR MIND ON YOUR HUNT, OLD MAN. YOU NEED STRONGER EYES TO COUNTER THOSE SHAKING OLD HANDS.

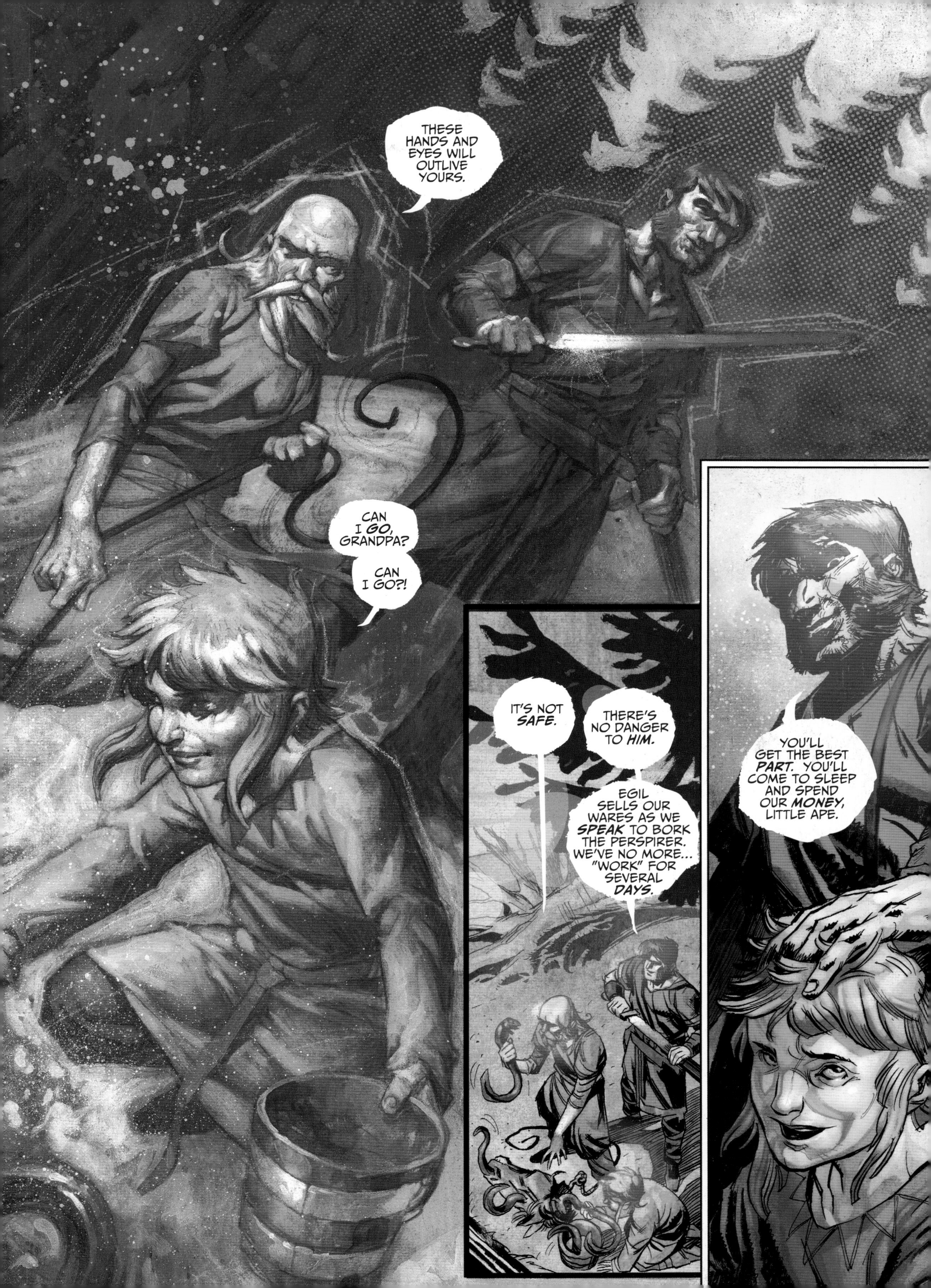
THESE HANDS AND EYES WILL OUTLIVE YOURS.
CAN I GO, GRANDPA?
CAN I GO?!
IT'S NOT SAFE.
THERE'S NO DANGER TO HIM.
EGIL SELLS OUR WARES AS WE SPEAK TO BORK THE PERSPIRER. WE'VE NO MORE... "WORK" FOR SEVERAL DAYS.
YOU'LL GET THE BEST PART. YOU'LL COME TO SLEEP AND SPEND OUR MONEY, LITTLE APE.

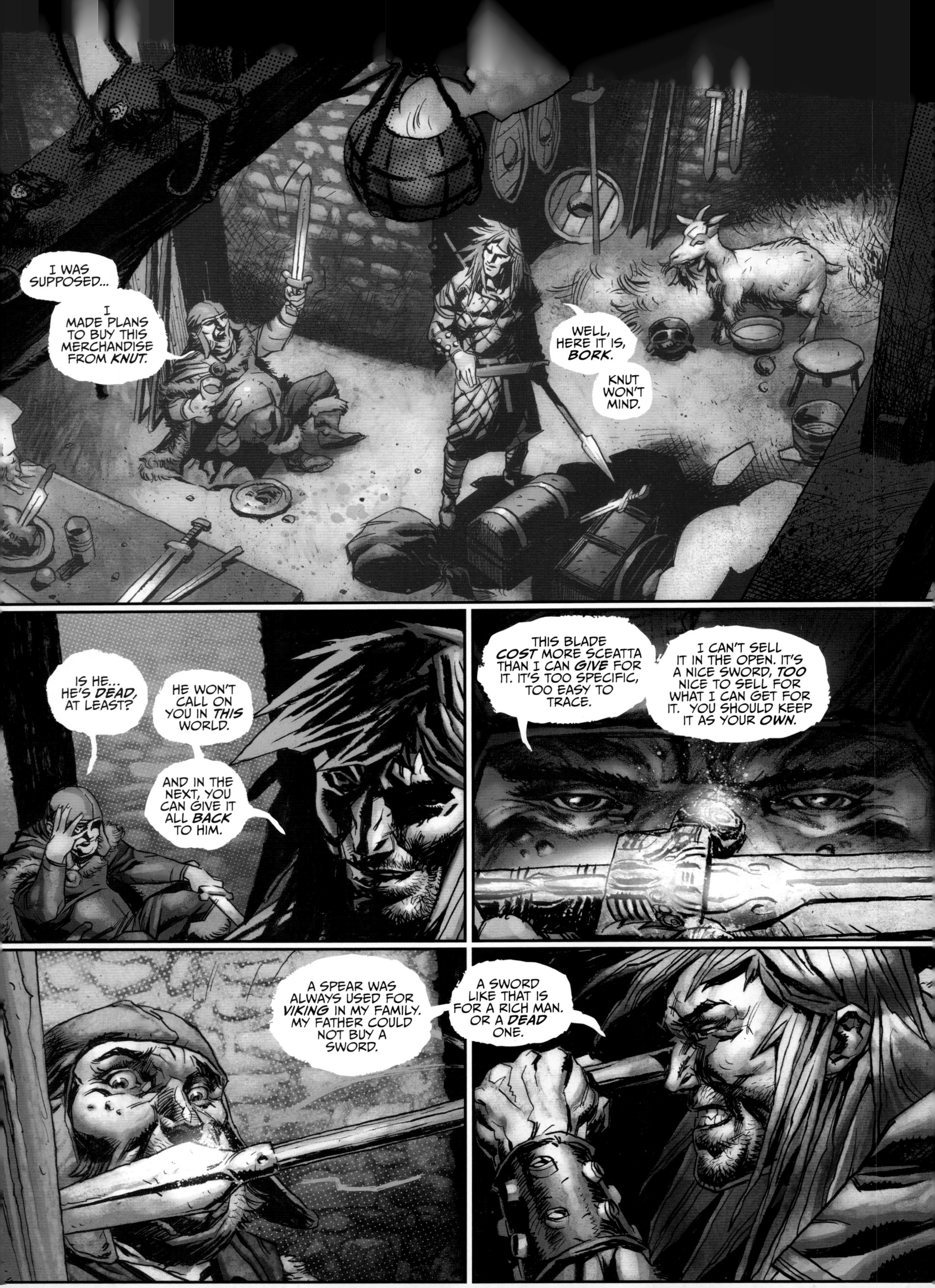

I WAS SUPPOSED...
I MADE PLANS TO BUY THIS MERCHANDISE FROM *KNUT.*
WELL, HERE IT IS, ***BORK.***
KNUT WON'T MIND.
IS HE... HE'S *DEAD,* AT LEAST?
HE WON'T CALL ON YOU IN *THIS* WORLD.
AND IN THE NEXT, YOU CAN GIVE IT ALL *BACK* TO HIM.
THIS BLADE *COST* MORE SCEATTA THAN I CAN *GIVE* FOR IT. IT'S TOO SPECIFIC, TOO EASY TO TRACE.
I CAN'T SELL IT IN THE OPEN. IT'S A NICE SWORD, *TOO* NICE TO SELL FOR WHAT I CAN GET FOR IT. YOU SHOULD KEEP IT AS YOUR *OWN.*
A SPEAR WAS ALWAYS USED FOR *VIKING* IN MY FAMILY. MY FATHER COULD NOT BUY A SWORD.
A SWORD LIKE THAT IS FOR A RICH MAN. OR A *DEAD* ONE.

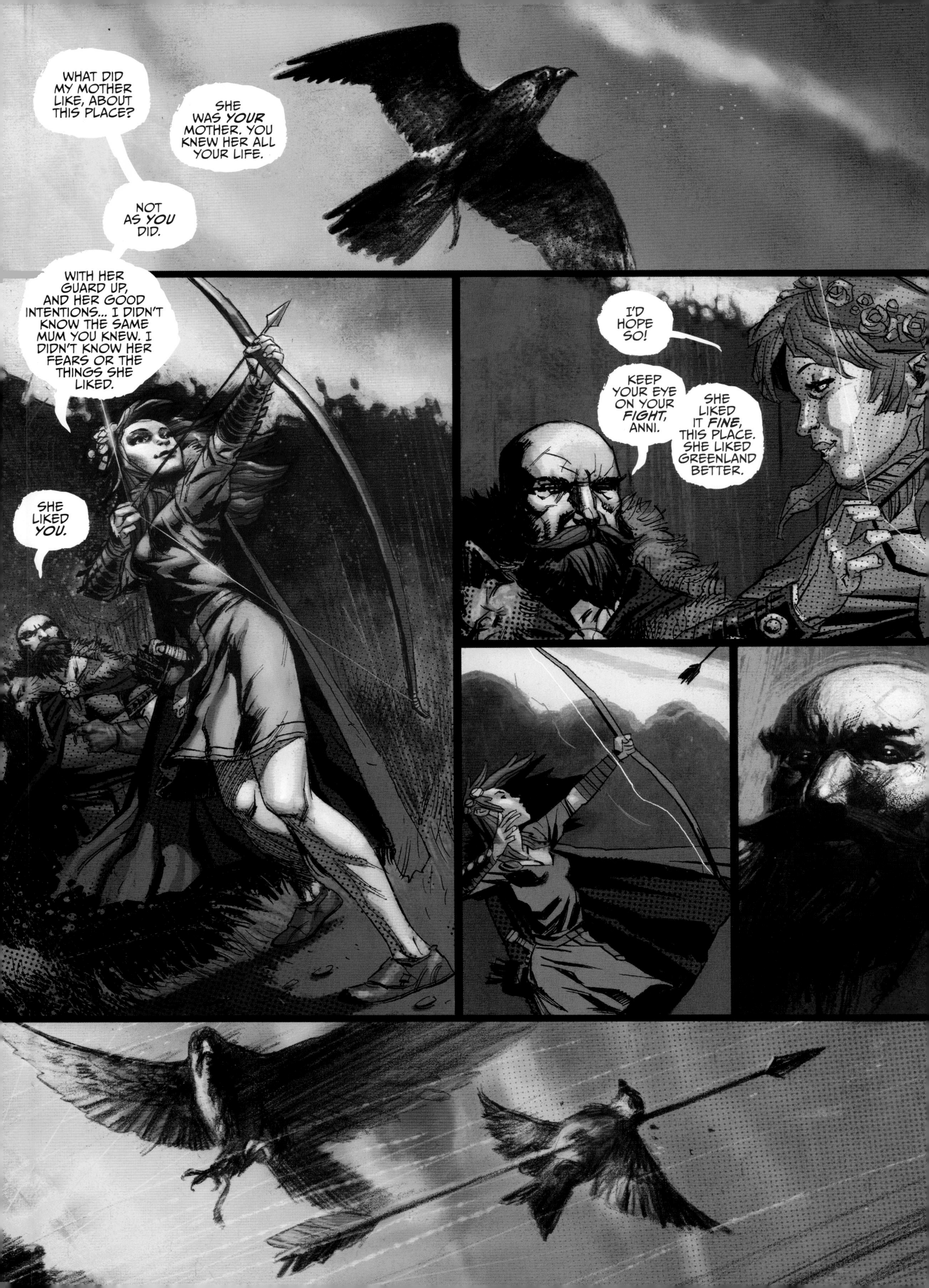
WHAT DID MY MOTHER LIKE, ABOUT THIS PLACE?
SHE WAS YOUR MOTHER. YOU KNEW HER ALL YOUR LIFE.
NOT AS YOU DID.
WITH HER GUARD UP, AND HER GOOD INTENTIONS... I DIDN'T KNOW THE SAME MUM YOU KNEW. I DIDN'T KNOW HER FEARS OR THE THINGS SHE LIKED.
SHE LIKED YOU.
I'D HOPE SO!
KEEP YOUR EYE ON YOUR FIGHT, ANNI.
SHE LIKED IT FINE, THIS PLACE. SHE LIKED GREENLAND BETTER.

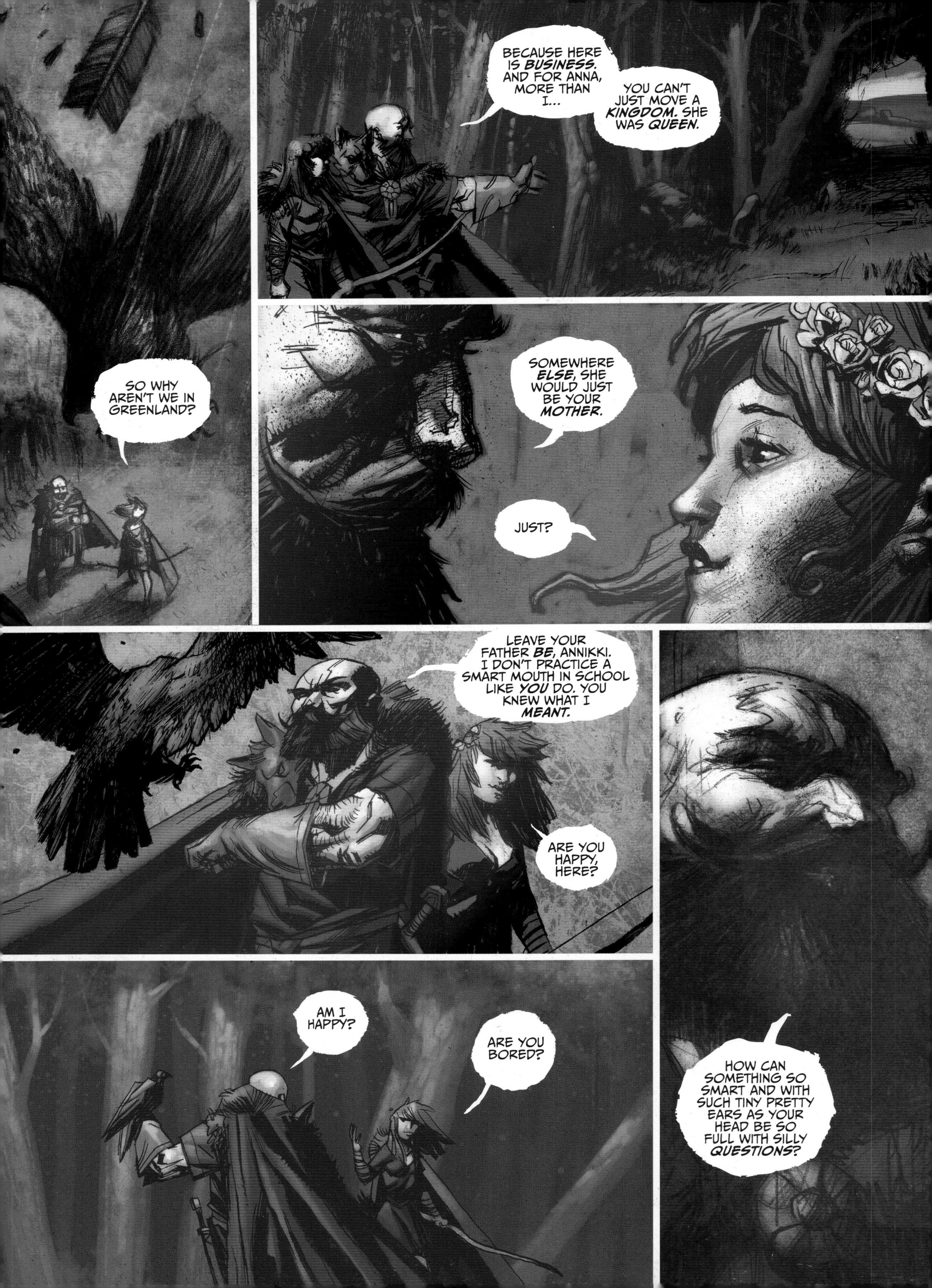

SO WHY AREN'T WE IN GREENLAND?
BECAUSE HERE IS BUSINESS. AND FOR ANNA, MORE THAN I...
YOU CAN'T JUST MOVE A KINGDOM. SHE WAS QUEEN.
SOMEWHERE ELSE, SHE WOULD JUST BE YOUR MOTHER.
JUST?
LEAVE YOUR FATHER BE, ANNIKKI. I DON'T PRACTICE A SMART MOUTH IN SCHOOL LIKE YOU DO. YOU KNEW WHAT I MEANT.
ARE YOU HAPPY, HERE?
AM I HAPPY?
ARE YOU BORED?
HOW CAN SOMETHING SO SMART AND WITH SUCH TINY PRETTY EARS AS YOUR HEAD BE SO FULL WITH SILLY QUESTIONS?

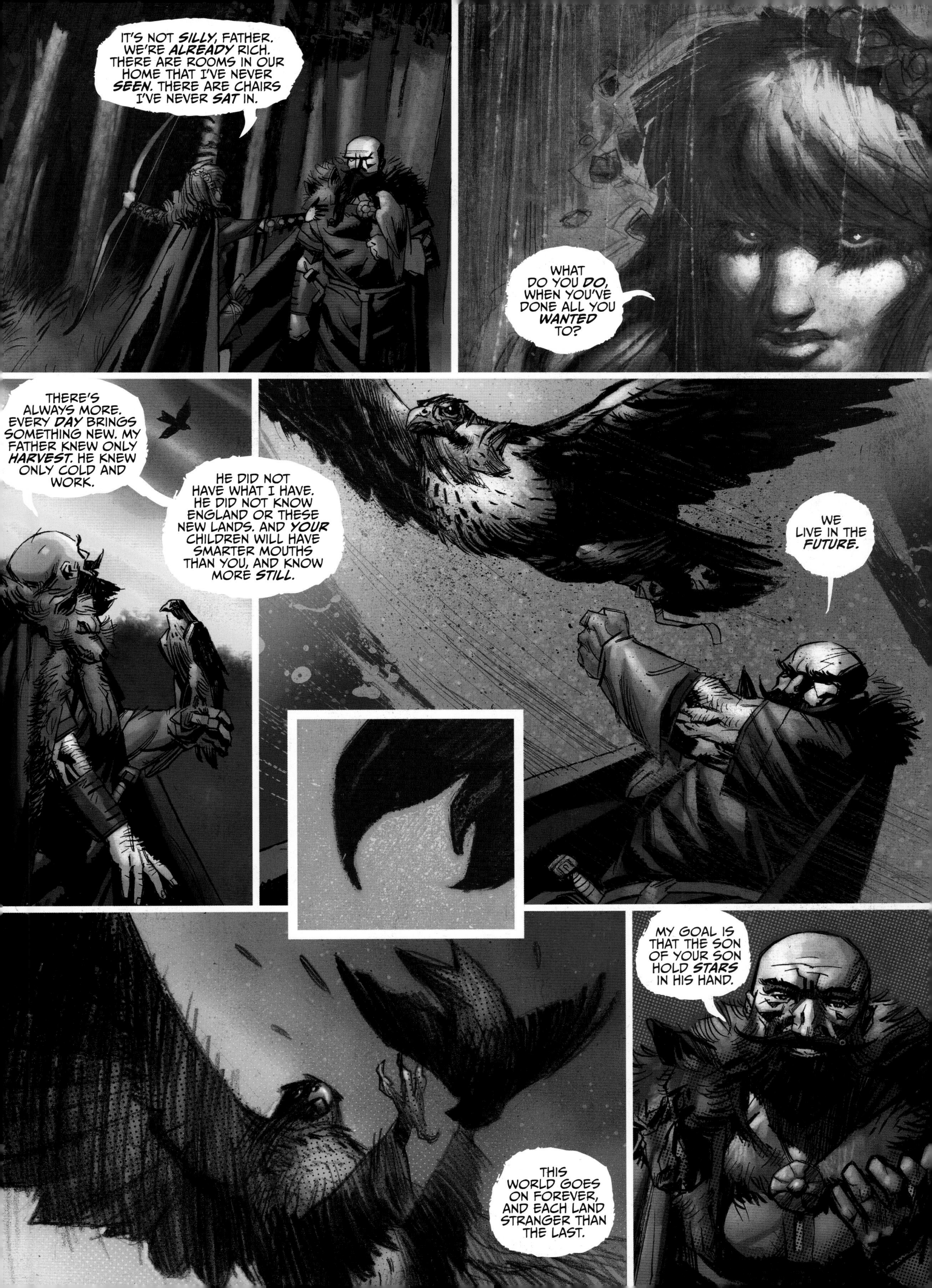
IT'S NOT SILLY, FATHER. WE'RE ALREADY RICH. THERE ARE ROOMS IN OUR HOME THAT I'VE NEVER SEEN. THERE ARE CHAIRS I'VE NEVER SAT IN.
WHAT DO YOU DO, WHEN YOU'VE DONE ALL YOU WANTED TO?
THERE'S ALWAYS MORE. EVERY DAY BRINGS SOMETHING NEW. MY FATHER KNEW ONLY HARVEST. HE KNEW ONLY COLD AND WORK.
HE DID NOT HAVE WHAT I HAVE. HE DID NOT KNOW ENGLAND OR THESE NEW LANDS. AND YOUR CHILDREN WILL HAVE SMARTER MOUTHS THAN YOU, AND KNOW MORE STILL.
WE LIVE IN THE FUTURE.
THIS WORLD GOES ON FOREVER, AND EACH LAND STRANGER THAN THE LAST.
MY GOAL IS THAT THE SON OF YOUR SON HOLD STARS IN HIS HAND.

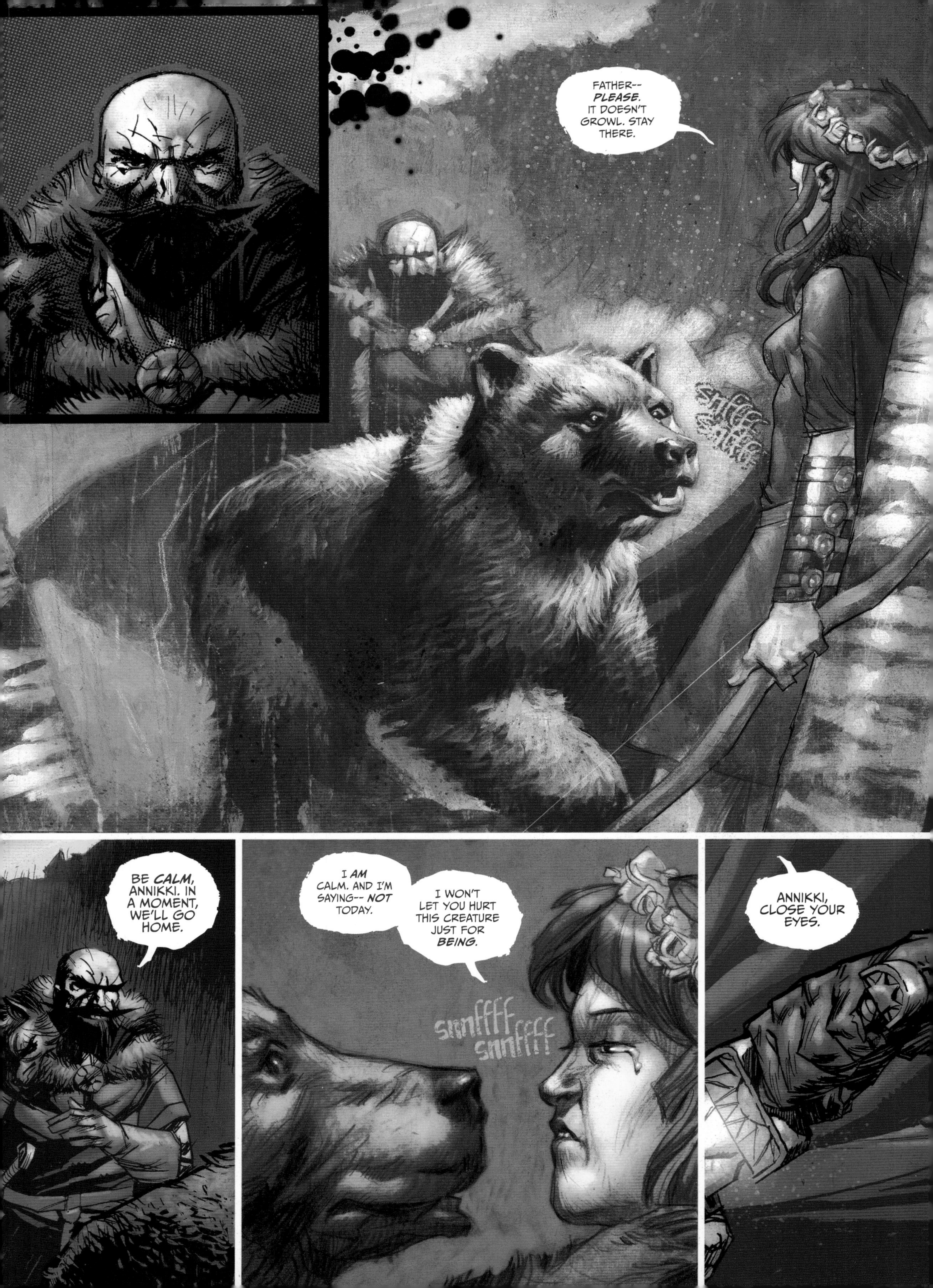
FATHER-- PLEASE. IT DOESN'T GROWL. STAY THERE.
BE CALM, ANNIKKI. IN A MOMENT, WE'LL GO HOME.
I AM CALM. AND I'M SAYING-- NOT TODAY.
I WON'T LET YOU HURT THIS CREATURE JUST FOR BEING.
snnfffff snnffff
ANNIKKI, CLOSE YOUR EYES.

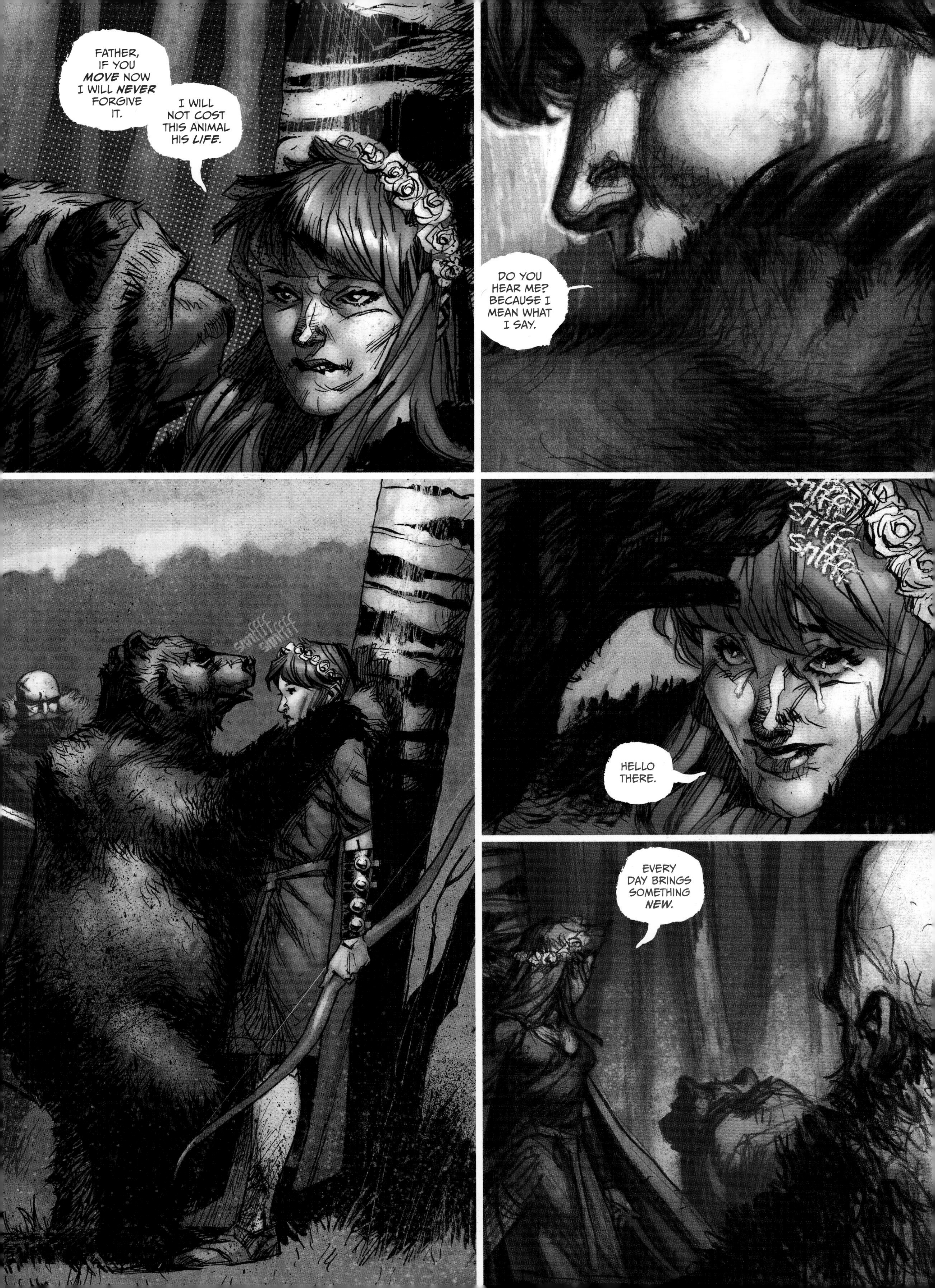
FATHER, IF YOU MOVE NOW I WILL NEVER FORGIVE IT.
I WILL NOT COST THIS ANIMAL HIS LIFE.
DO YOU HEAR ME? BECAUSE I MEAN WHAT I SAY.
SNIFFF SNIFFF
SNIFF SNIFF SNIFF
HELLO THERE.
EVERY DAY BRINGS SOMETHING NEW.

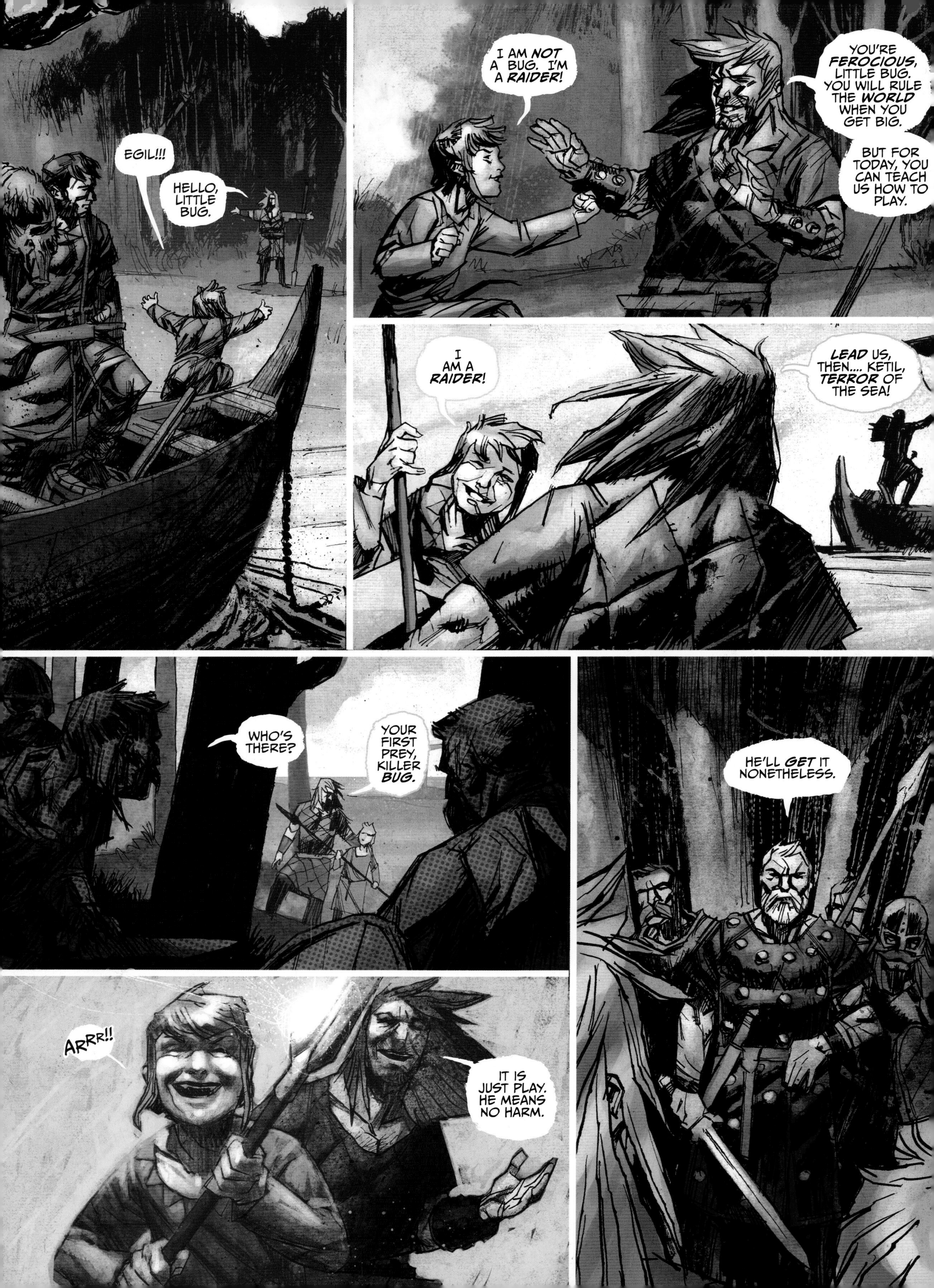
EGIL!!!
HELLO, LITTLE BUG.
I AM NOT A BUG. I'M A RAIDER!
YOU'RE FEROCIOUS, LITTLE BUG. YOU WILL RULE THE WORLD WHEN YOU GET BIG.
BUT FOR TODAY, YOU CAN TEACH US HOW TO PLAY.
I AM A RAIDER!
LEAD US, THEN.... KETIL, TERROR OF THE SEA!
WHO'S THERE?
YOUR FIRST PREY, KILLER BUG.
ARRR!!
IT IS JUST PLAY. HE MEANS NO HARM.
HE'LL GET IT NONETHELESS.

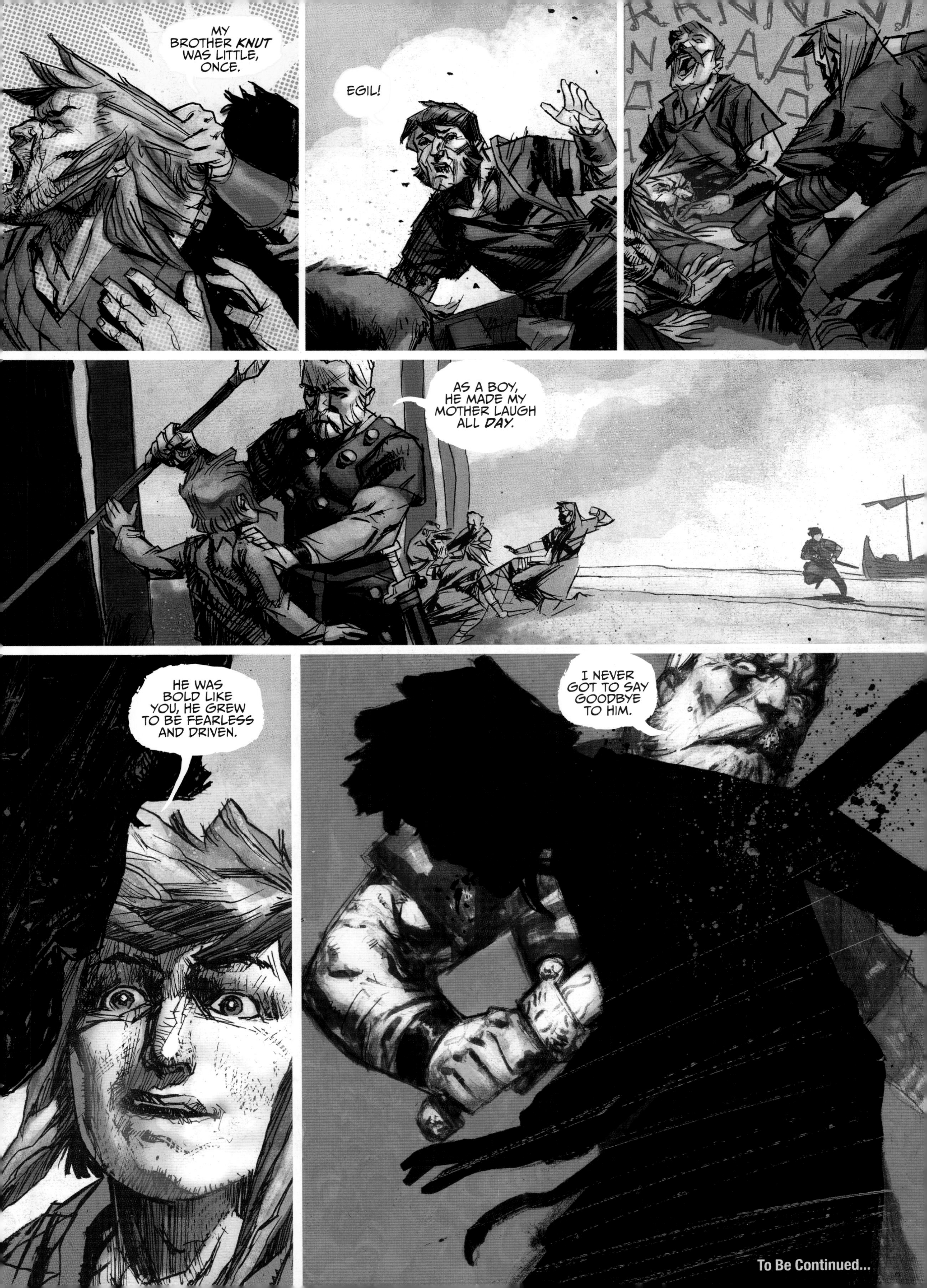
MY BROTHER KNUT WAS LITTLE, ONCE.
EGIL!
AS A BOY, HE MADE MY MOTHER LAUGH ALL DAY.
HE WAS BOLD LIKE YOU, HE GREW TO BE FEARLESS AND DRIVEN.
I NEVER GOT TO SAY GOODBYE TO HIM.
To Be Continued...

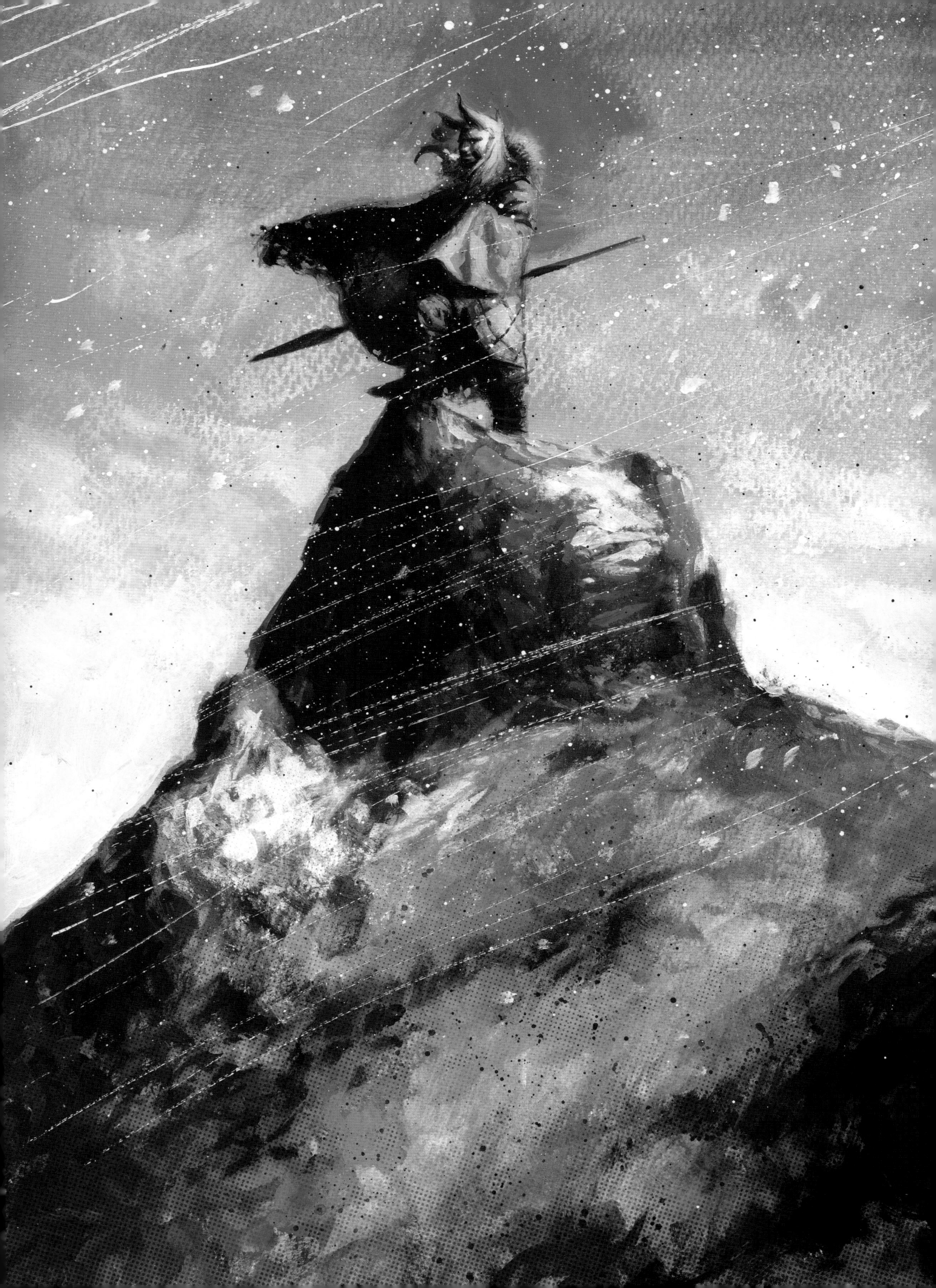

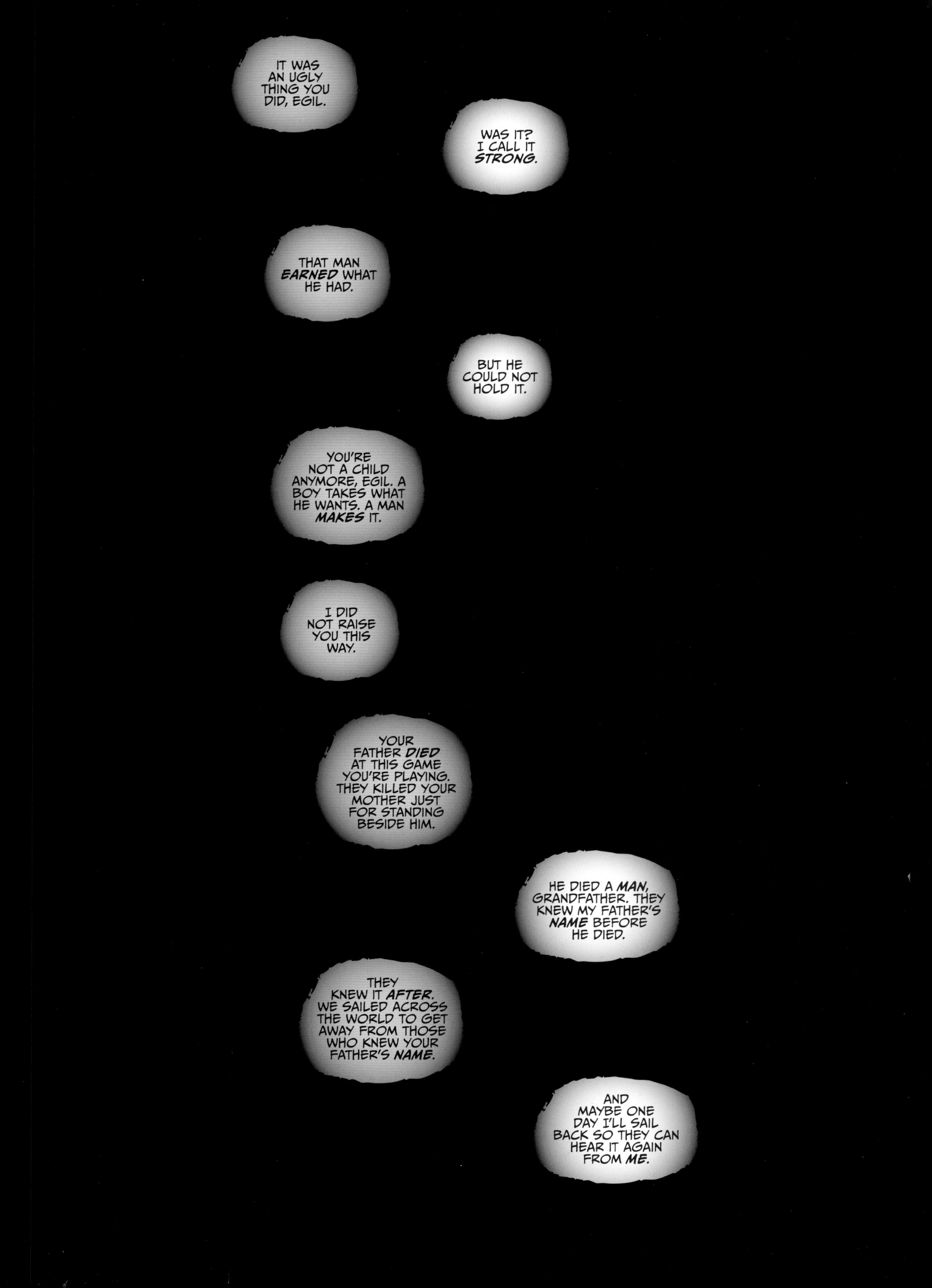
IT WAS AN UGLY THING YOU DID, EGIL.
WAS IT? I CALL IT *STRONG.*
THAT MAN *EARNED* WHAT HE HAD.
BUT HE COULD NOT HOLD IT.
YOU'RE NOT A CHILD ANYMORE, EGIL. A BOY TAKES WHAT HE WANTS. A MAN *MAKES* IT.
I DID NOT RAISE YOU THIS WAY.
YOUR FATHER *DIED* AT THIS GAME YOU'RE PLAYING. THEY KILLED YOUR MOTHER JUST FOR STANDING BESIDE HIM.
HE DIED A *MAN*, GRANDFATHER. THEY KNEW MY FATHER'S *NAME* BEFORE HE DIED.
THEY KNEW IT *AFTER*. WE SAILED ACROSS THE WORLD TO GET AWAY FROM THOSE WHO KNEW YOUR FATHER'S *NAME.*
AND MAYBE ONE DAY I'LL SAIL BACK SO THEY CAN HEAR IT AGAIN FROM *ME.*

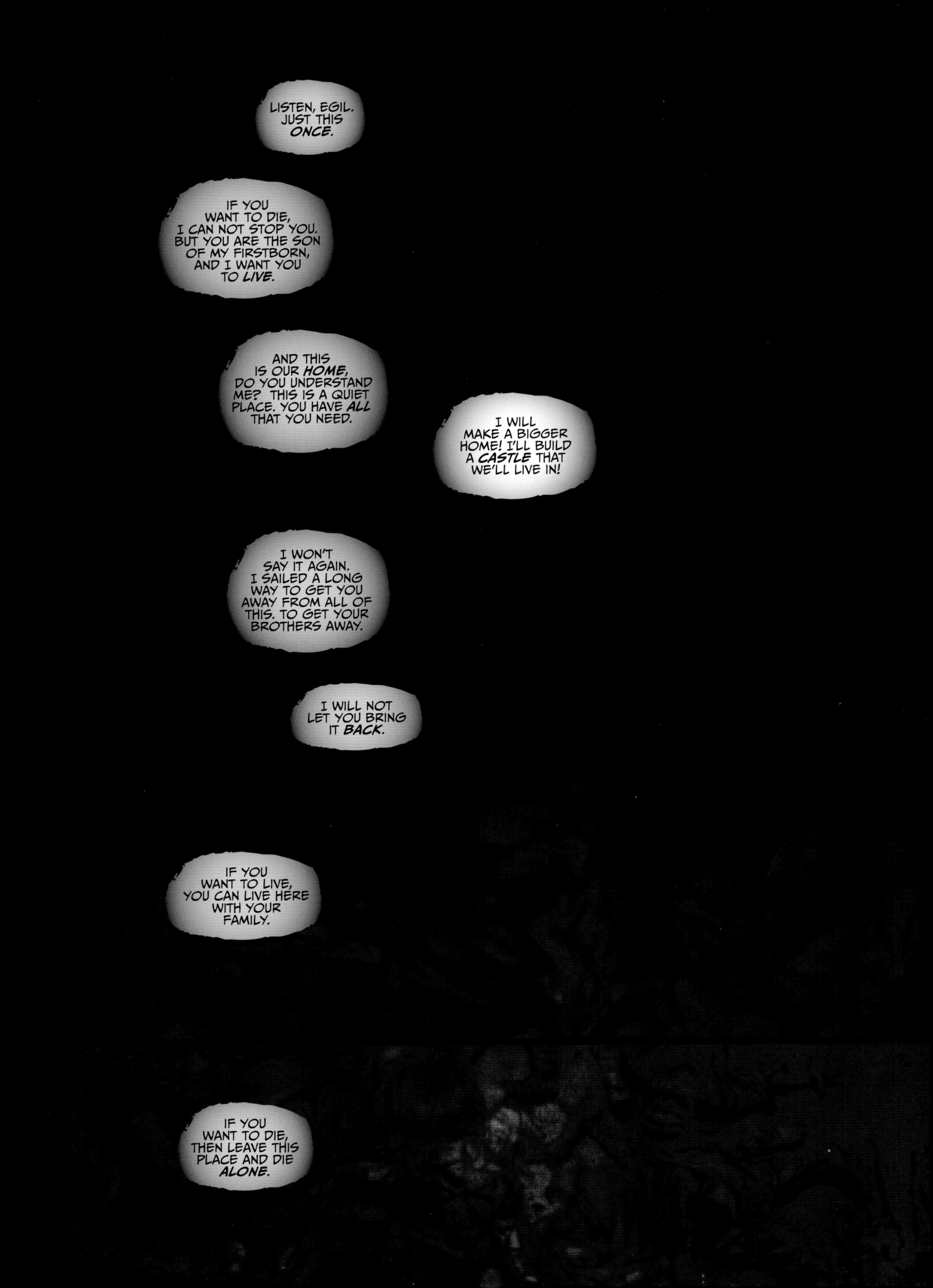
LISTEN, EGIL. JUST THIS ONCE.
IF YOU WANT TO DIE, I CAN NOT STOP YOU. BUT YOU ARE THE SON OF MY FIRSTBORN, AND I WANT YOU TO LIVE.
AND THIS IS OUR HOME, DO YOU UNDERSTAND ME? THIS IS A QUIET PLACE. YOU HAVE ALL THAT YOU NEED.
I WILL MAKE A BIGGER HOME! I'LL BUILD A CASTLE THAT WE'LL LIVE IN!
I WON'T SAY IT AGAIN. I SAILED A LONG WAY TO GET YOU AWAY FROM ALL OF THIS. TO GET YOUR BROTHERS AWAY.
I WILL NOT LET YOU BRING IT BACK.
IF YOU WANT TO LIVE, YOU CAN LIVE HERE WITH YOUR FAMILY.
IF YOU WANT TO DIE, THEN LEAVE THIS PLACE AND DIE ALONE.

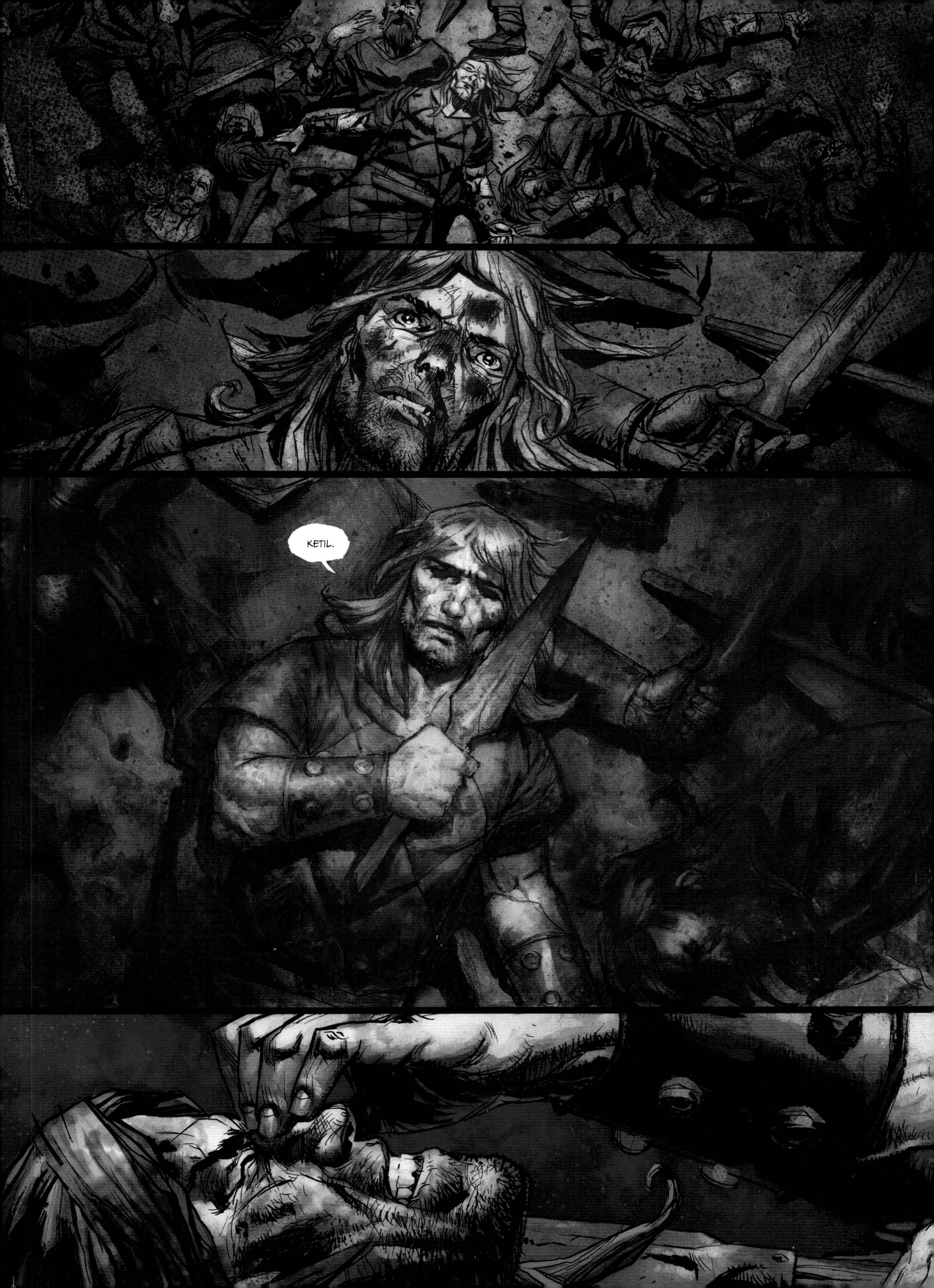
KETIL.

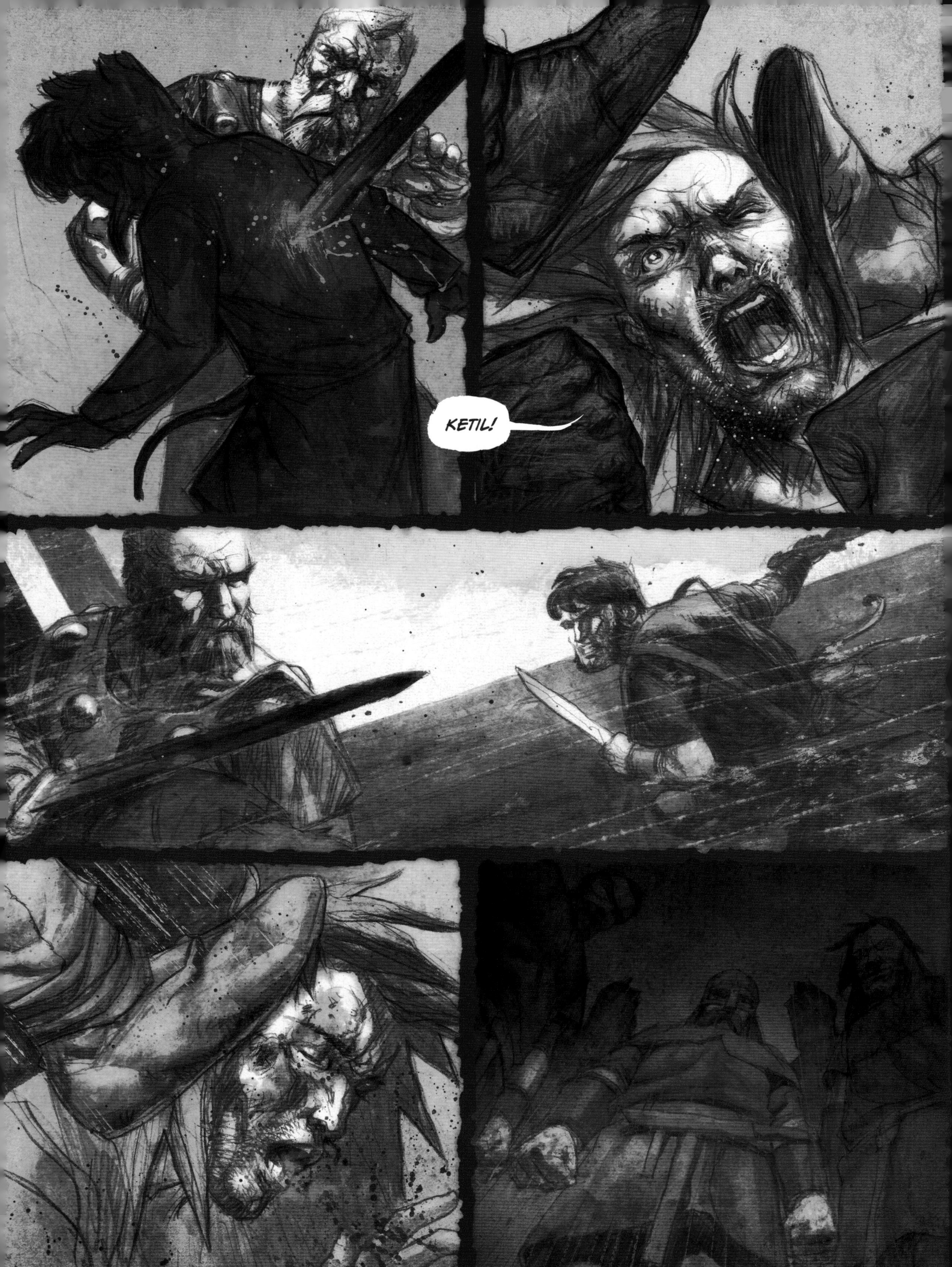
KETIL!

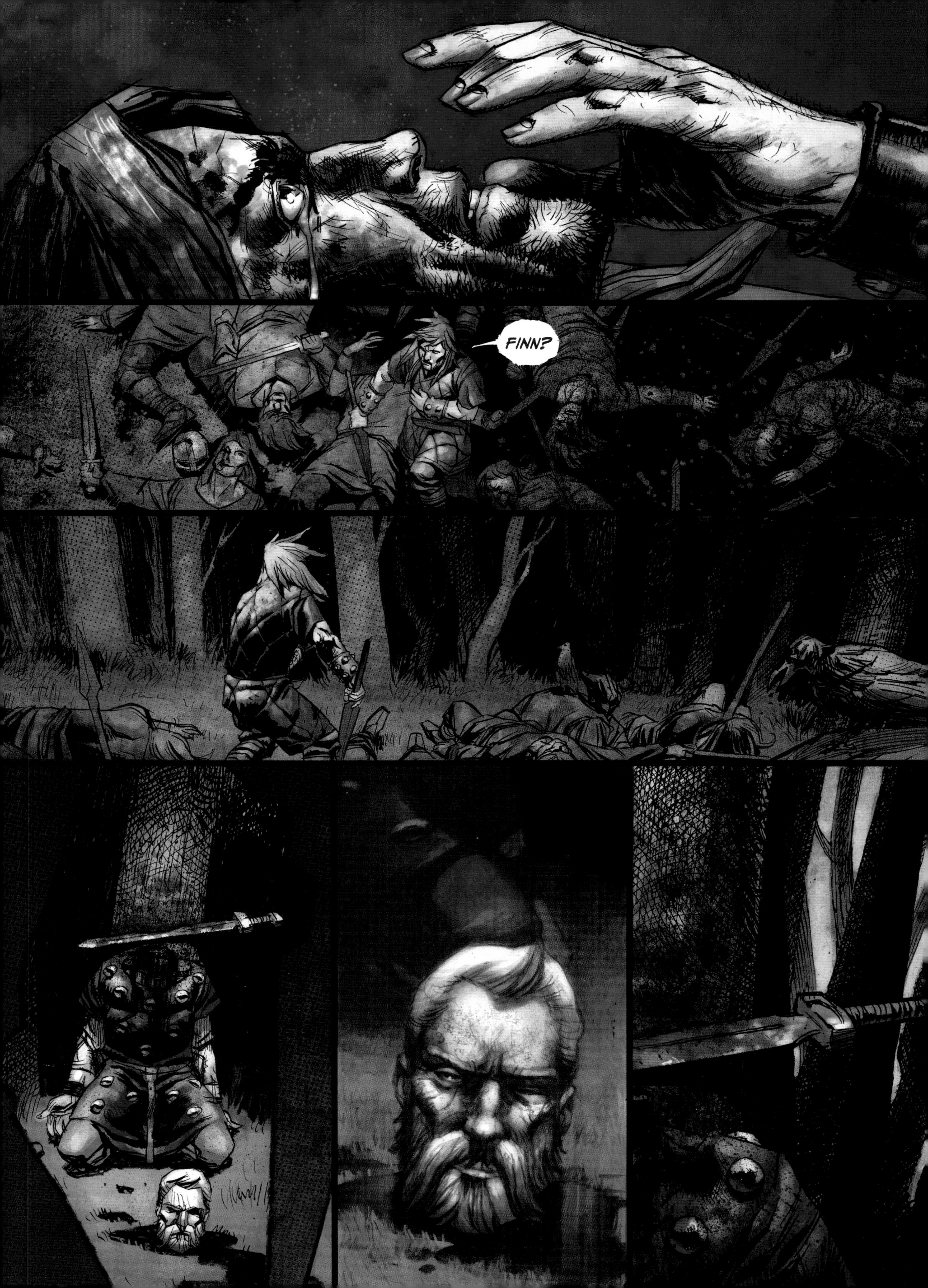
FINN?

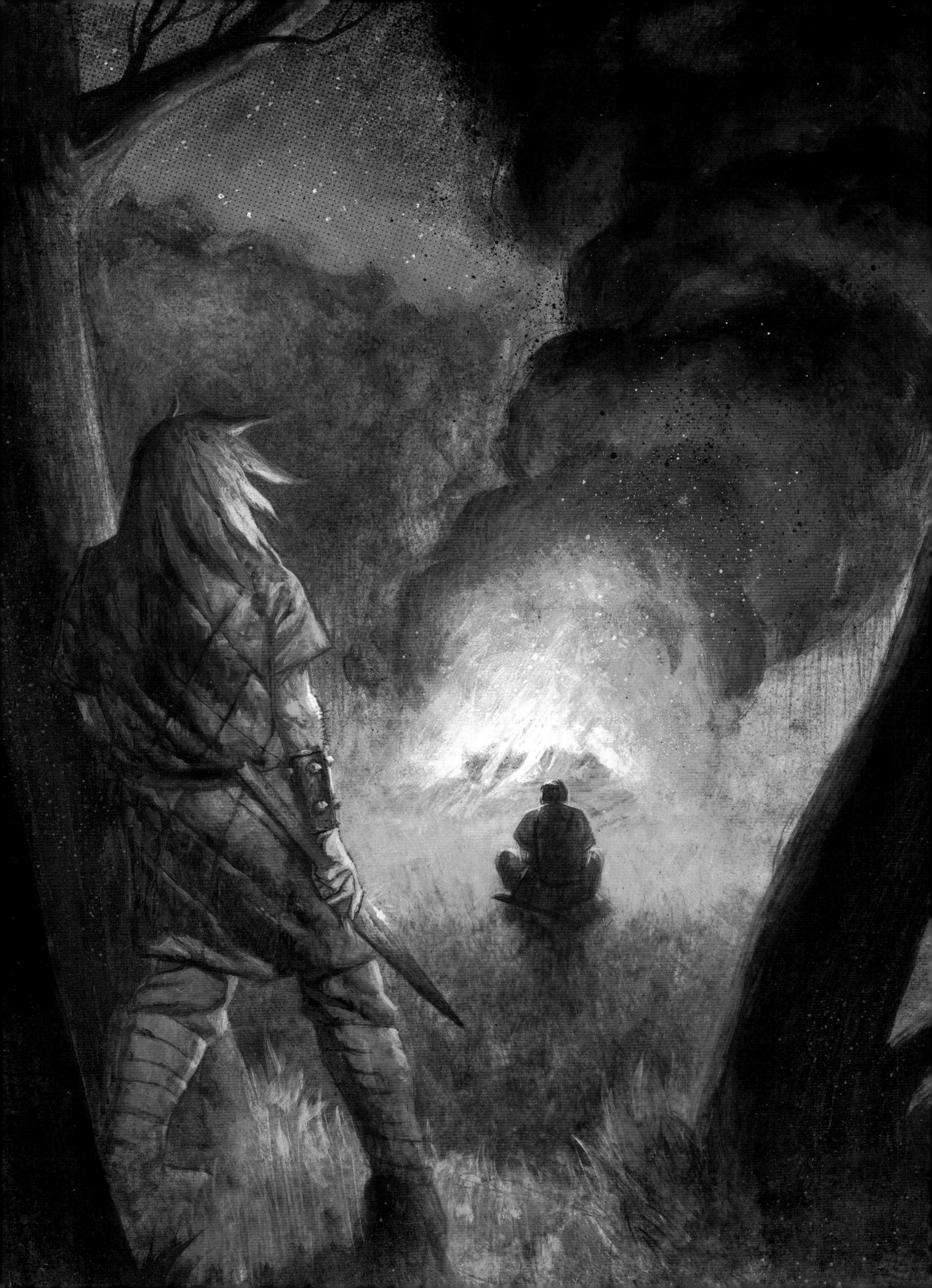

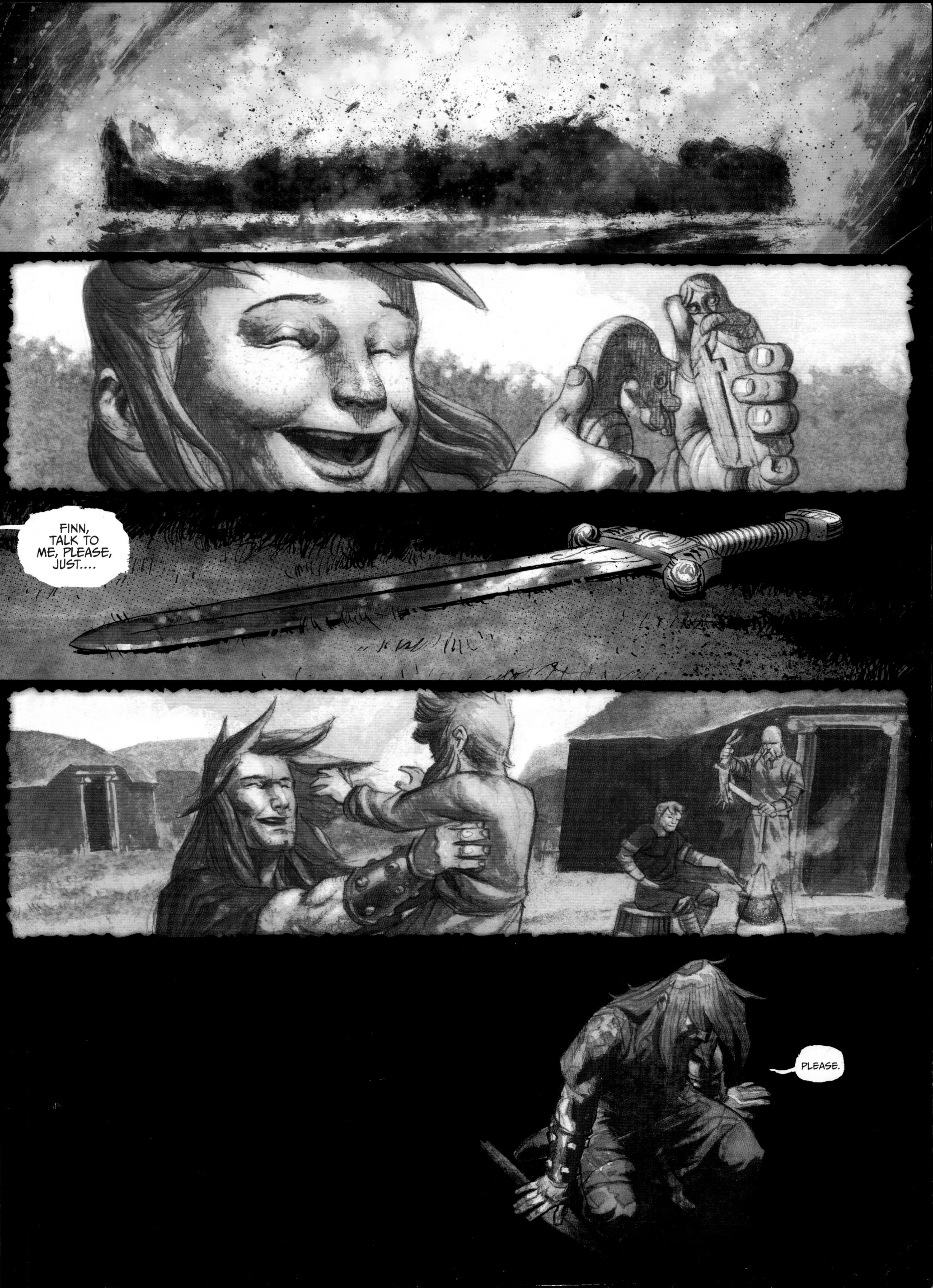
FINN, TALK TO ME, PLEASE, JUST....
PLEASE.

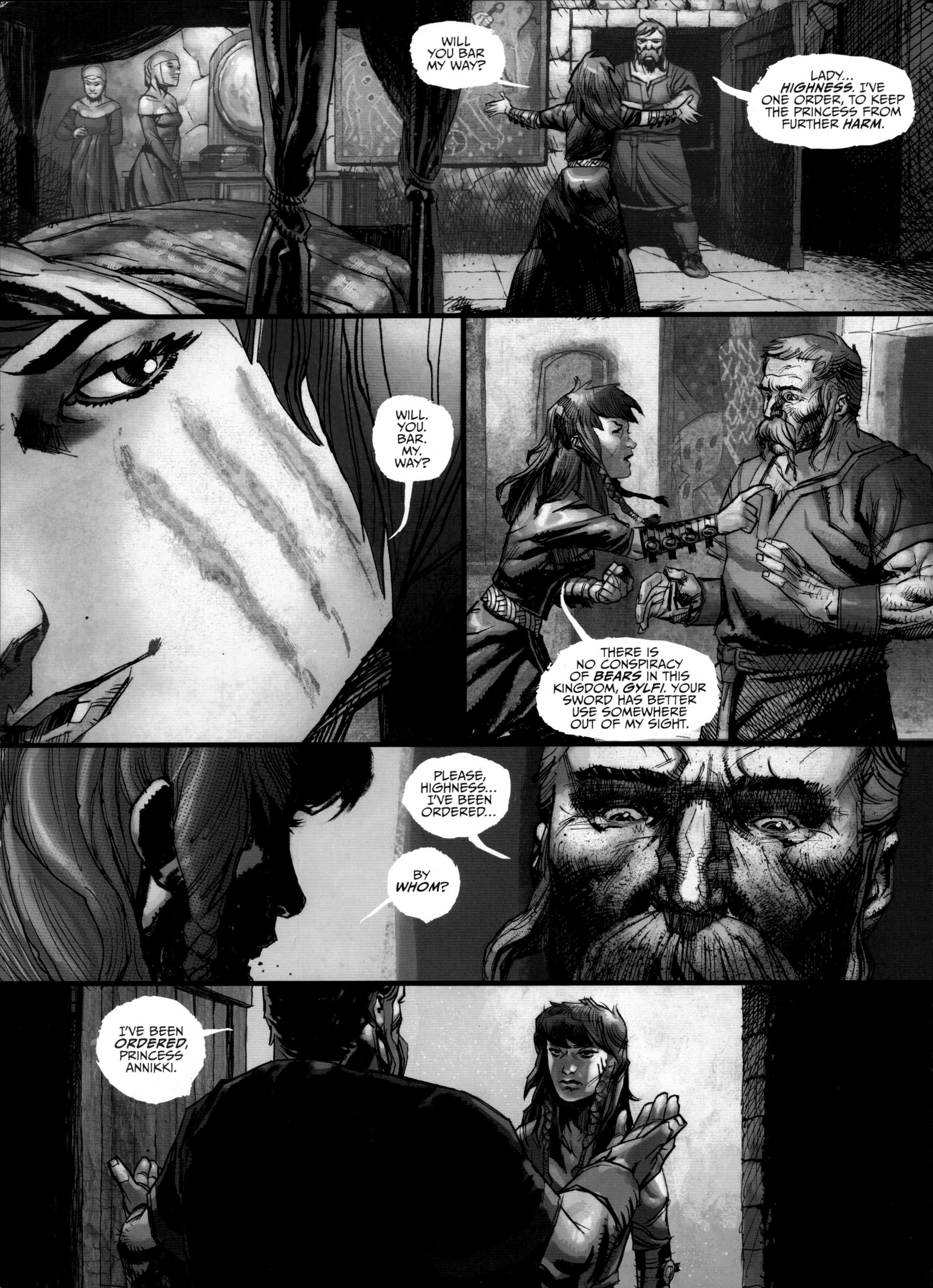
WILL YOU BAR MY WAY?
LADY... HIGHNESS. I'VE ONE ORDER, TO KEEP THE PRINCESS FROM FURTHER HARM.
WILL. YOU. BAR. MY. WAY?
THERE IS NO CONSPIRACY OF BEARS IN THIS KINGDOM, GYLFI. YOUR SWORD HAS BETTER USE SOMEWHERE OUT OF MY SIGHT.
PLEASE, HIGHNESS... I'VE BEEN ORDERED...
BY WHOM?
I'VE BEEN ORDERED, PRINCESS ANNIKKI.

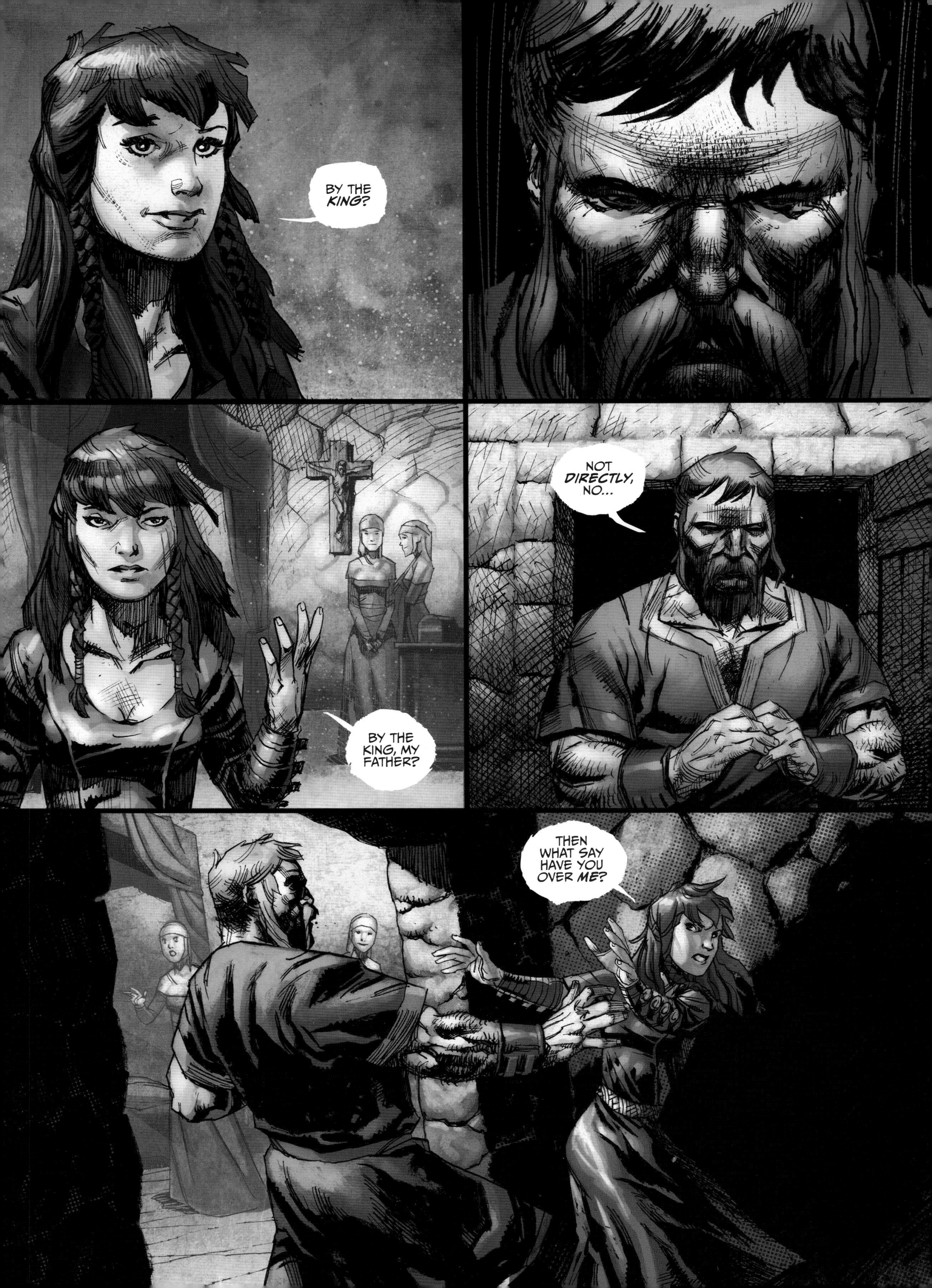
BY THE KING?
BY THE KING, MY FATHER?
NOT DIRECTLY, NO...
THEN WHAT SAY HAVE YOU OVER ME?

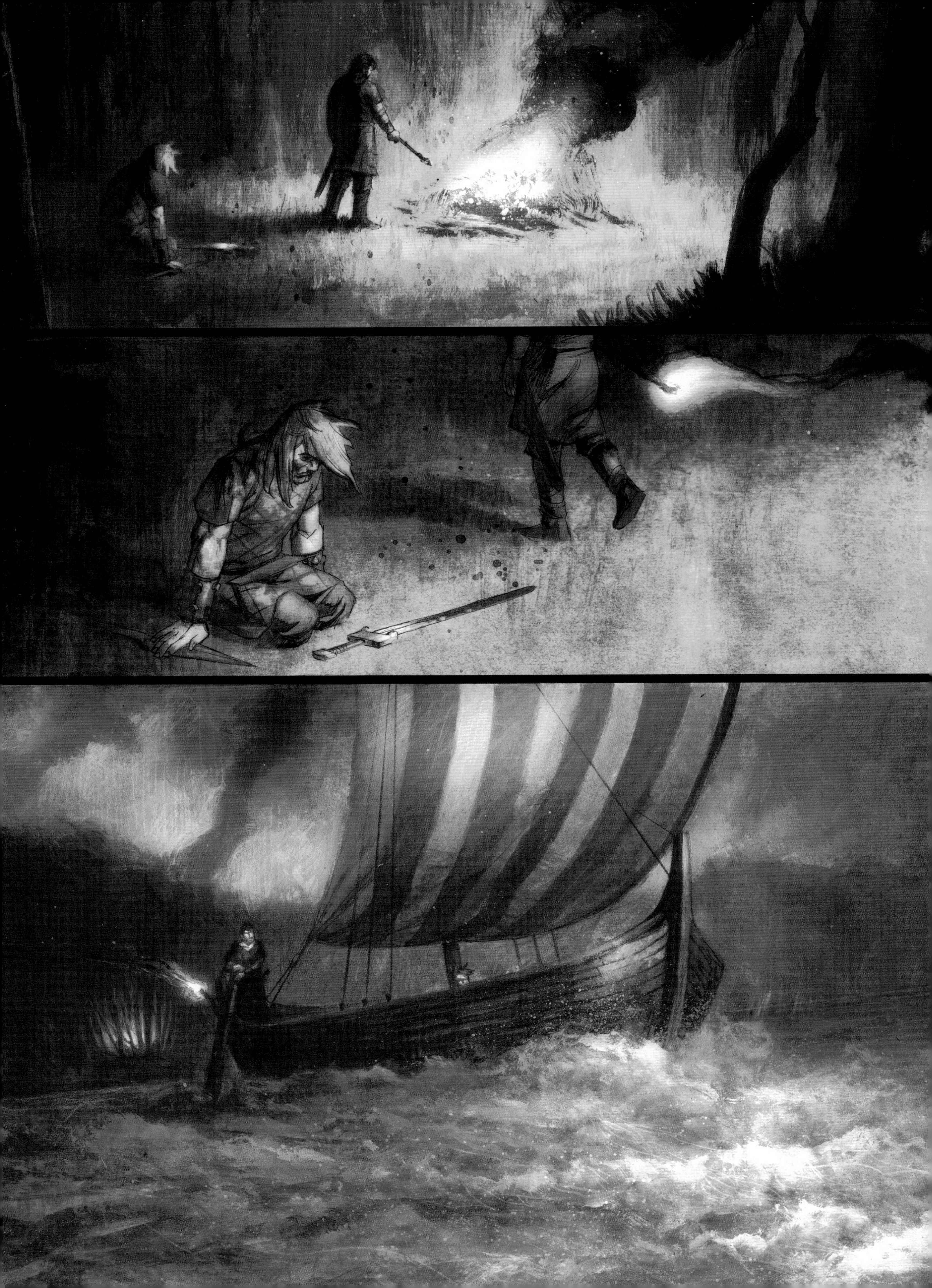

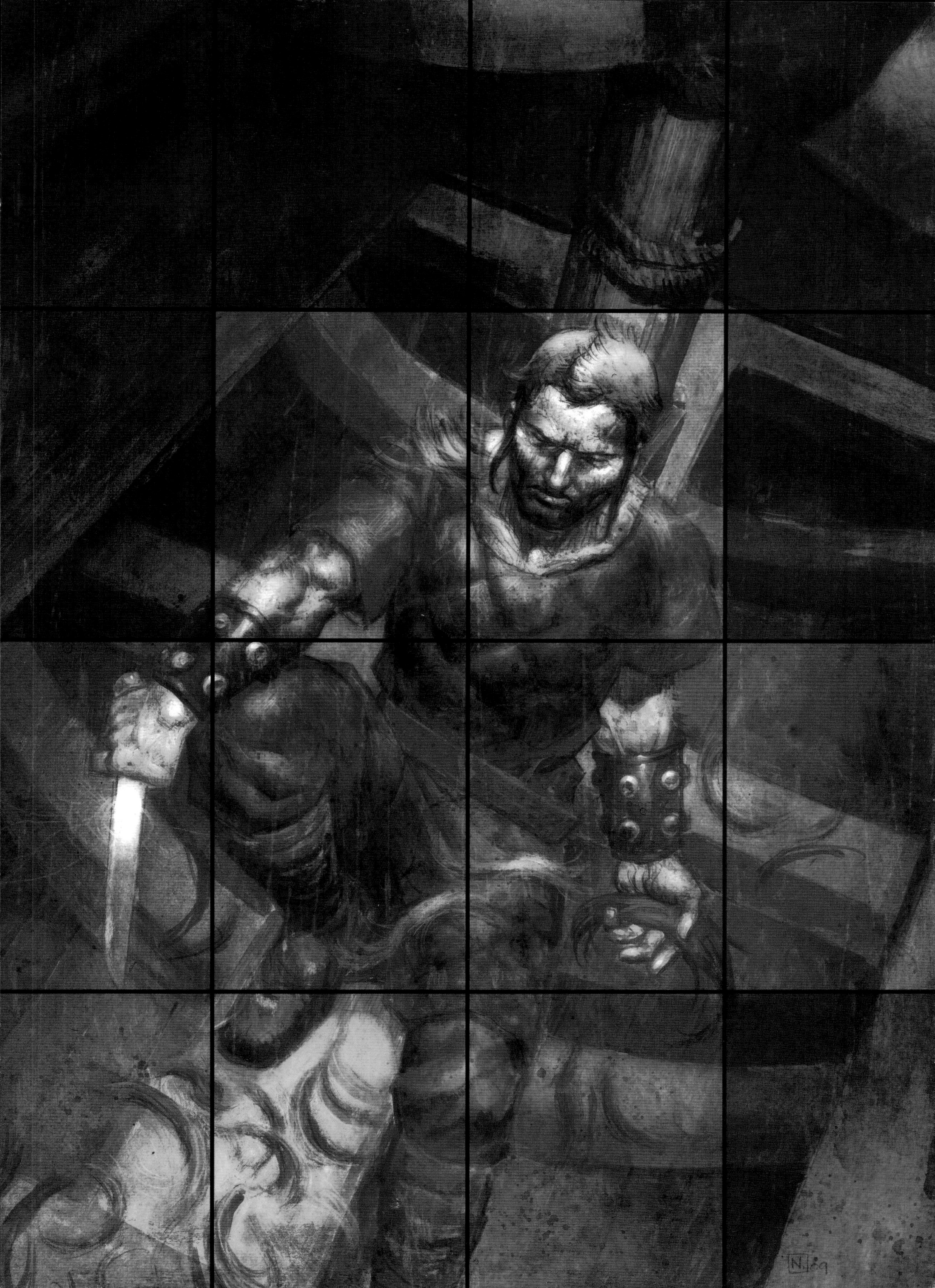

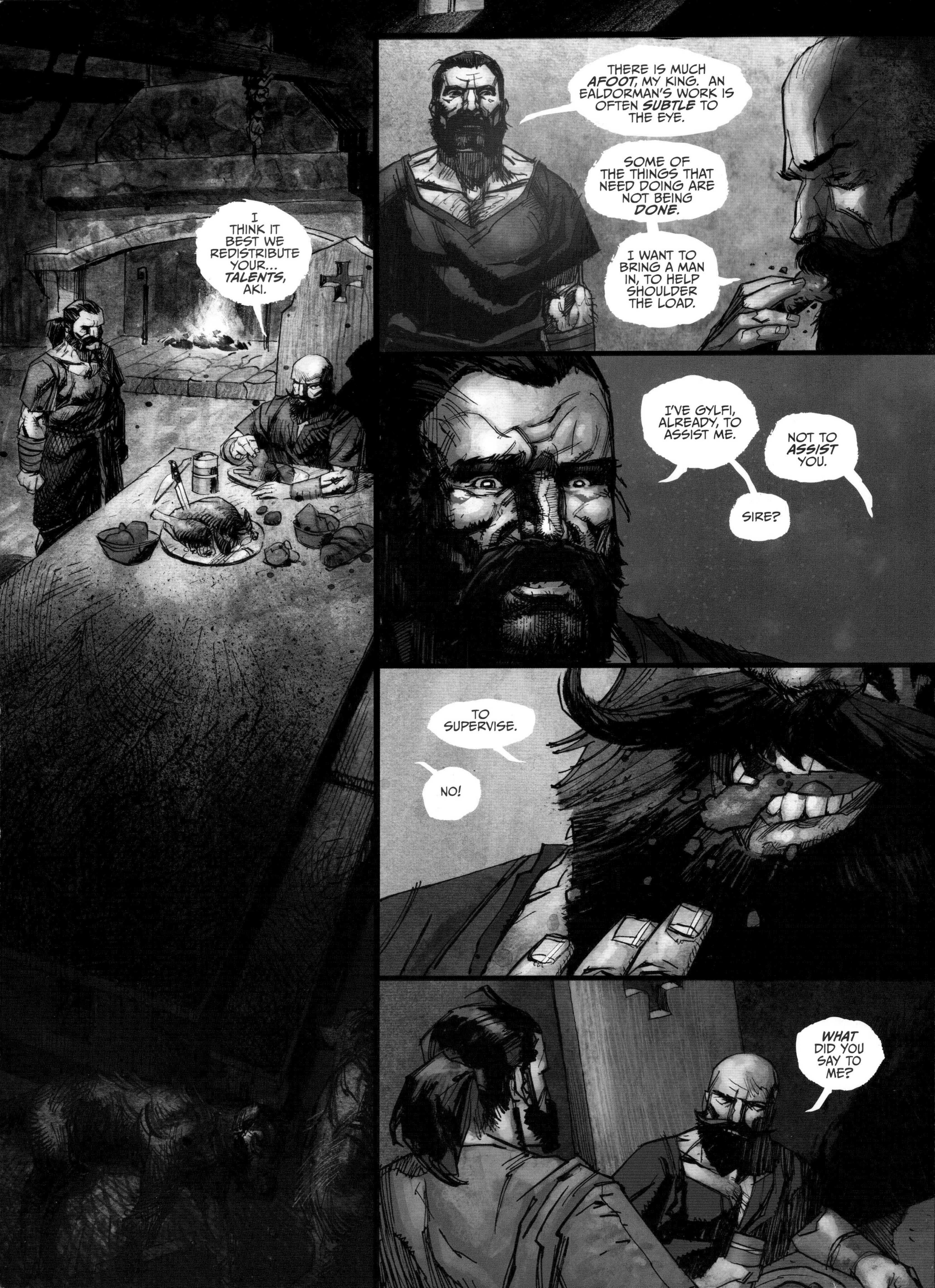

I THINK IT BEST WE REDISTRIBUTE YOUR... TALENTS, AKI.
THERE IS MUCH AFOOT, MY KING. AN EALDORMAN'S WORK IS OFTEN SUBTLE TO THE EYE.
SOME OF THE THINGS THAT NEED DOING ARE NOT BEING DONE.
I WANT TO BRING A MAN IN, TO HELP SHOULDER THE LOAD.
I'VE GYLFI, ALREADY, TO ASSIST ME.
SIRE?
NOT TO ASSIST YOU.
TO SUPERVISE.
NO!
WHAT DID YOU SAY TO ME?

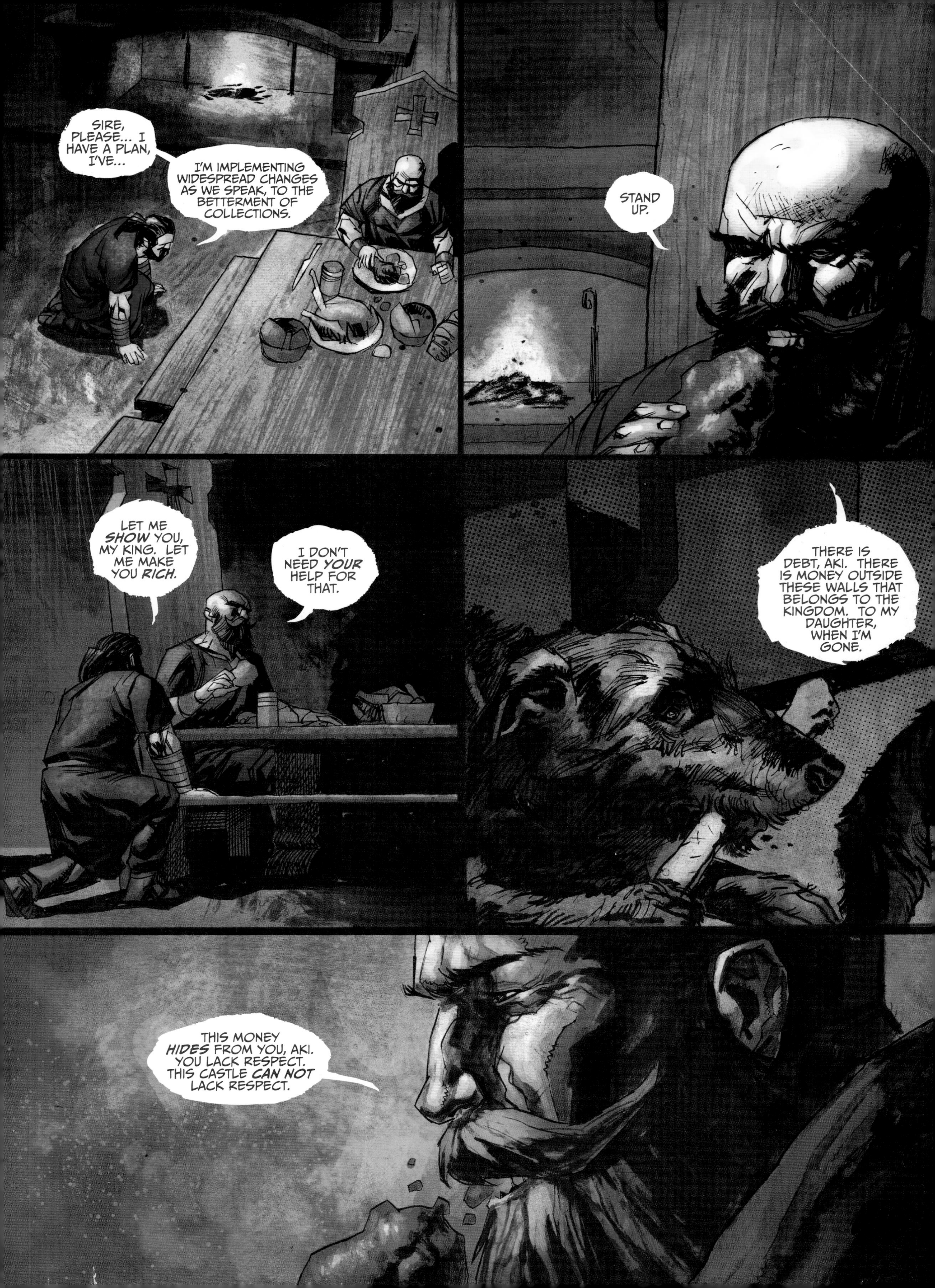
SIRE, PLEASE... I HAVE A PLAN, I'VE...
I'M IMPLEMENTING WIDESPREAD CHANGES AS WE SPEAK, TO THE BETTERMENT OF COLLECTIONS.
STAND UP.
LET ME *SHOW* YOU, MY KING. LET ME MAKE YOU *RICH*.
I DON'T NEED *YOUR* HELP FOR THAT.
THERE IS DEBT, AKI. THERE IS MONEY OUTSIDE THESE WALLS THAT BELONGS TO THE KINGDOM. TO MY DAUGHTER, WHEN I'M GONE.
THIS MONEY *HIDES* FROM YOU, AKI. YOU LACK RESPECT. THIS CASTLE *CAN NOT* LACK RESPECT.

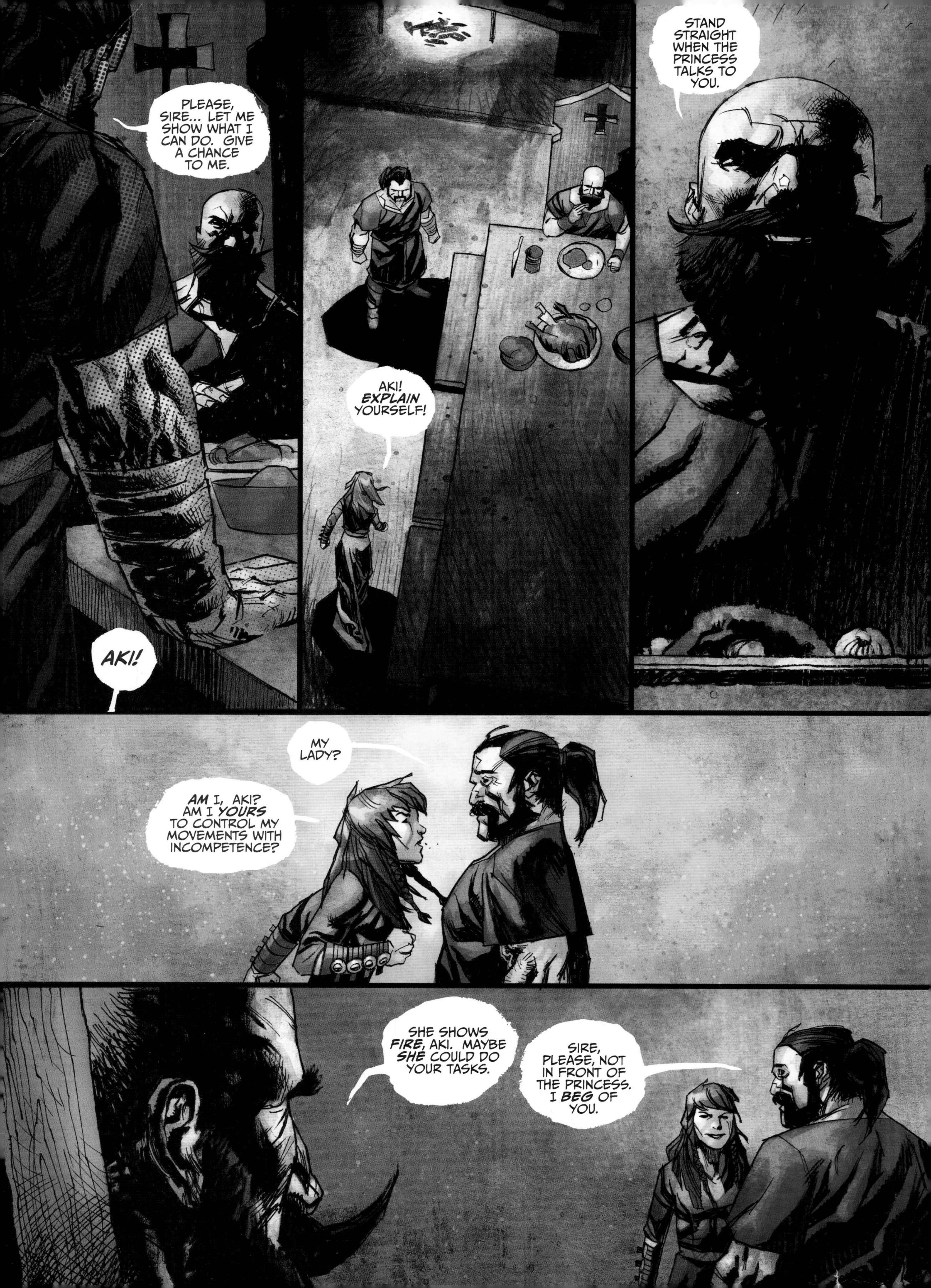

PLEASE, SIRE... LET ME SHOW WHAT I CAN DO. GIVE A CHANCE TO ME.
AKI!
AKI! EXPLAIN YOURSELF!
STAND STRAIGHT WHEN THE PRINCESS TALKS TO YOU.
MY LADY?
AM I, AKI? AM I YOURS TO CONTROL MY MOVEMENTS WITH INCOMPETENCE?
SHE SHOWS FIRE, AKI. MAYBE SHE COULD DO YOUR TASKS.
SIRE, PLEASE, NOT IN FRONT OF THE PRINCESS. I BEG OF YOU.

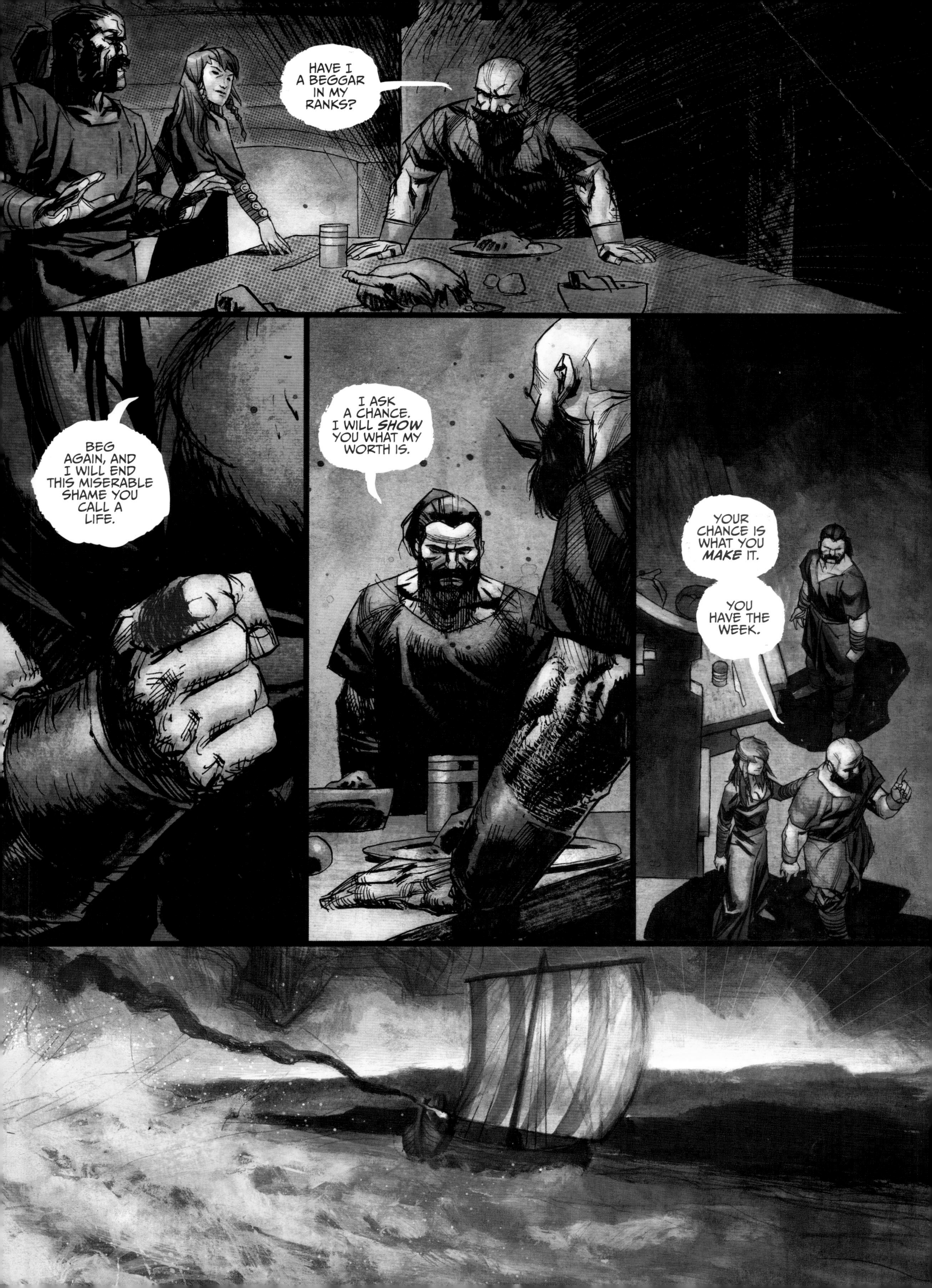
HAVE I A BEGGAR IN MY RANKS?
BEG AGAIN, AND I WILL END THIS MISERABLE SHAME YOU CALL A LIFE.
I ASK A CHANCE. I WILL SHOW YOU WHAT MY WORTH IS.
YOUR CHANCE IS WHAT YOU MAKE IT.
YOU HAVE THE WEEK.

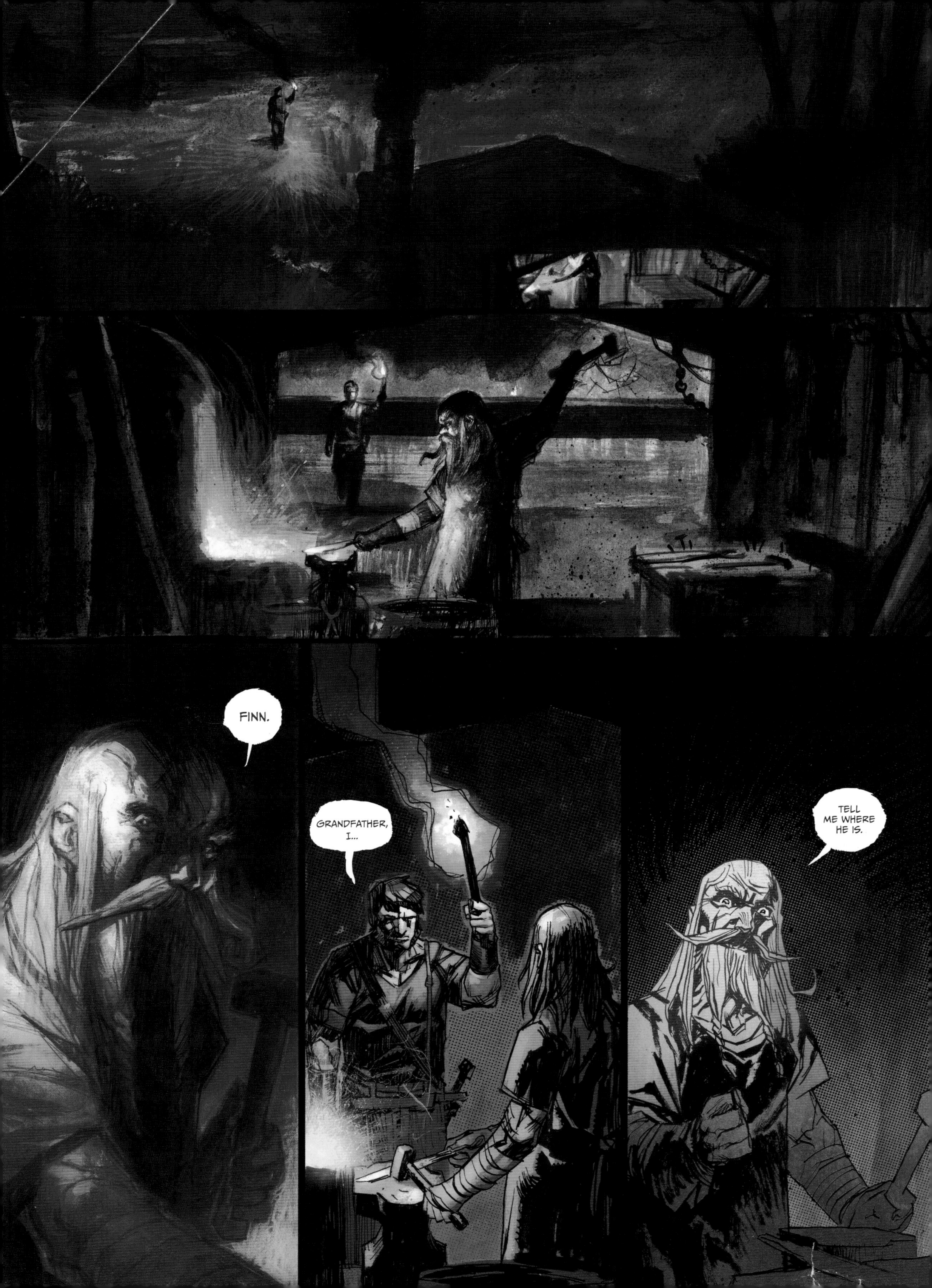
FINN.
GRANDFATHER, I...
TELL ME WHERE HE IS.

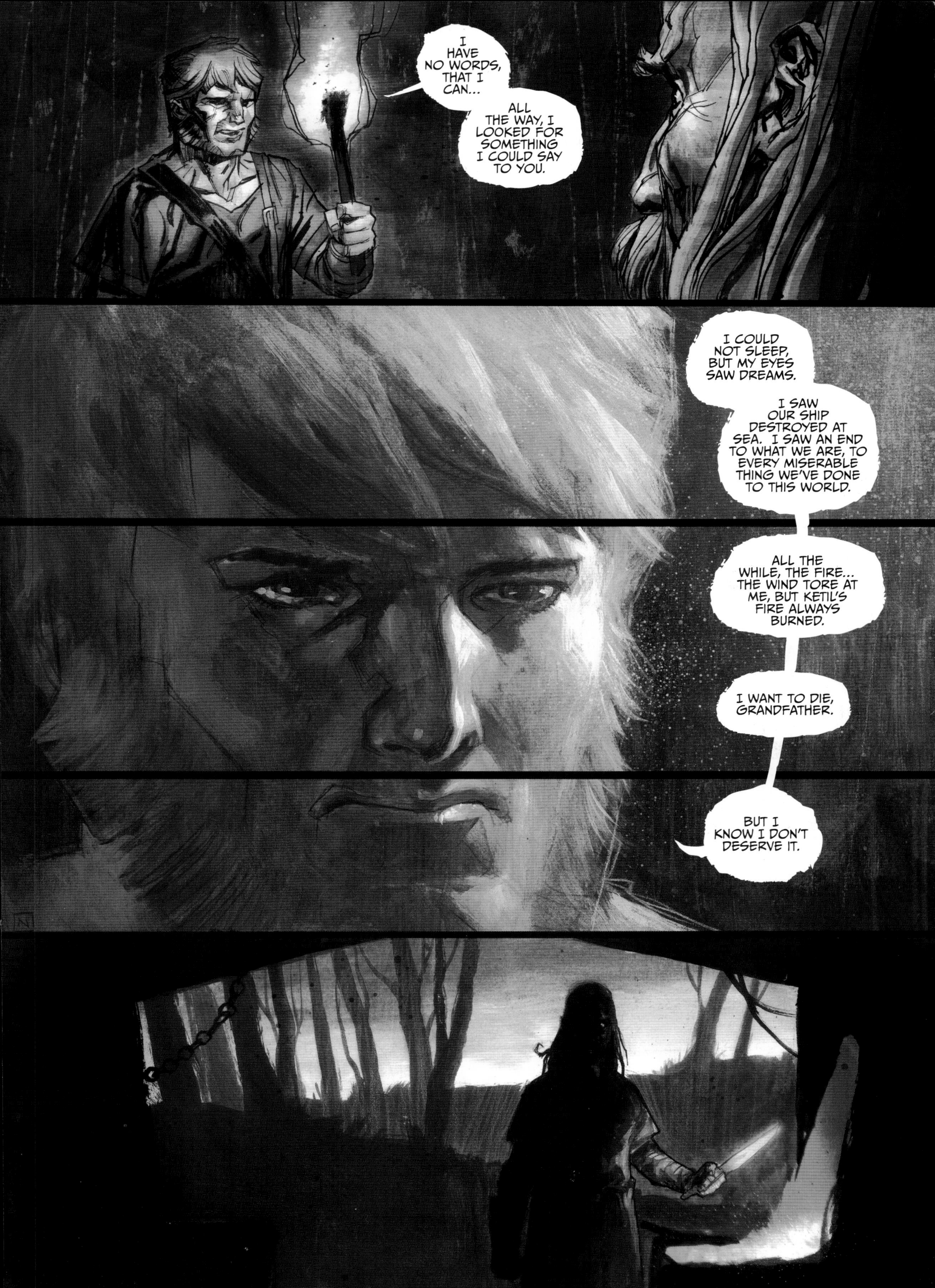
I HAVE NO WORDS, THAT I CAN...
ALL THE WAY, I LOOKED FOR SOMETHING I COULD SAY TO YOU.
I COULD NOT SLEEP, BUT MY EYES SAW DREAMS.
I SAW OUR SHIP DESTROYED AT SEA. I SAW AN END TO WHAT WE ARE, TO EVERY MISERABLE THING WE'VE DONE TO THIS WORLD.
ALL THE WHILE, THE FIRE... THE WIND TORE AT ME, BUT KETIL'S FIRE ALWAYS BURNED.
I WANT TO DIE, GRANDFATHER.
BUT I KNOW I DON'T DESERVE IT.

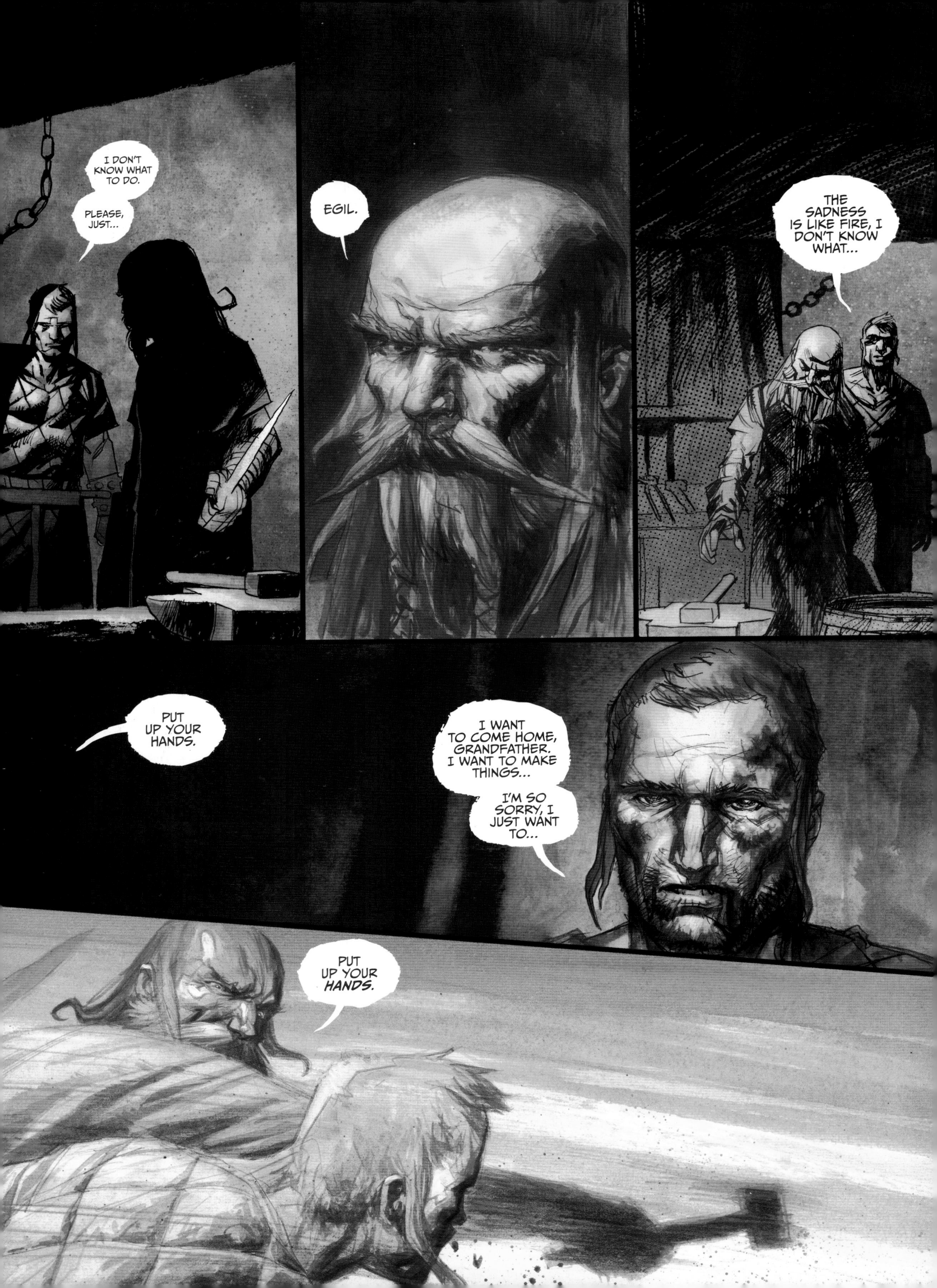
I DON'T KNOW WHAT TO DO.
PLEASE, JUST...
EGIL.
THE SADNESS IS LIKE FIRE, I DON'T KNOW WHAT...
PUT UP YOUR HANDS.
I WANT TO COME HOME, GRANDFATHER. I WANT TO MAKE THINGS...
I'M SO SORRY, I JUST WANT TO...
PUT UP YOUR *HANDS*.

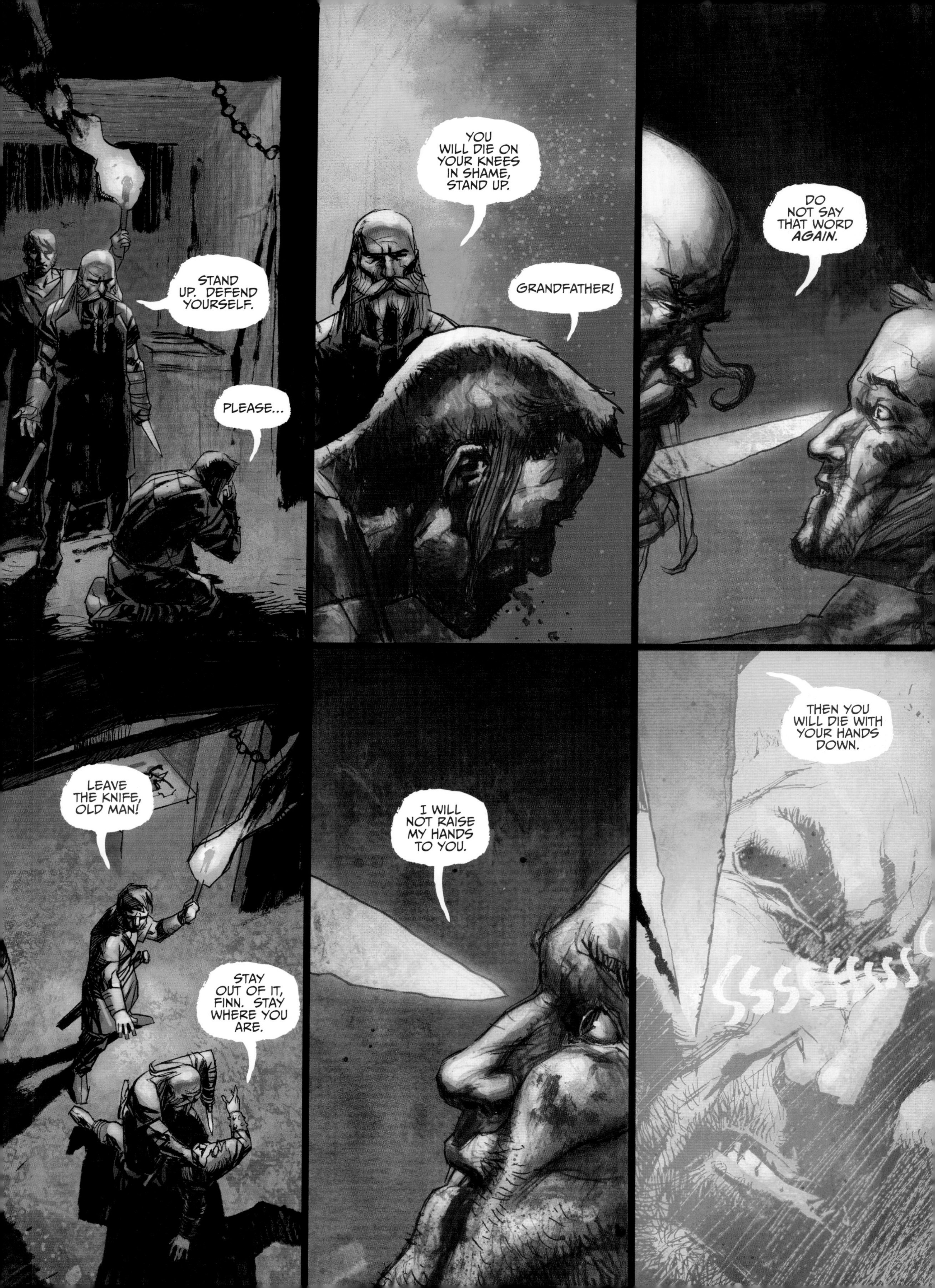
STAND UP. DEFEND YOURSELF.
PLEASE...
YOU WILL DIE ON YOUR KNEES IN SHAME, STAND UP.
GRANDFATHER!
DO NOT SAY THAT WORD *AGAIN.*
LEAVE THE KNIFE, OLD MAN!
STAY OUT OF IT, FINN. STAY WHERE YOU ARE.
I WILL NOT RAISE MY HANDS TO YOU.
THEN YOU WILL DIE WITH YOUR HANDS DOWN.

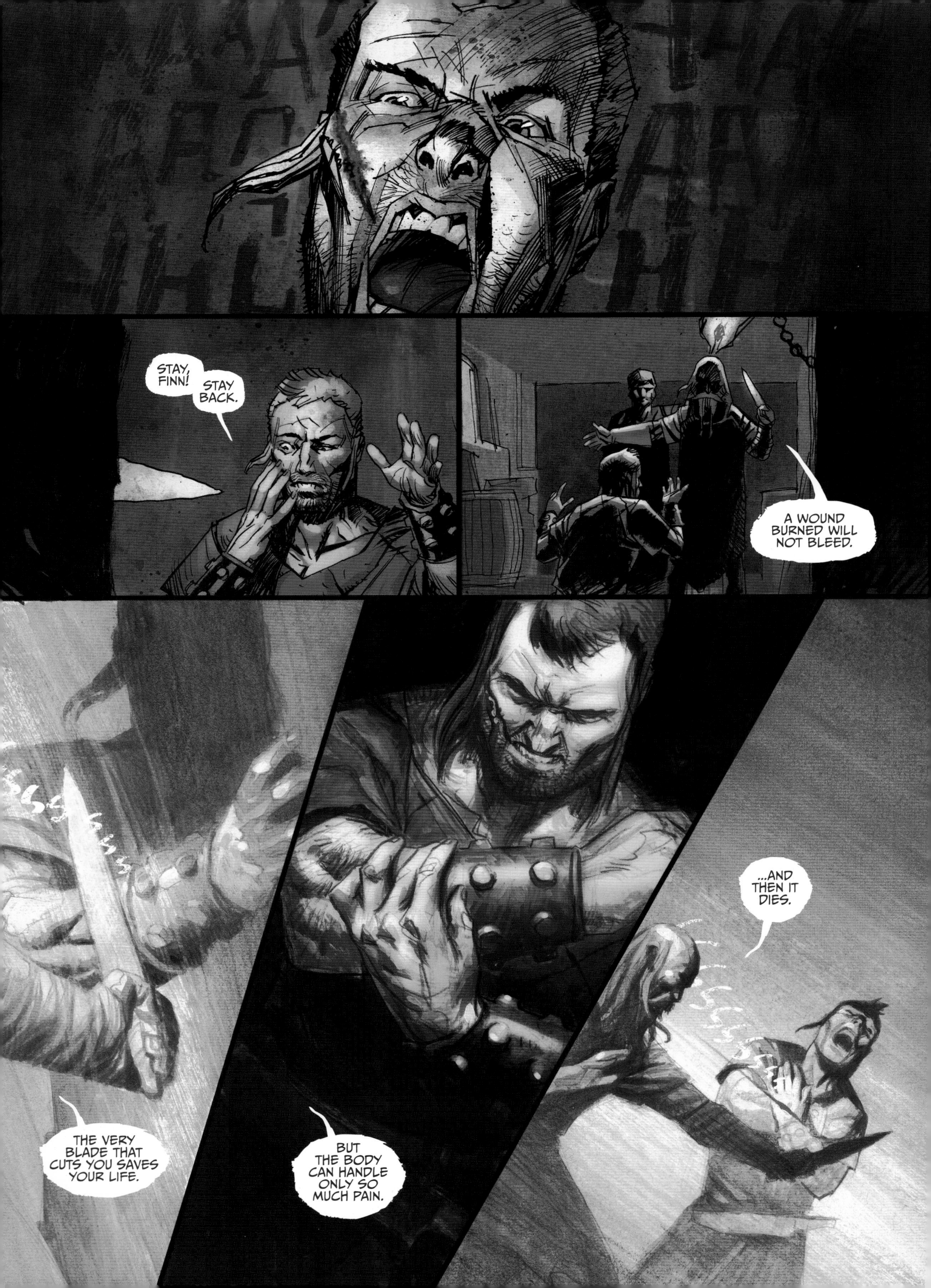
STAY, FINN!
STAY BACK.
A WOUND BURNED WILL NOT BLEED.
THE VERY BLADE THAT CUTS YOU SAVES YOUR LIFE.
BUT THE BODY CAN HANDLE ONLY SO MUCH PAIN.
...AND THEN IT DIES.

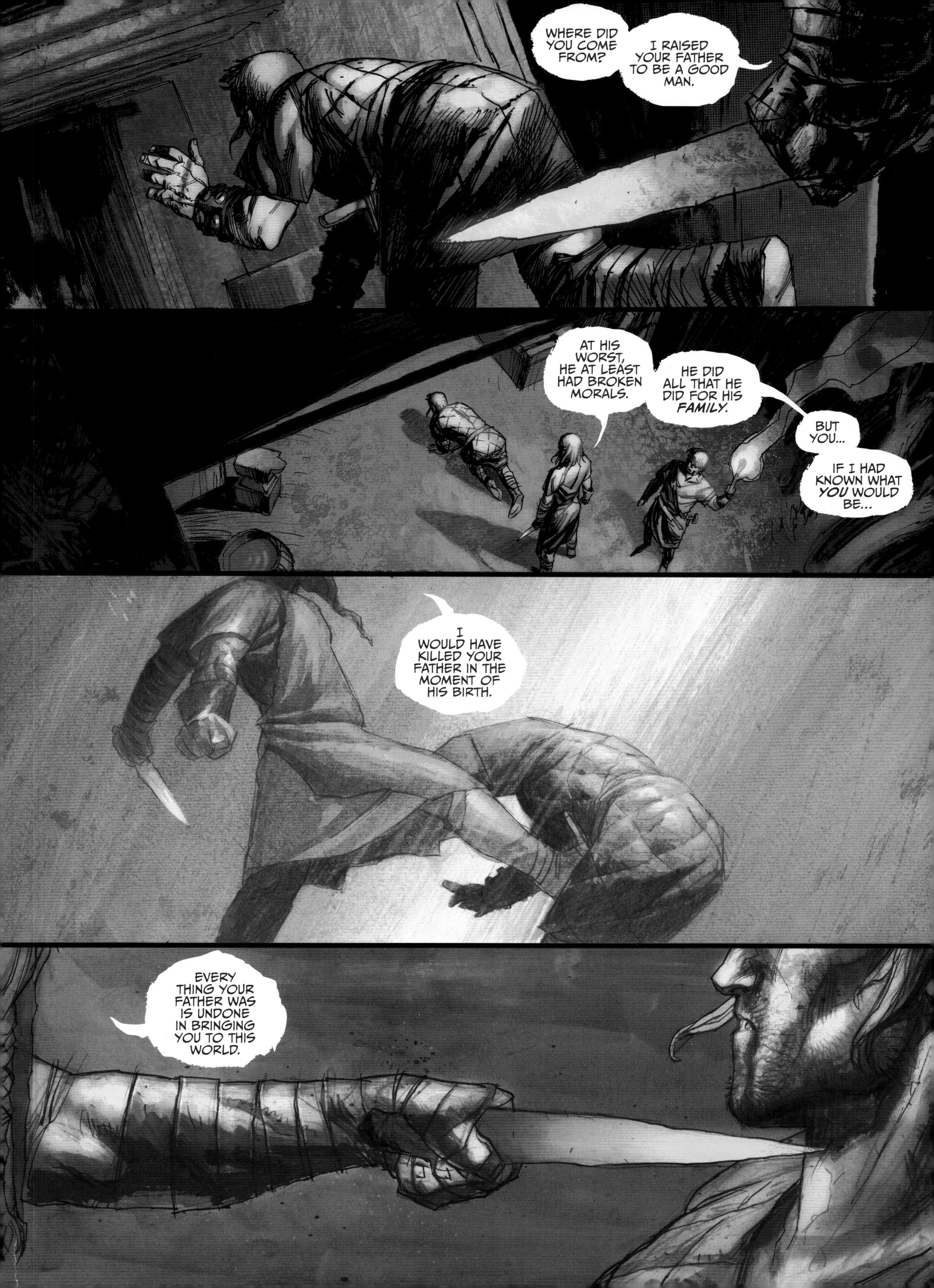

WHERE DID YOU COME FROM?
I RAISED YOUR FATHER TO BE A GOOD MAN.
AT HIS WORST, HE AT LEAST HAD BROKEN MORALS.
HE DID ALL THAT HE DID FOR HIS *FAMILY.*
BUT YOU...
IF I HAD KNOWN WHAT *YOU* WOULD BE...
I WOULD HAVE KILLED YOUR FATHER IN THE MOMENT OF HIS BIRTH.
EVERY THING YOUR FATHER WAS IS UNDONE IN BRINGING YOU TO THIS WORLD.

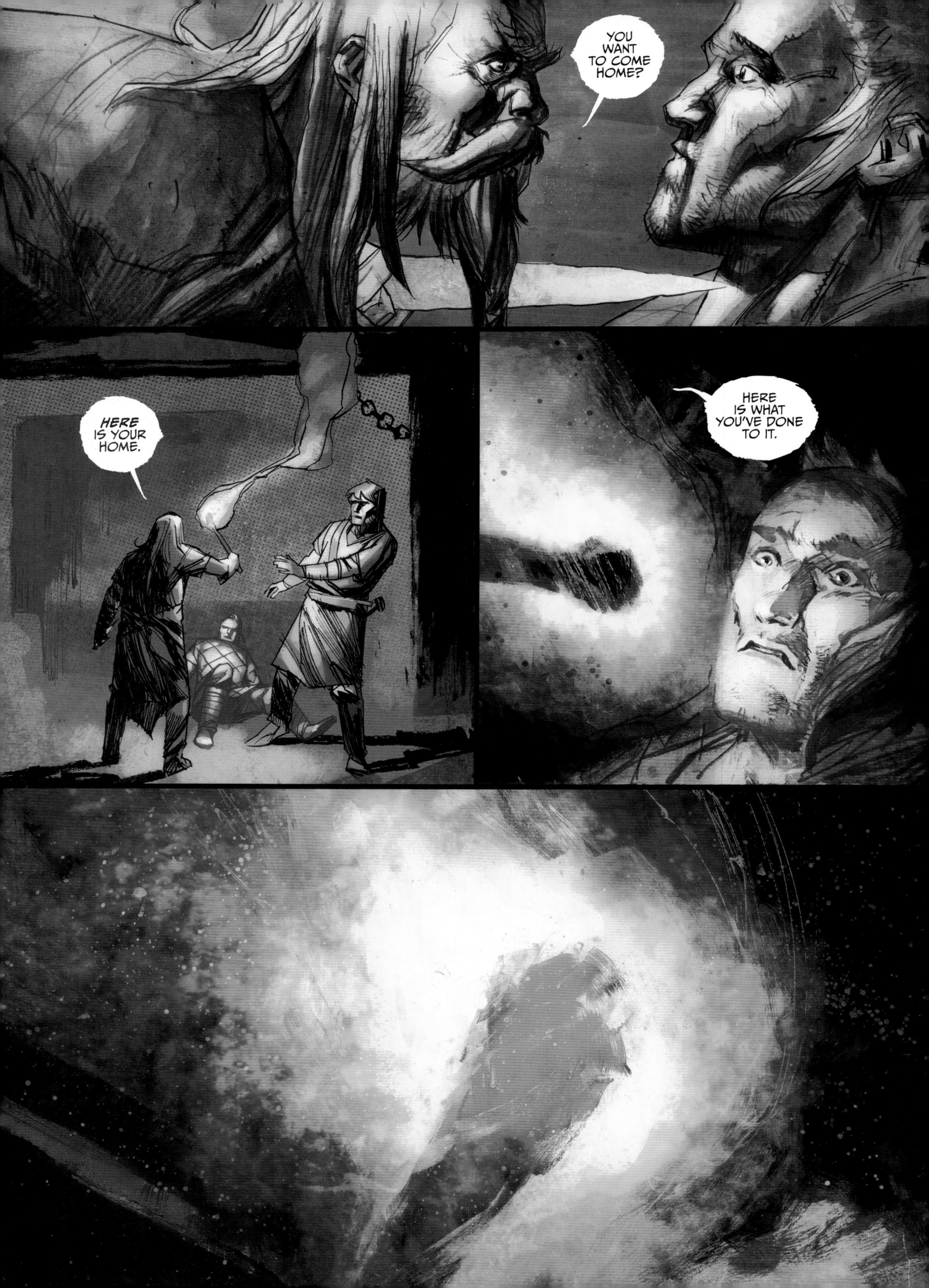
YOU WANT TO COME HOME?
HERE IS YOUR HOME.
HERE IS WHAT YOU'VE DONE TO IT.

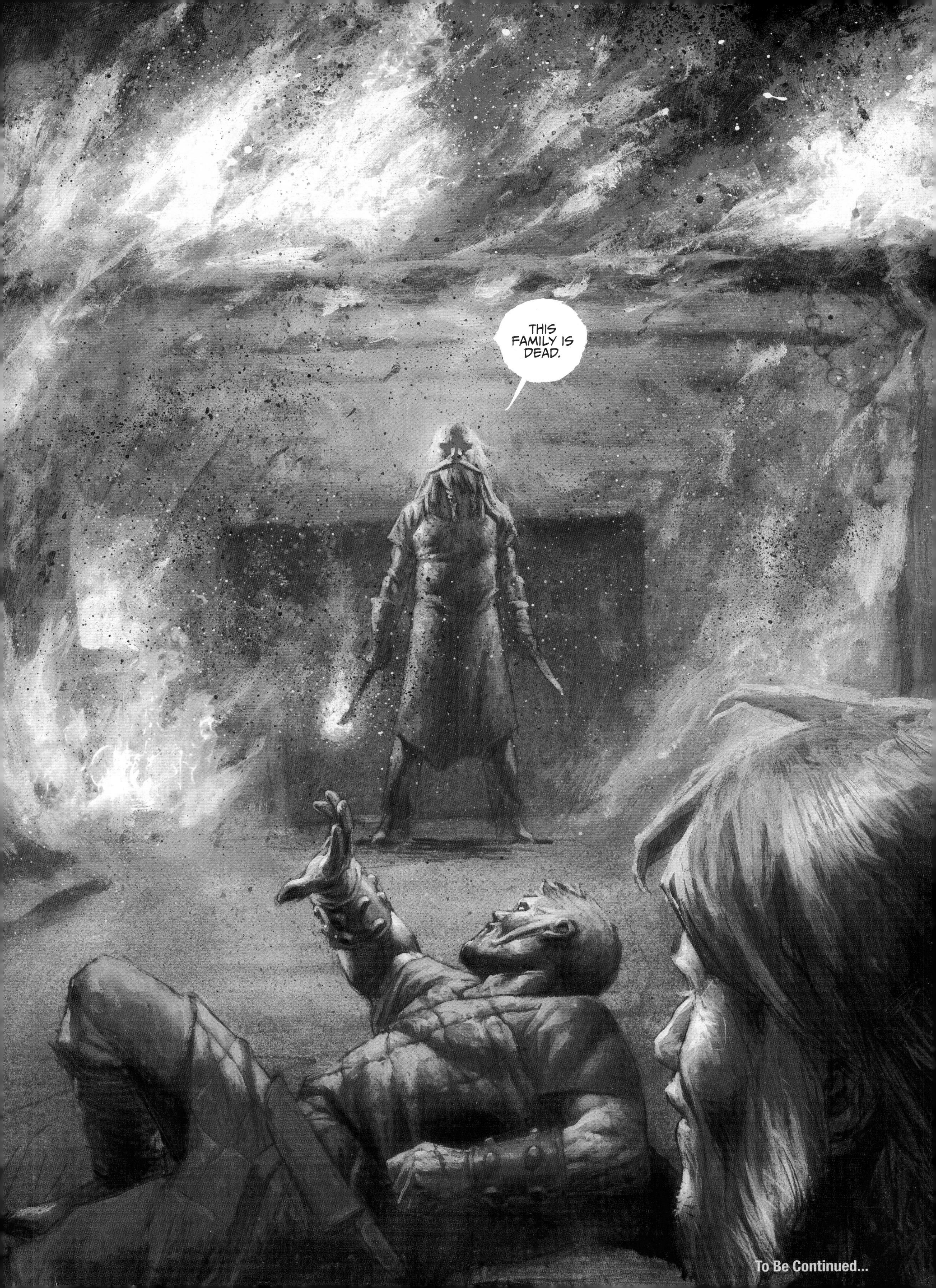
THIS FAMILY IS DEAD.
To Be Continued...

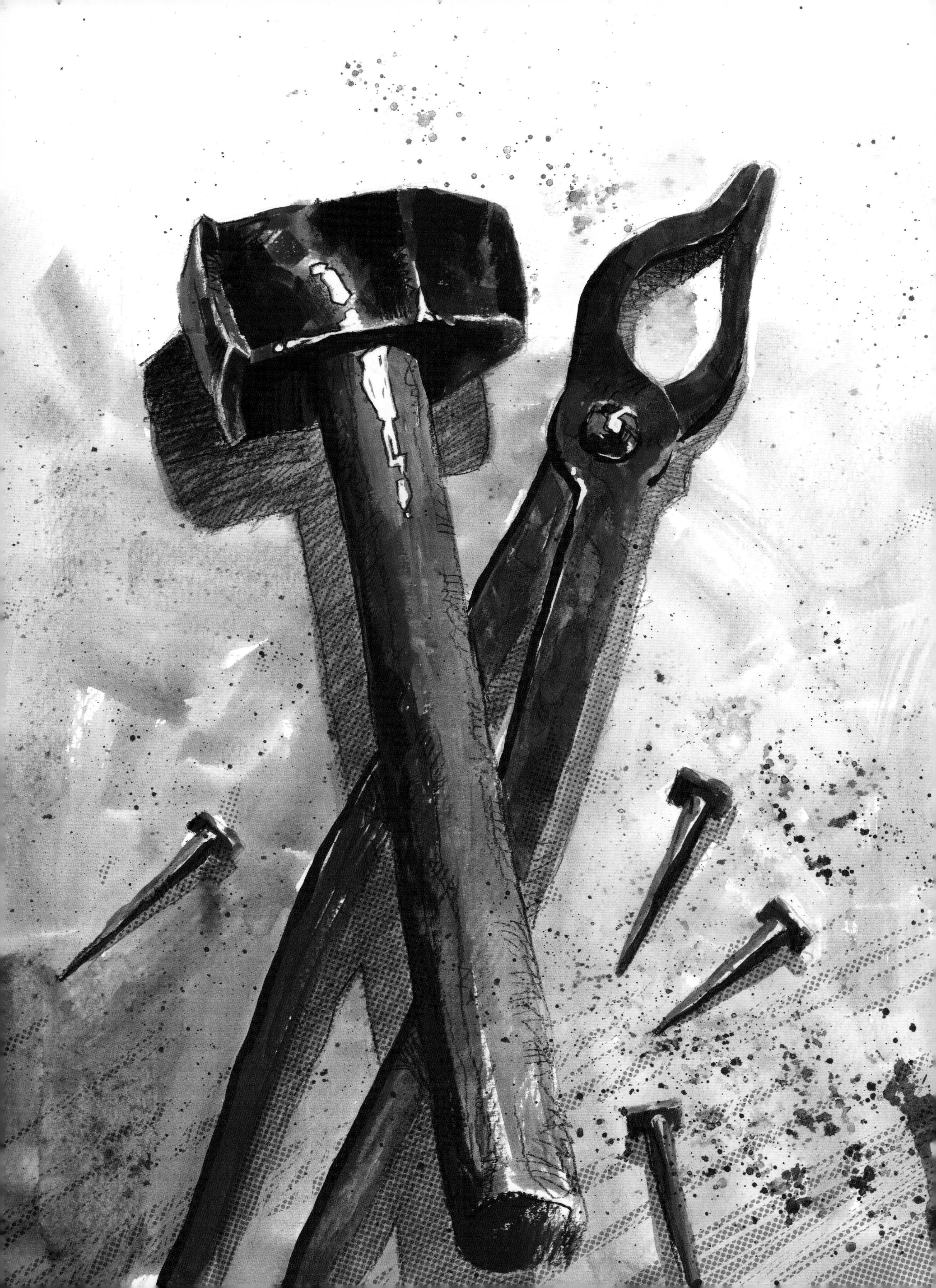

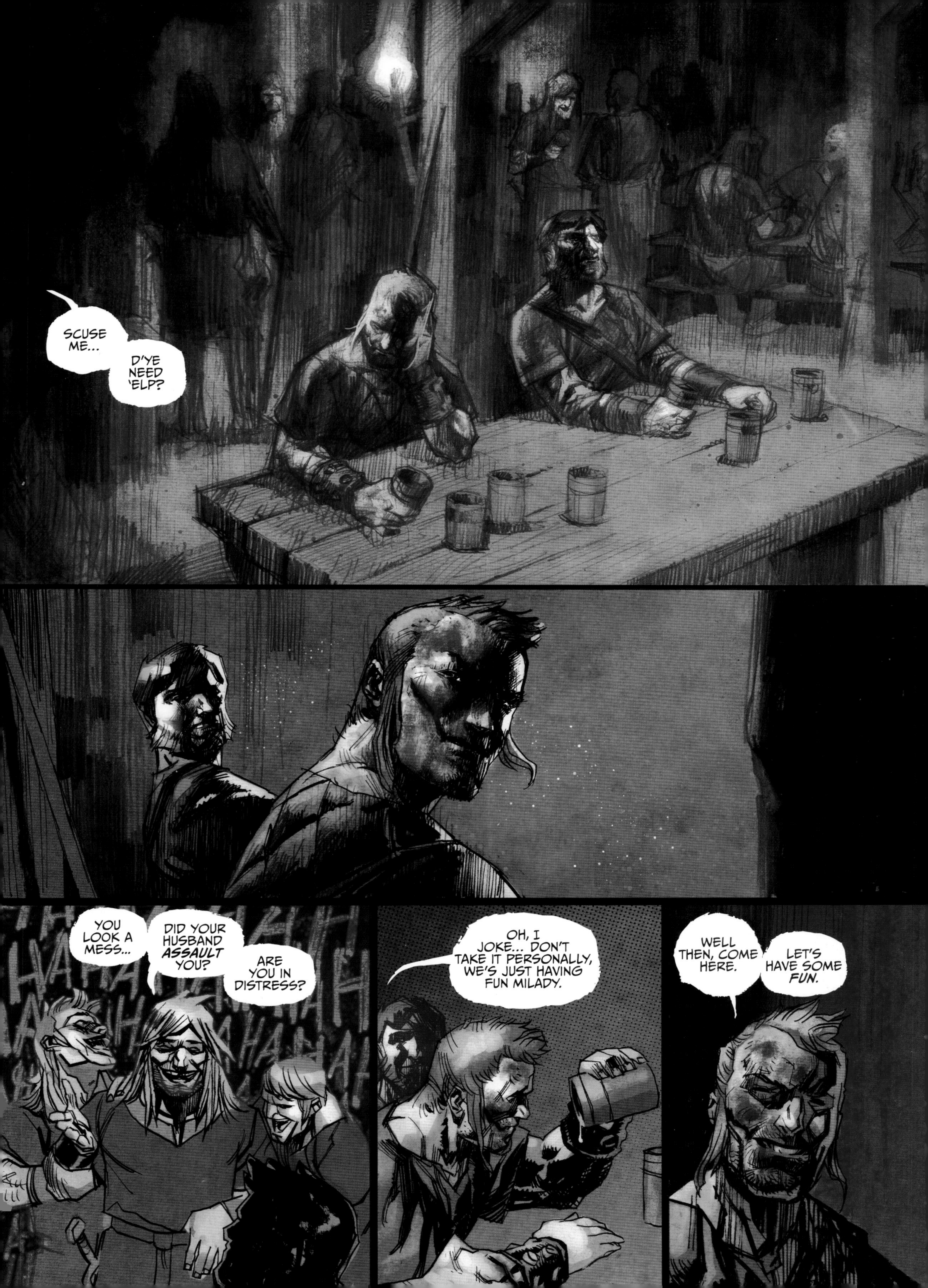
SCUSE ME...
D'YE NEED 'ELP?
YOU LOOK A MESS...
DID YOUR HUSBAND ASSAULT YOU?
ARE YOU IN DISTRESS?
OH, I JOKE... DON'T TAKE IT PERSONALLY, WE'S JUST HAVING FUN MILADY.
WELL THEN, COME HERE.
LET'S HAVE SOME FUN.

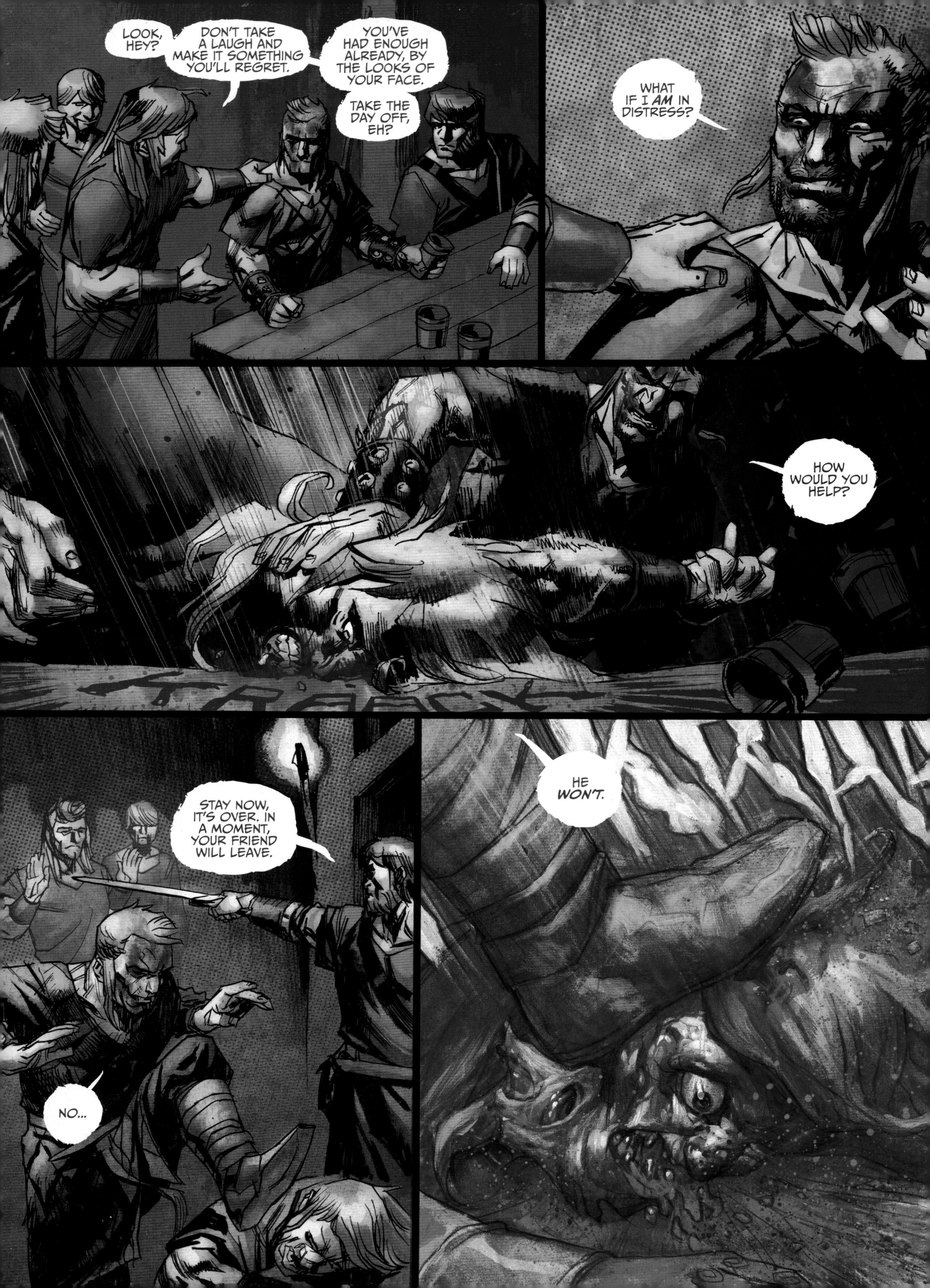
LOOK, HEY?
DON'T TAKE A LAUGH AND MAKE IT SOMETHING YOU'LL REGRET.
YOU'VE HAD ENOUGH ALREADY, BY THE LOOKS OF YOUR FACE.
TAKE THE DAY OFF, EH?
WHAT IF I *AM* IN DISTRESS?
HOW WOULD YOU HELP?
STAY NOW, IT'S OVER. IN A MOMENT, YOUR FRIEND WILL LEAVE.
NO...
HE *WON'T*.

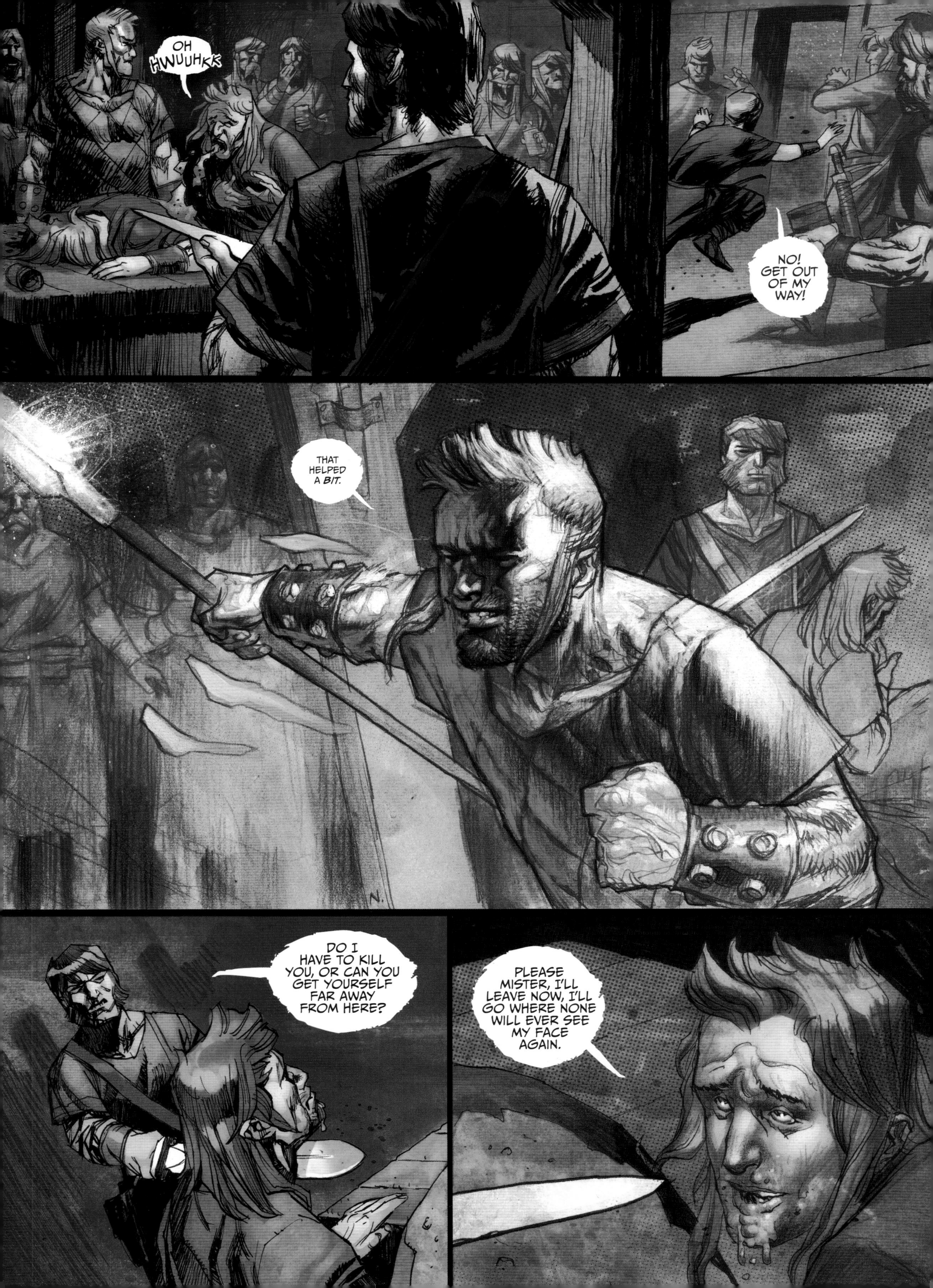

OH HWUUHKK
NO! GET OUT OF MY WAY!
THAT HELPED A *BIT*.
DO I HAVE TO KILL YOU, OR CAN YOU GET YOURSELF FAR AWAY FROM HERE?
PLEASE MISTER, I'LL LEAVE NOW, I'LL GO WHERE NONE WILL EVER SEE MY FACE AGAIN.

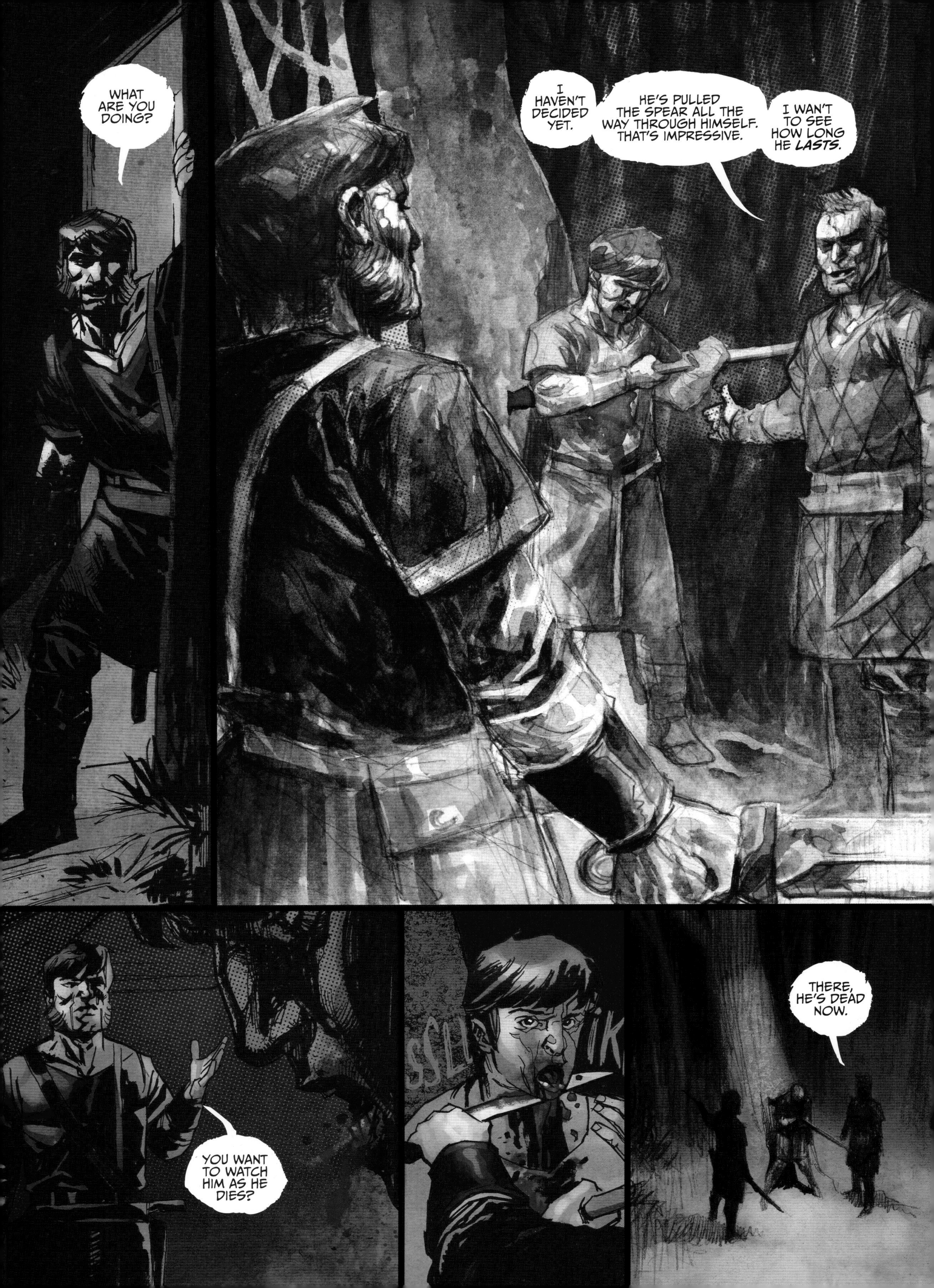
WHAT ARE YOU DOING?
I HAVEN'T DECIDED YET.
HE'S PULLED THE SPEAR ALL THE WAY THROUGH HIMSELF. THAT'S IMPRESSIVE.
I WAN'T TO SEE HOW LONG HE *LASTS*.
YOU WANT TO WATCH HIM AS HE DIES?
THERE, HE'S DEAD NOW.

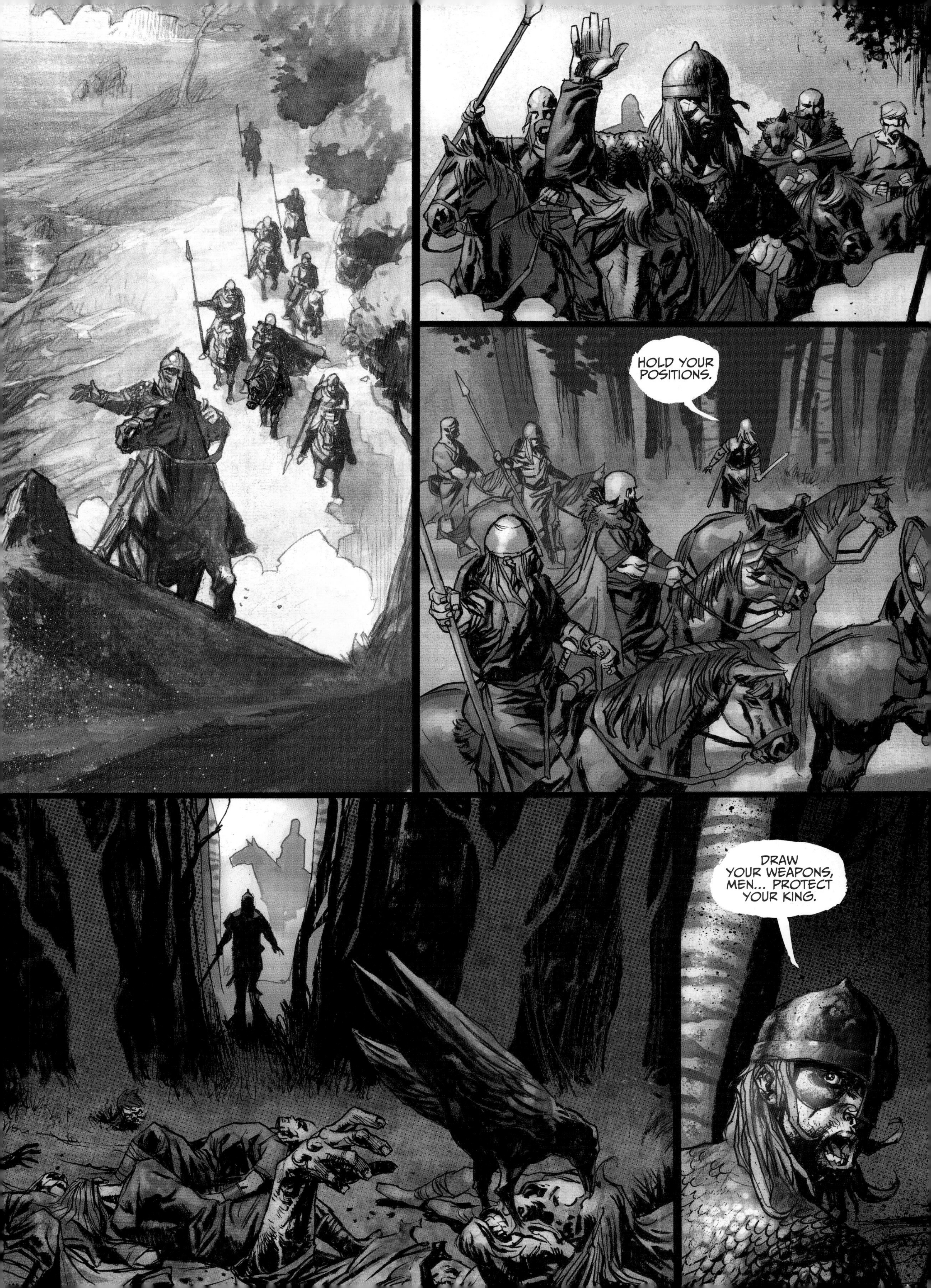
HOLD YOUR POSITIONS.
DRAW YOUR WEAPONS, MEN... PROTECT YOUR KING.

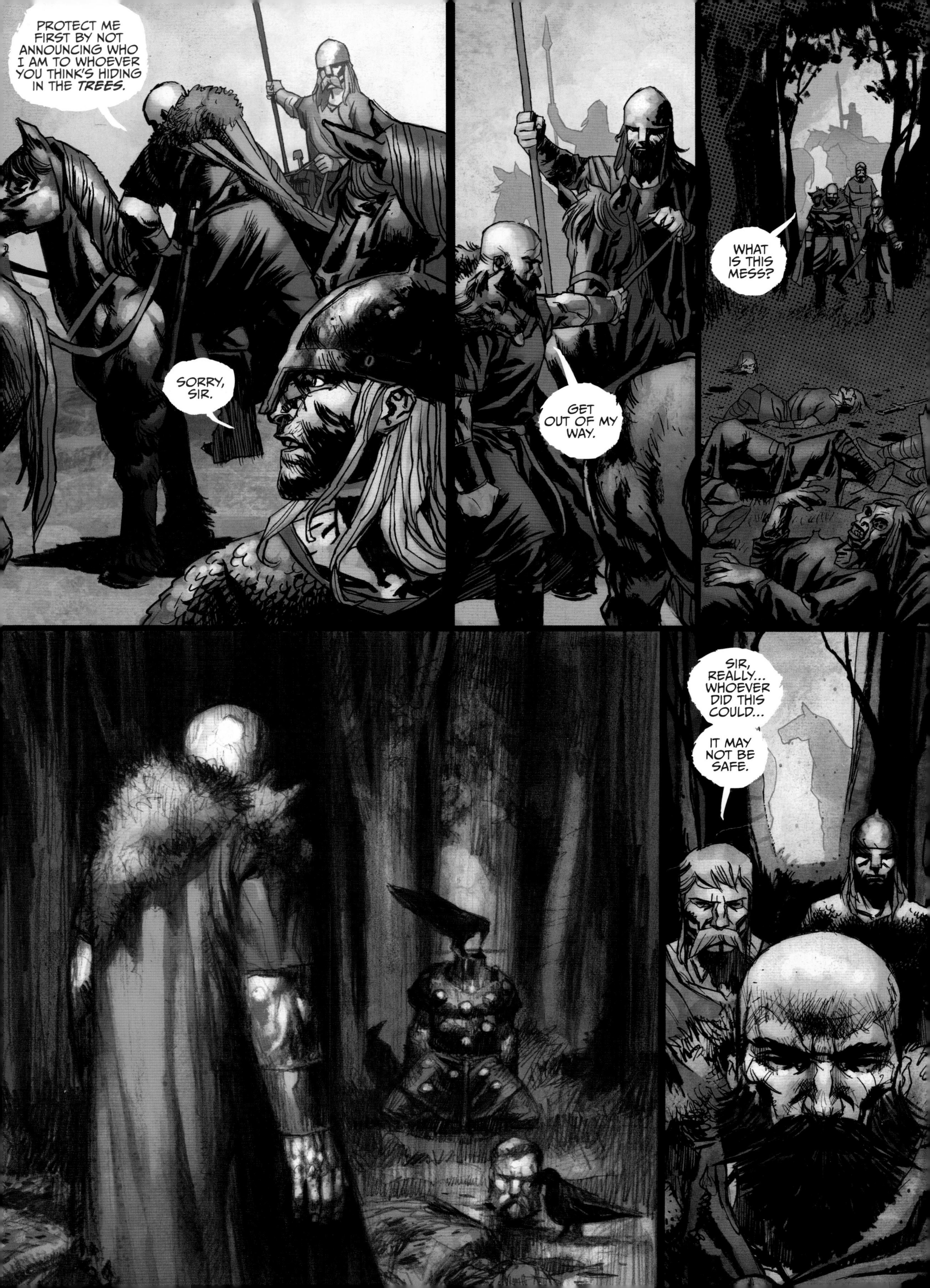
PROTECT ME FIRST BY NOT ANNOUNCING WHO I AM TO WHOEVER YOU THINK'S HIDING IN THE *TREES*.
SORRY, SIR.
GET OUT OF MY WAY.
WHAT IS THIS MESS?
SIR, REALLY... WHOEVER DID THIS COULD...
IT MAY NOT BE SAFE.

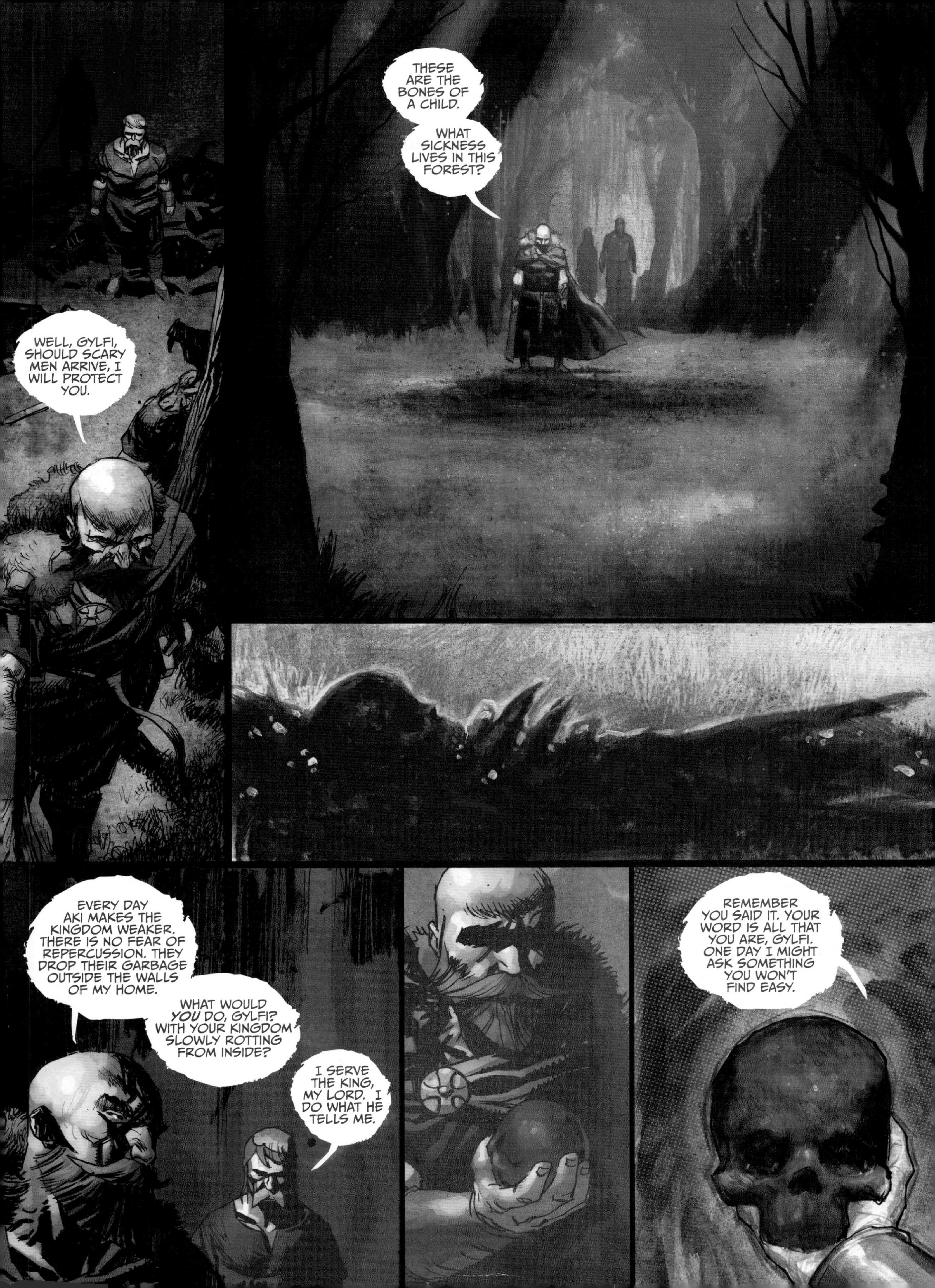
WELL, GYLFI, SHOULD SCARY MEN ARRIVE, I WILL PROTECT YOU.
THESE ARE THE BONES OF A CHILD.
WHAT SICKNESS LIVES IN THIS FOREST?
EVERY DAY AKI MAKES THE KINGDOM WEAKER. THERE IS NO FEAR OF REPERCUSSION. THEY DROP THEIR GARBAGE OUTSIDE THE WALLS OF MY HOME.
WHAT WOULD *YOU* DO, GYLFI? WITH YOUR KINGDOM SLOWLY ROTTING FROM INSIDE?
I SERVE THE KING, MY LORD. I DO WHAT HE TELLS ME.
REMEMBER YOU SAID IT. YOUR WORD IS ALL THAT YOU ARE, GYLFI. ONE DAY I MIGHT ASK SOMETHING YOU WON'T FIND EASY.

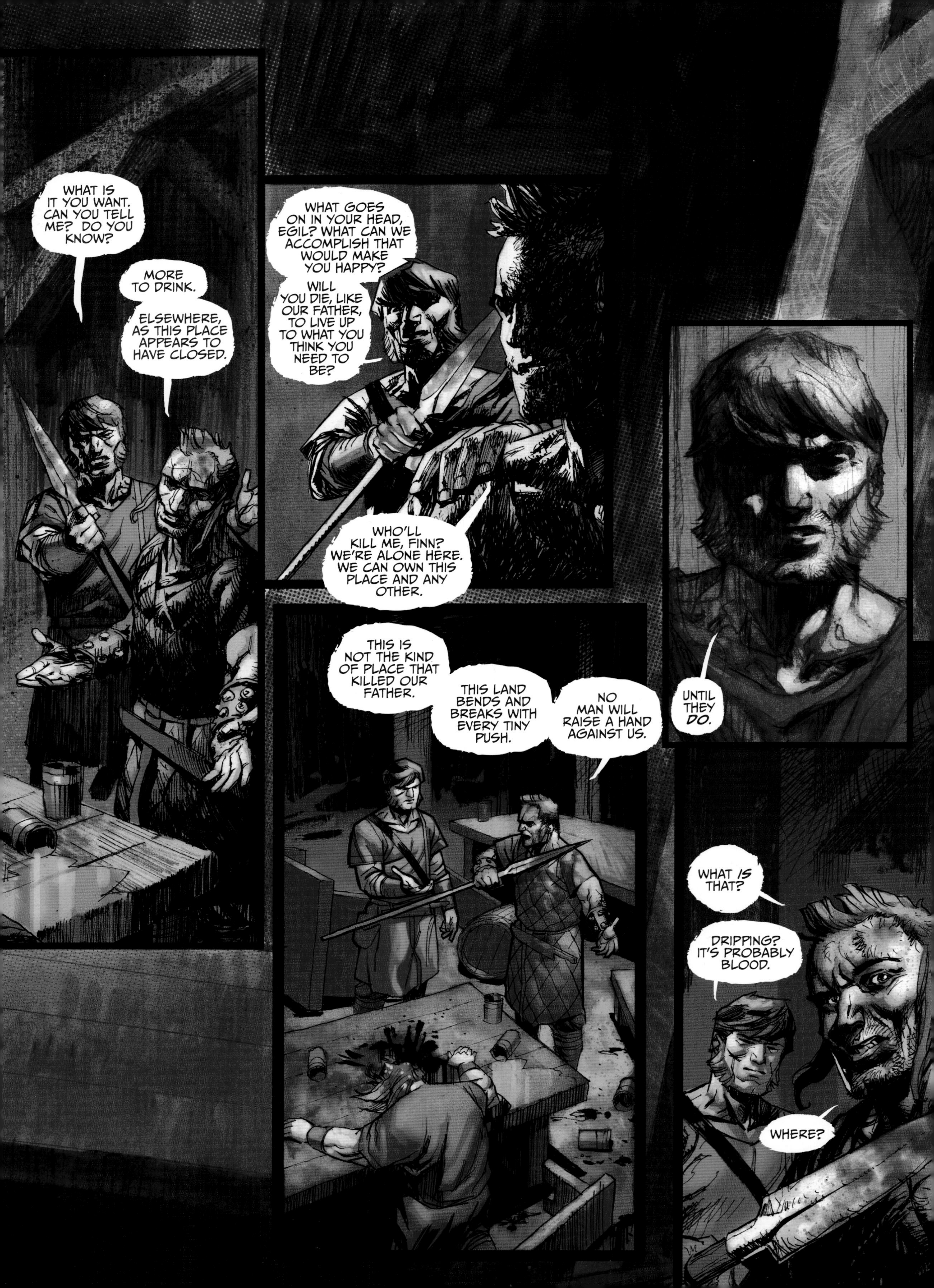
WHAT IS IT YOU WANT. CAN YOU TELL ME? DO YOU KNOW?
MORE TO DRINK.
ELSEWHERE, AS THIS PLACE APPEARS TO HAVE CLOSED.
WHAT GOES ON IN YOUR HEAD, EGIL? WHAT CAN WE ACCOMPLISH THAT WOULD MAKE YOU HAPPY?
WILL YOU DIE, LIKE OUR FATHER, TO LIVE UP TO WHAT YOU THINK YOU NEED TO BE?
WHO'LL KILL ME, FINN? WE'RE ALONE HERE. WE CAN OWN THIS PLACE AND ANY OTHER.
UNTIL THEY DO.
THIS IS NOT THE KIND OF PLACE THAT KILLED OUR FATHER.
THIS LAND BENDS AND BREAKS WITH EVERY TINY PUSH.
NO MAN WILL RAISE A HAND AGAINST US.
WHAT IS THAT?
DRIPPING? IT'S PROBABLY BLOOD.
WHERE?

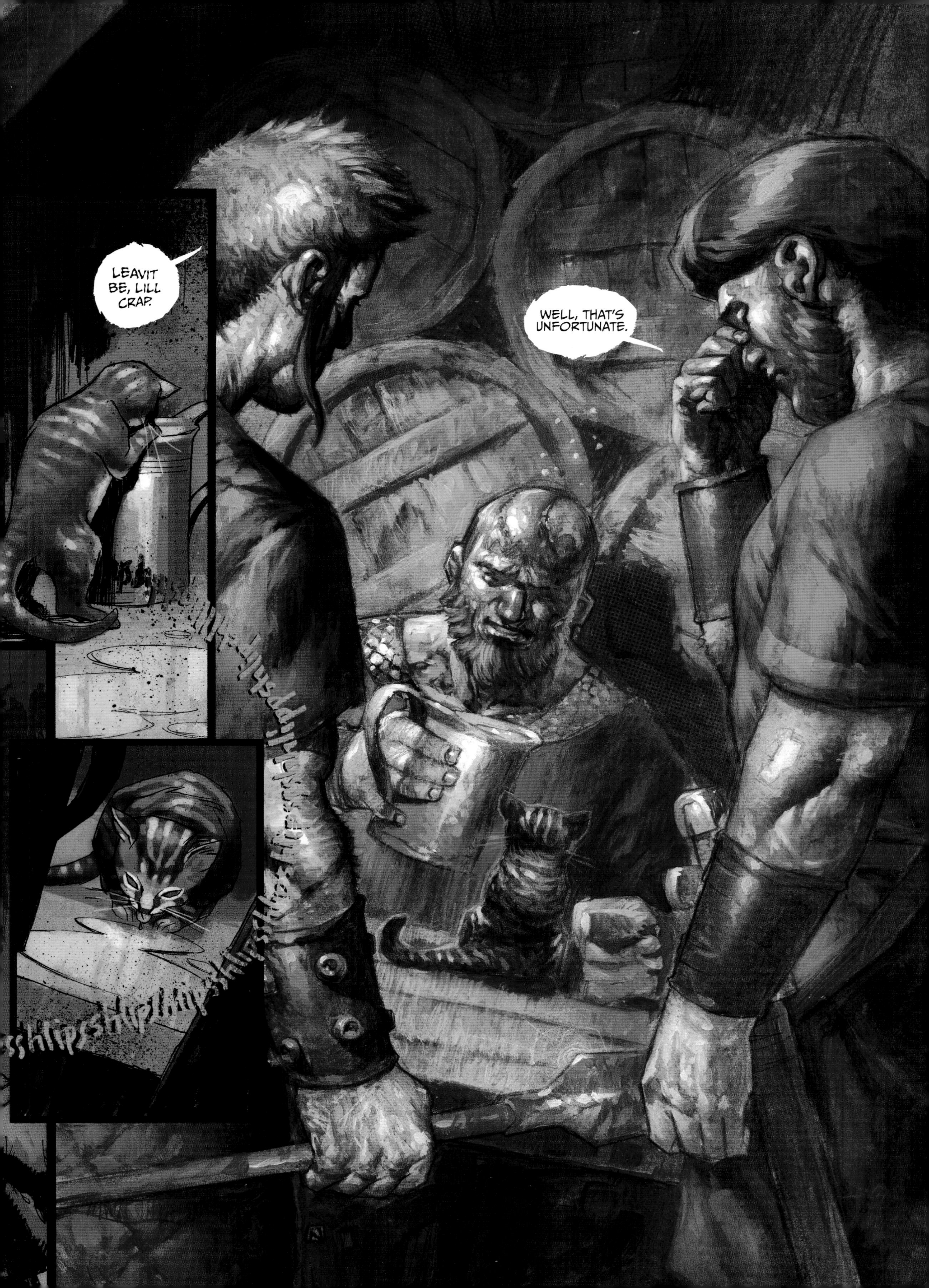
LEAVIT BE, LILL CRAP.
WELL, THAT'S UNFORTUNATE.

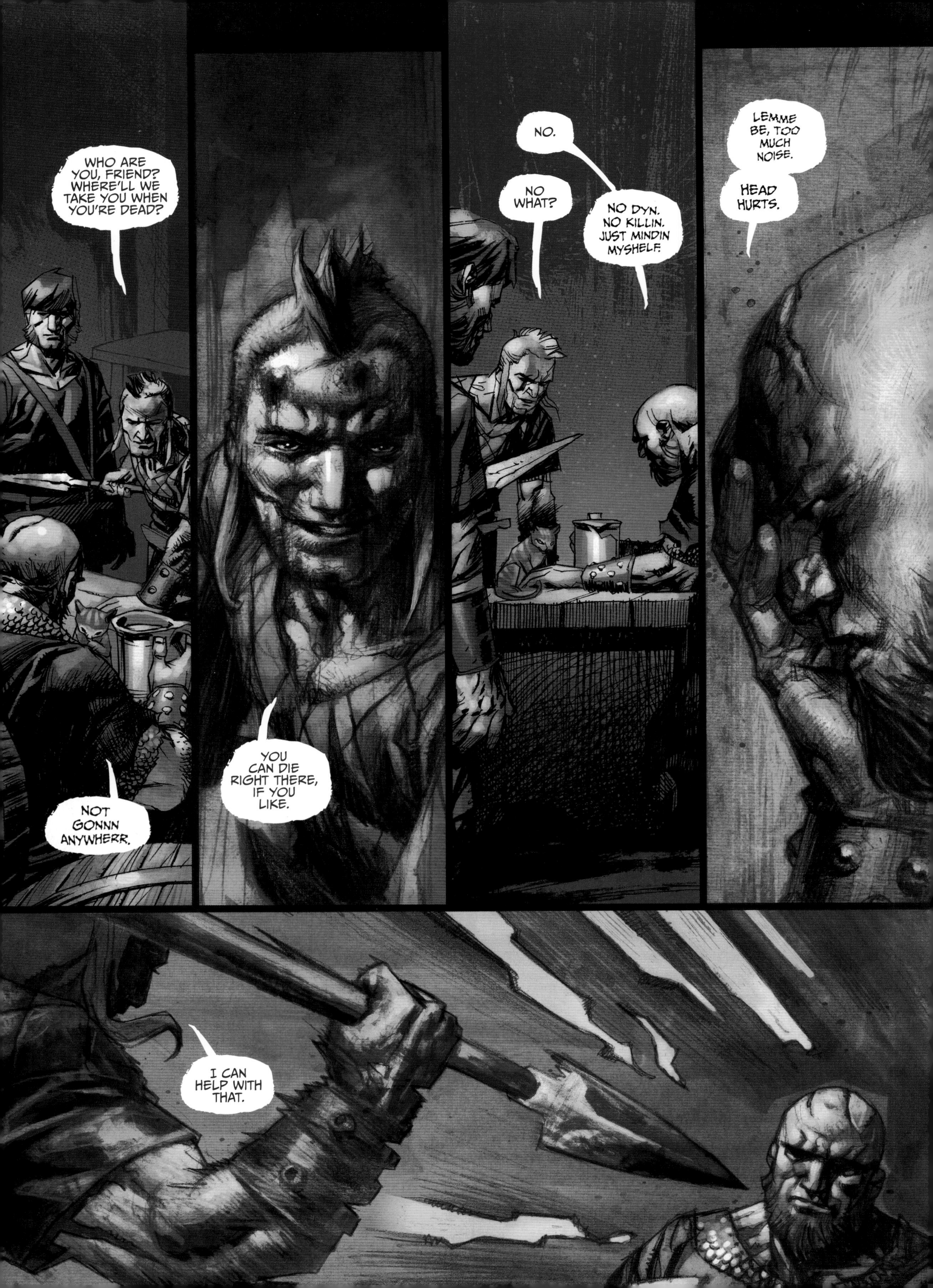
WHO ARE YOU, FRIEND? WHERE'LL WE TAKE YOU WHEN YOU'RE DEAD?
NOT GONNN ANYWHERR.
YOU CAN DIE RIGHT THERE, IF YOU LIKE.
NO.
NO WHAT?
NO DYN. NO KILLIN. JUST MINDIN MYSHELF.
LEMME BE, TOO MUCH NOISE.
HEAD HURTS.
I CAN HELP WITH THAT.

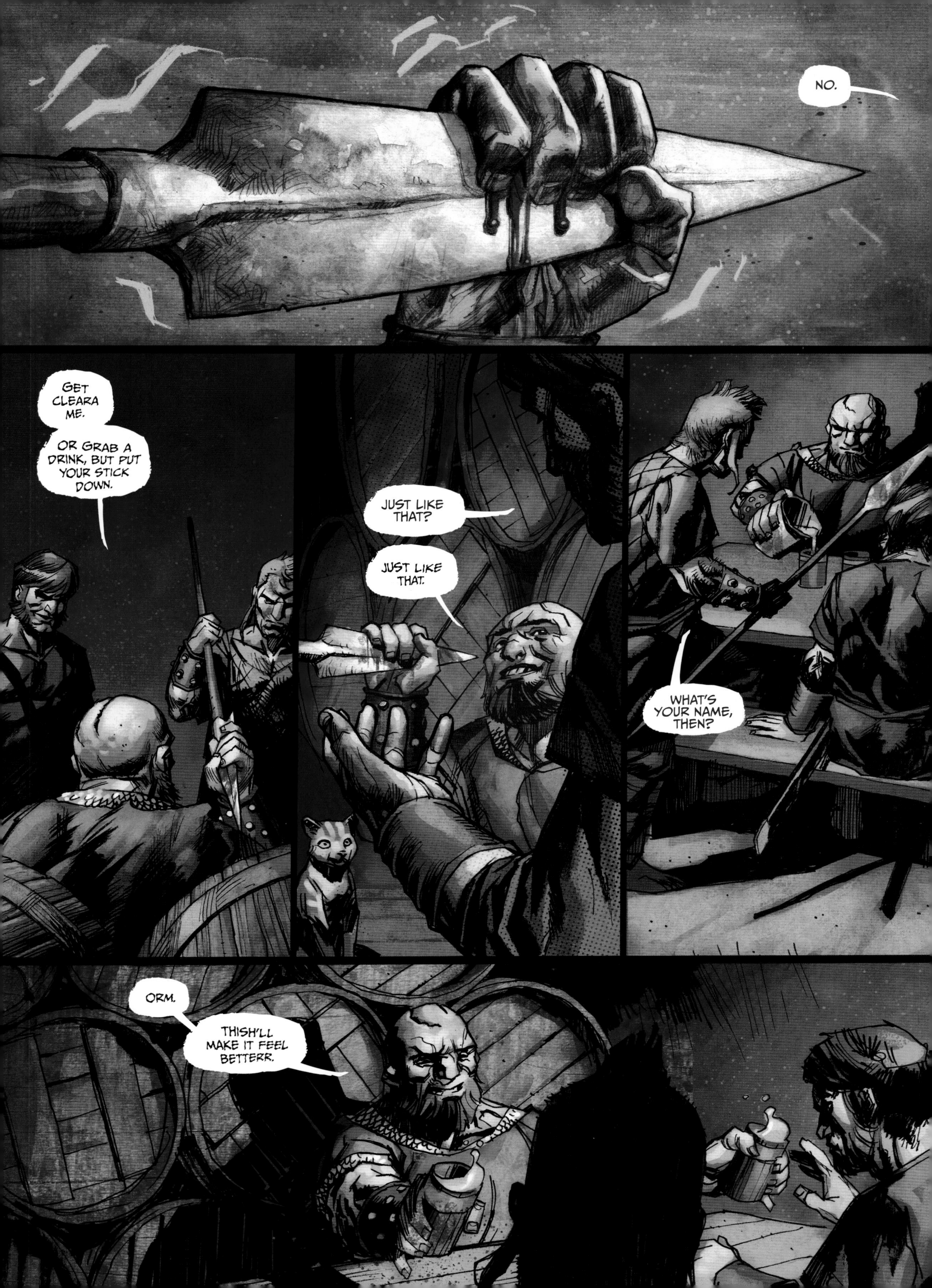
NO.
GET CLEARA ME.
OR GRAB A DRINK, BUT PUT YOUR STICK DOWN.
JUST LIKE THAT?
JUST LIKE THAT.
WHAT'S YOUR NAME, THEN?
ORM.
THISH'LL MAKE IT FEEL BETTERR.

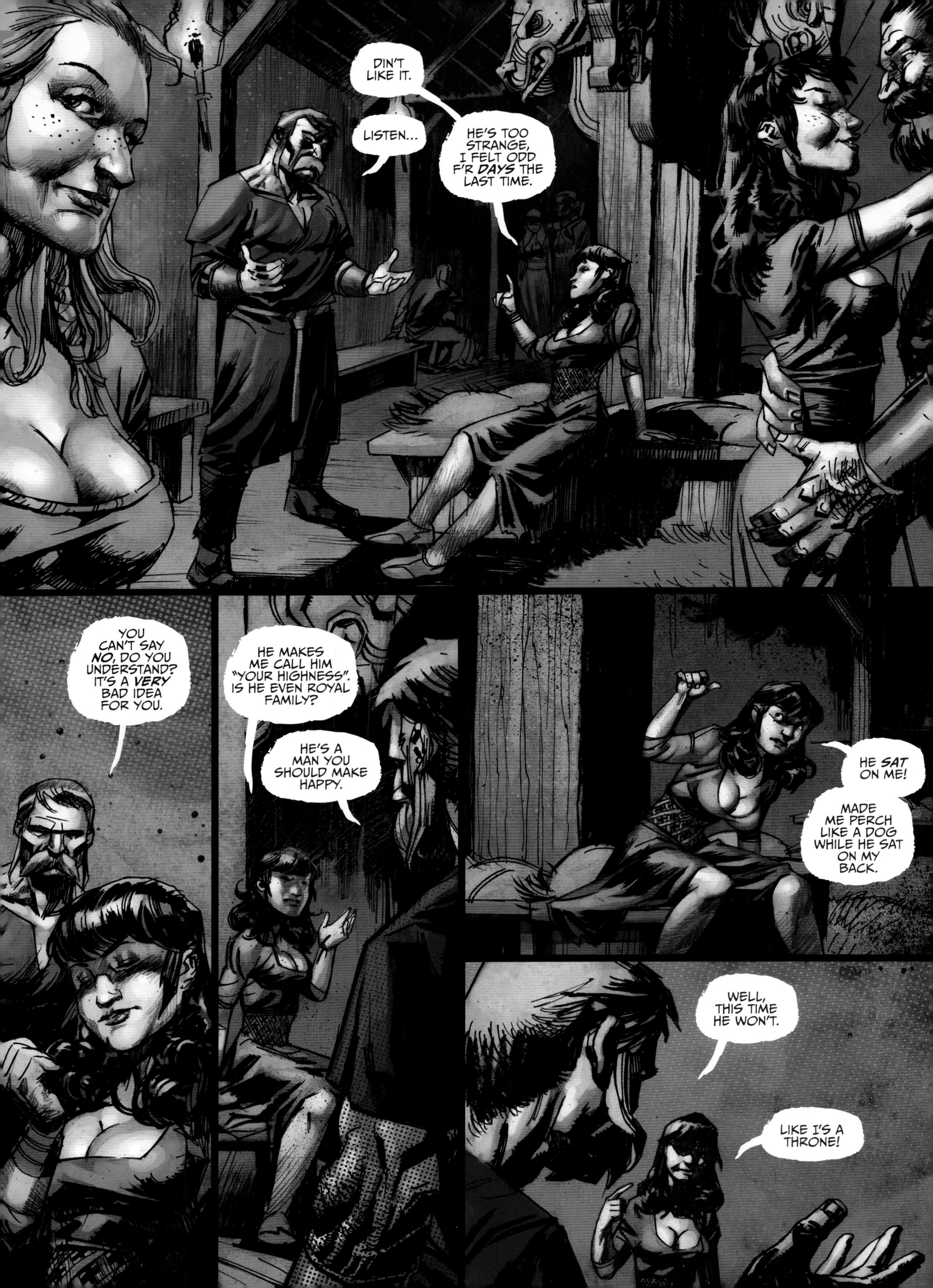
DIN'T LIKE IT.
LISTEN...
HE'S TOO STRANGE, I FELT ODD F'R DAYS THE LAST TIME.
YOU CAN'T SAY NO, DO YOU UNDERSTAND? IT'S A VERY BAD IDEA FOR YOU.
HE MAKES ME CALL HIM "YOUR HIGHNESS". IS HE EVEN ROYAL FAMILY?
HE'S A MAN YOU SHOULD MAKE HAPPY.
HE SAT ON ME!
MADE ME PERCH LIKE A DOG WHILE HE SAT ON MY BACK.
WELL, THIS TIME HE WON'T.
LIKE I'S A THRONE!

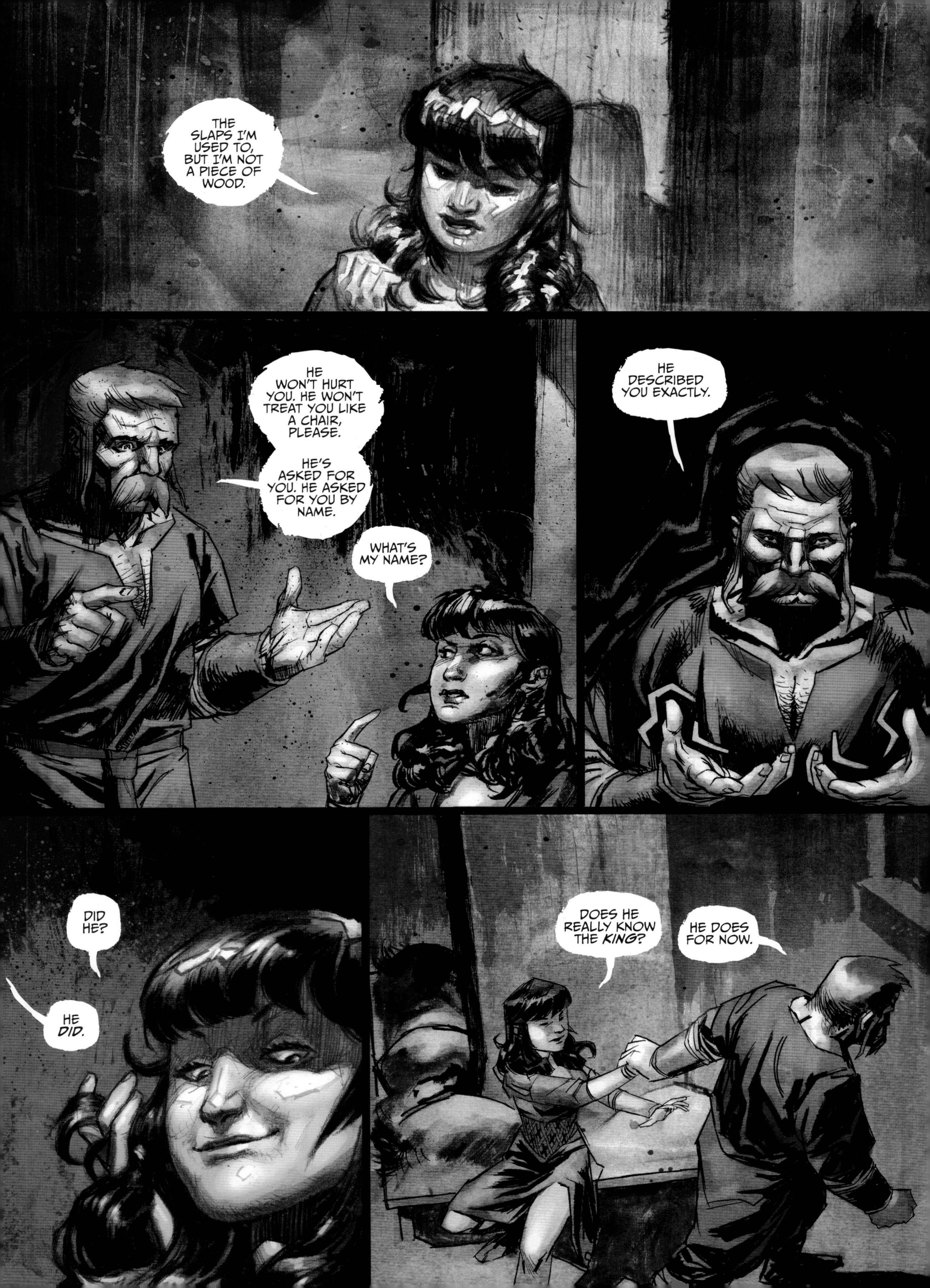
THE SLAPS I'M USED TO, BUT I'M NOT A PIECE OF WOOD.
HE WON'T HURT YOU. HE WON'T TREAT YOU LIKE A CHAIR, PLEASE.
HE'S ASKED FOR YOU. HE ASKED FOR YOU BY NAME.
WHAT'S MY NAME?
HE DESCRIBED YOU EXACTLY.
DID HE?
HE *DID*.
DOES HE REALLY KNOW THE *KING*?
HE DOES FOR NOW.

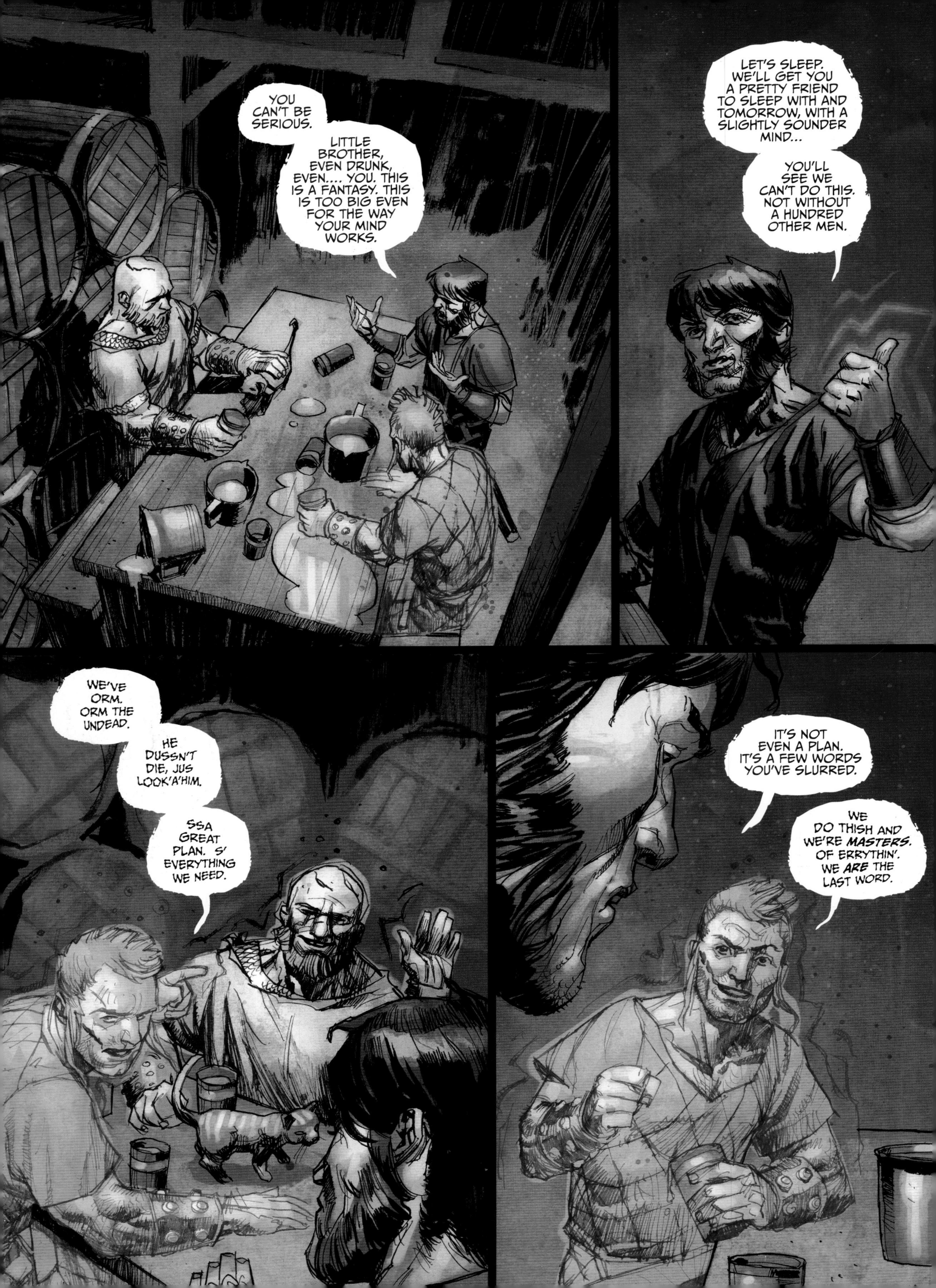
YOU CAN'T BE SERIOUS.
LITTLE BROTHER, EVEN DRUNK, EVEN.... YOU. THIS IS A FANTASY. THIS IS TOO BIG EVEN FOR THE WAY YOUR MIND WORKS.
LET'S SLEEP. WE'LL GET YOU A PRETTY FRIEND TO SLEEP WITH AND TOMORROW, WITH A SLIGHTLY SOUNDER MIND...
YOU'LL SEE WE CAN'T DO THIS. NOT WITHOUT A HUNDRED OTHER MEN.
WE'VE ORM. ORM THE UNDEAD.
HE DUSSN'T DIE, JUS LOOK'A'HIM.
SSA GREAT PLAN. S' EVERYTHING WE NEED.
IT'S NOT EVEN A PLAN. IT'S A FEW WORDS YOU'VE SLURRED.
WE DO THISH AND WE'RE *MASTERS.* OF ERRYTHIN'. WE *ARE* THE LAST WORD.

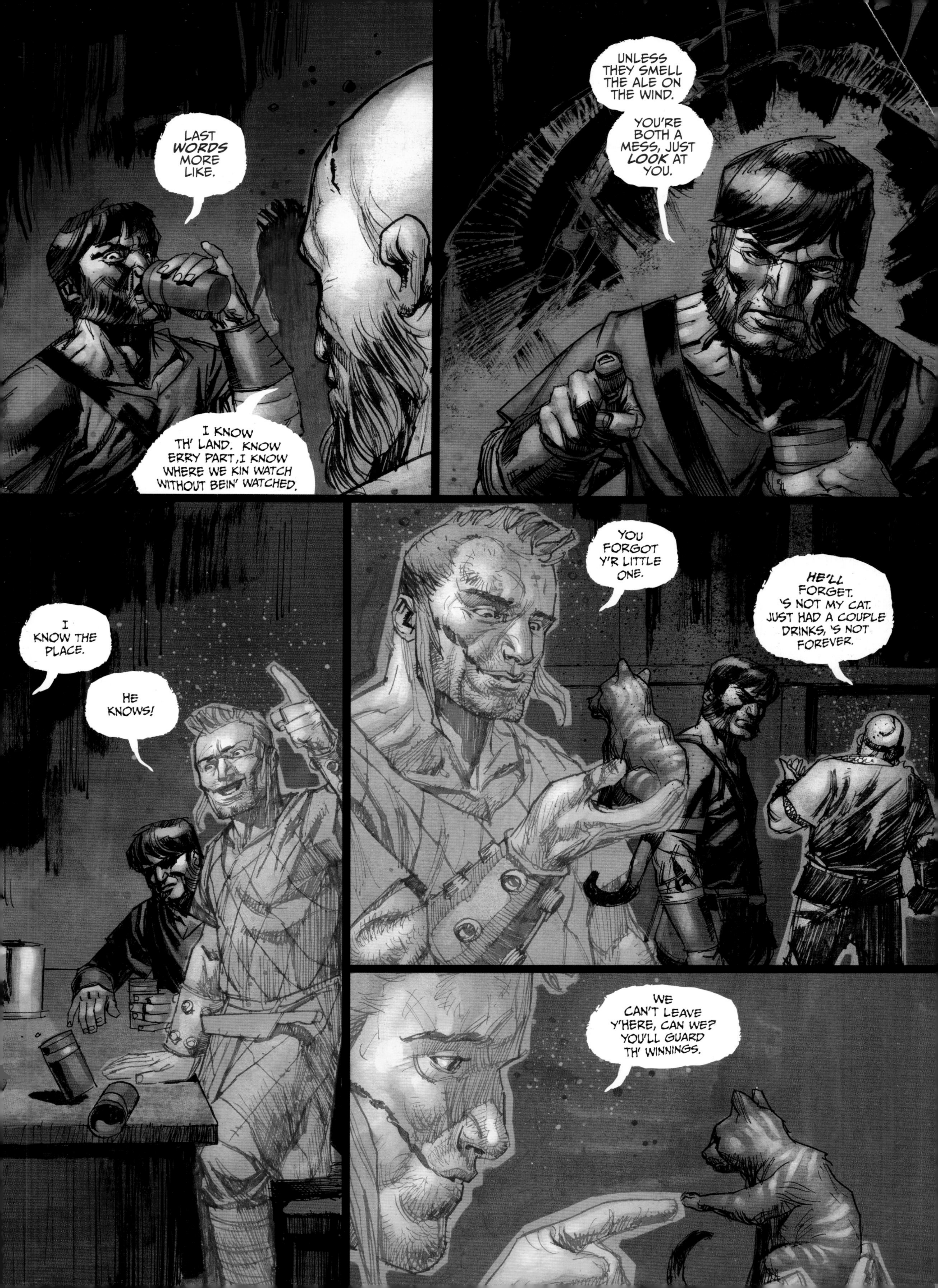
LAST WORDS MORE LIKE.
I KNOW TH' LAND. KNOW ERRY PART, I KNOW WHERE WE KIN WATCH WITHOUT BEIN' WATCHED.
UNLESS THEY SMELL THE ALE ON THE WIND.
YOU'RE BOTH A MESS, JUST LOOK AT YOU.
I KNOW THE PLACE.
HE KNOWS!
YOU FORGOT Y'R LITTLE ONE.
HE'LL FORGET. 'S NOT MY CAT. JUST HAD A COUPLE DRINKS, 'S NOT FOREVER.
WE CAN'T LEAVE Y'HERE, CAN WE? YOU'LL GUARD TH' WINNINGS.

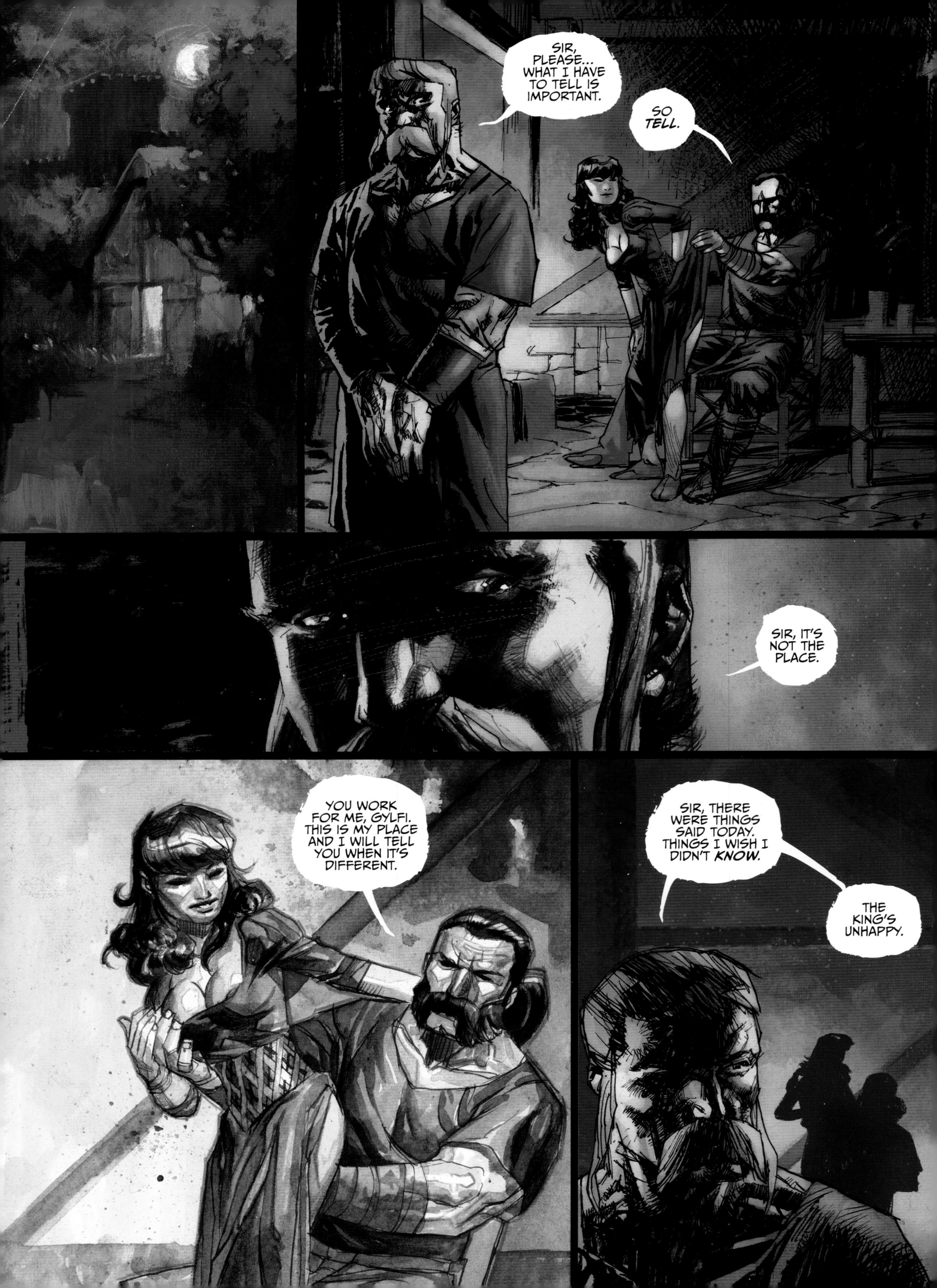
SIR, PLEASE... WHAT I HAVE TO TELL IS IMPORTANT.
SO TELL.
SIR, IT'S NOT THE PLACE.
YOU WORK FOR ME, GYLFI. THIS IS MY PLACE AND I WILL TELL YOU WHEN IT'S DIFFERENT.
SIR, THERE WERE THINGS SAID TODAY. THINGS I WISH I DIDN'T KNOW.
THE KING'S UNHAPPY.

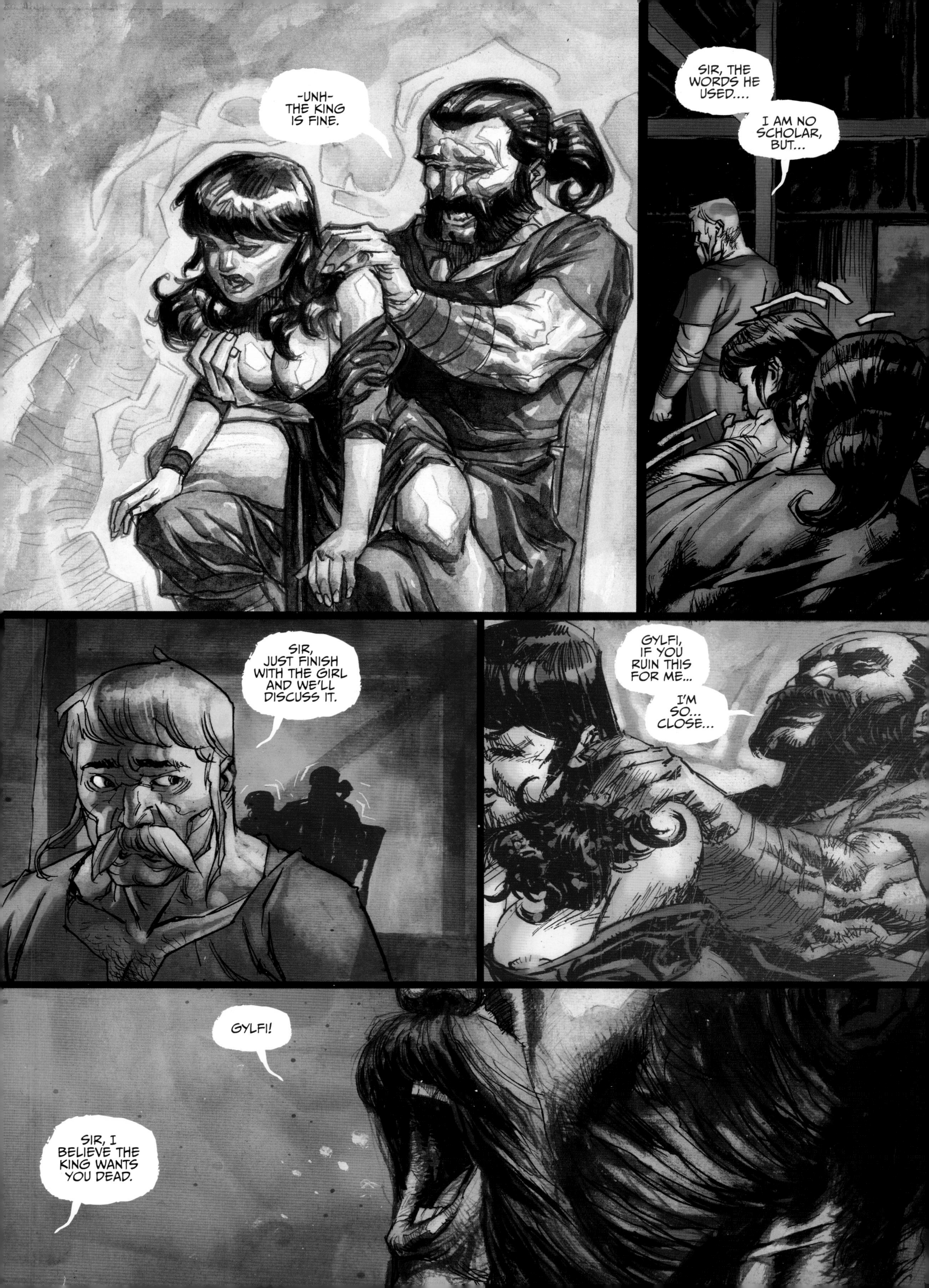
-UNH- THE KING IS FINE.
SIR, THE WORDS HE USED....
I AM NO SCHOLAR, BUT...
SIR, JUST FINISH WITH THE GIRL AND WE'LL DISCUSS IT.
GYLFI, IF YOU RUIN THIS FOR ME...
I'M SO... CLOSE...
GYLFI!
SIR, I BELIEVE THE KING WANTS YOU DEAD.

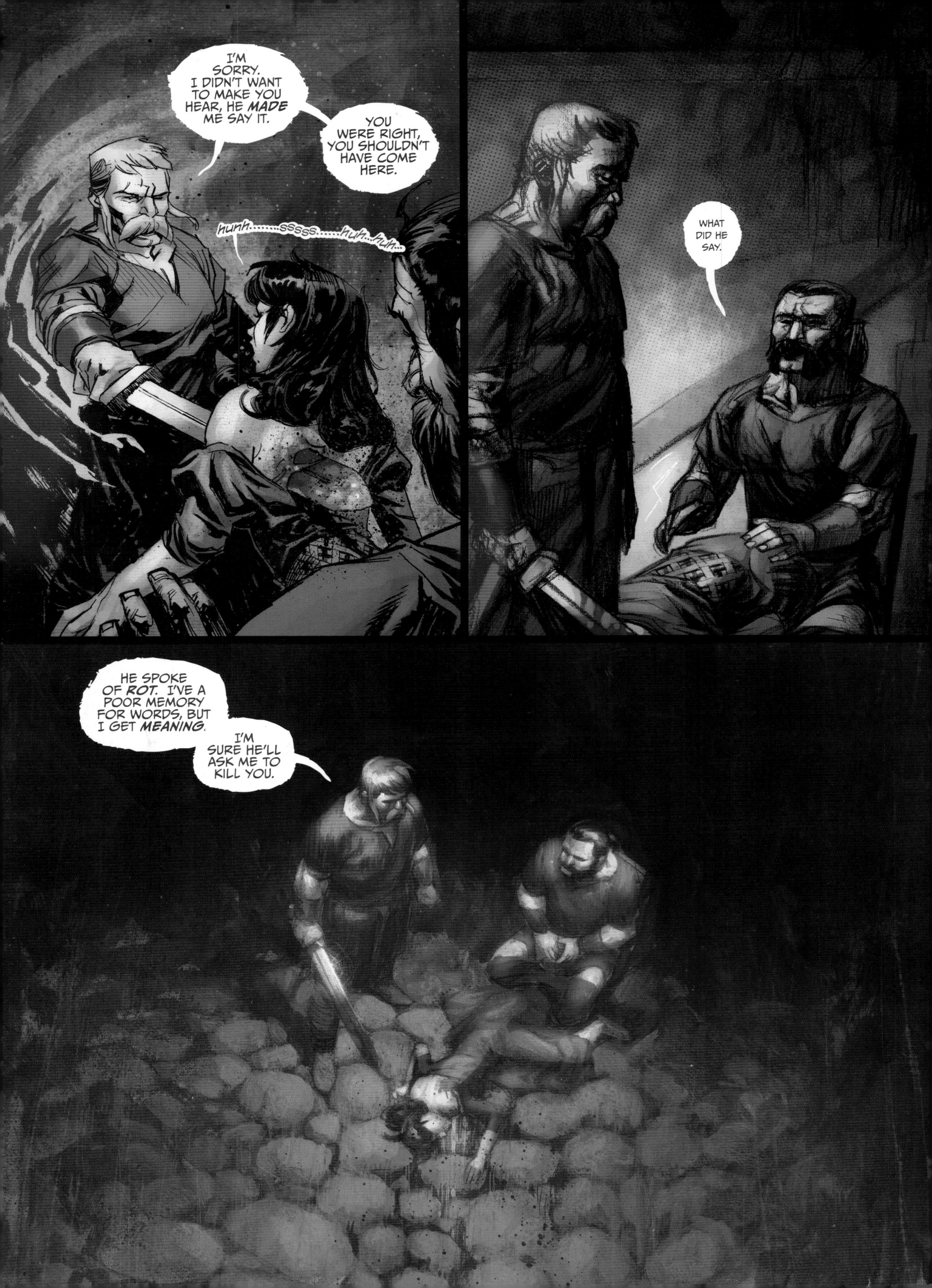
I'M SORRY. I DIDN'T WANT TO MAKE YOU HEAR, HE **MADE** ME SAY IT.
YOU WERE RIGHT, YOU SHOULDN'T HAVE COME HERE.
hunh.......sssss......huh...huh...
WHAT DID HE SAY.
HE SPOKE OF **ROT**. I'VE A POOR MEMORY FOR WORDS, BUT I GET **MEANING**.
I'M SURE HE'LL ASK ME TO KILL YOU.

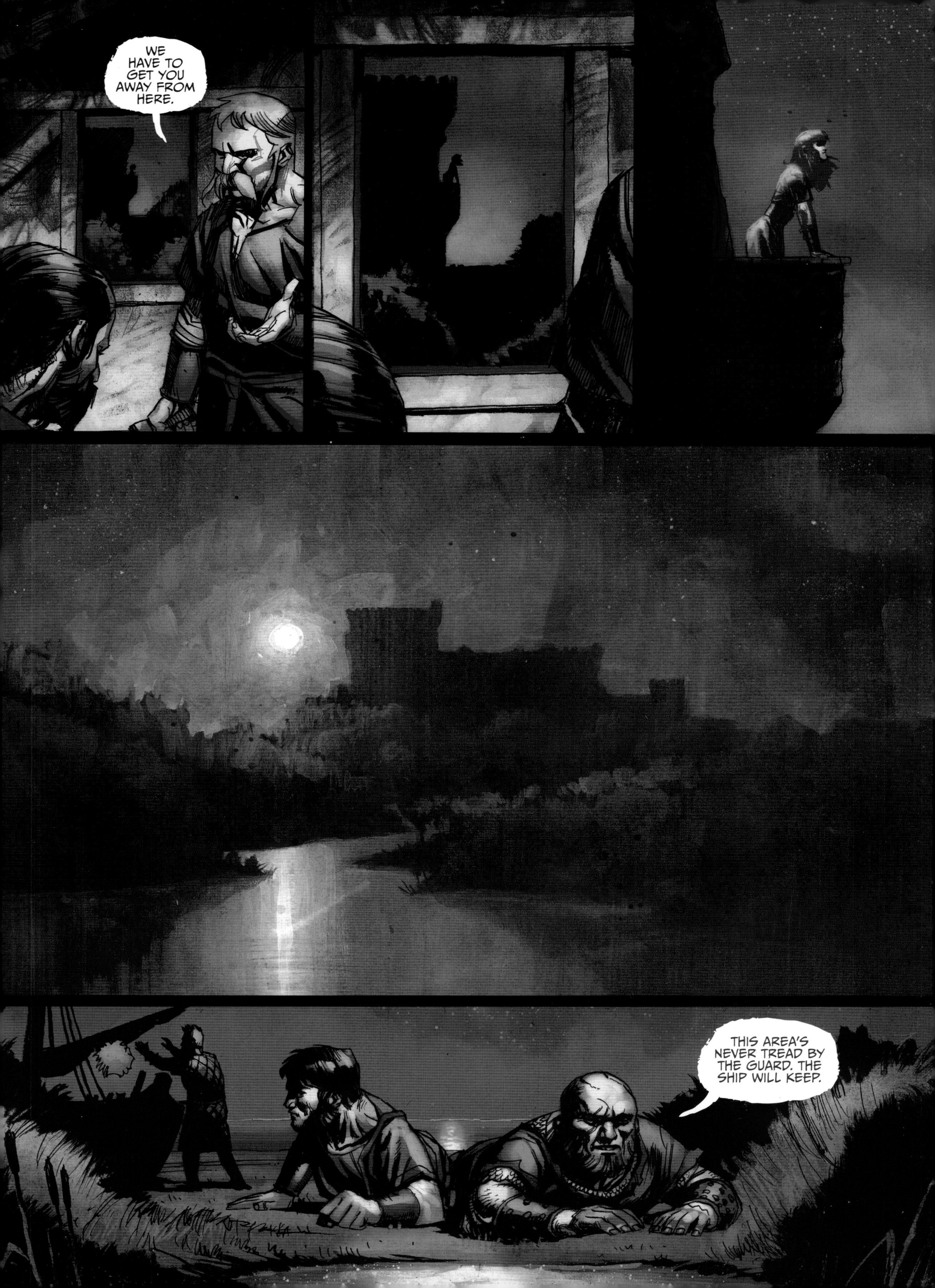
WE HAVE TO GET YOU AWAY FROM HERE.
THIS AREA'S NEVER TREAD BY THE GUARD. THE SHIP WILL KEEP.

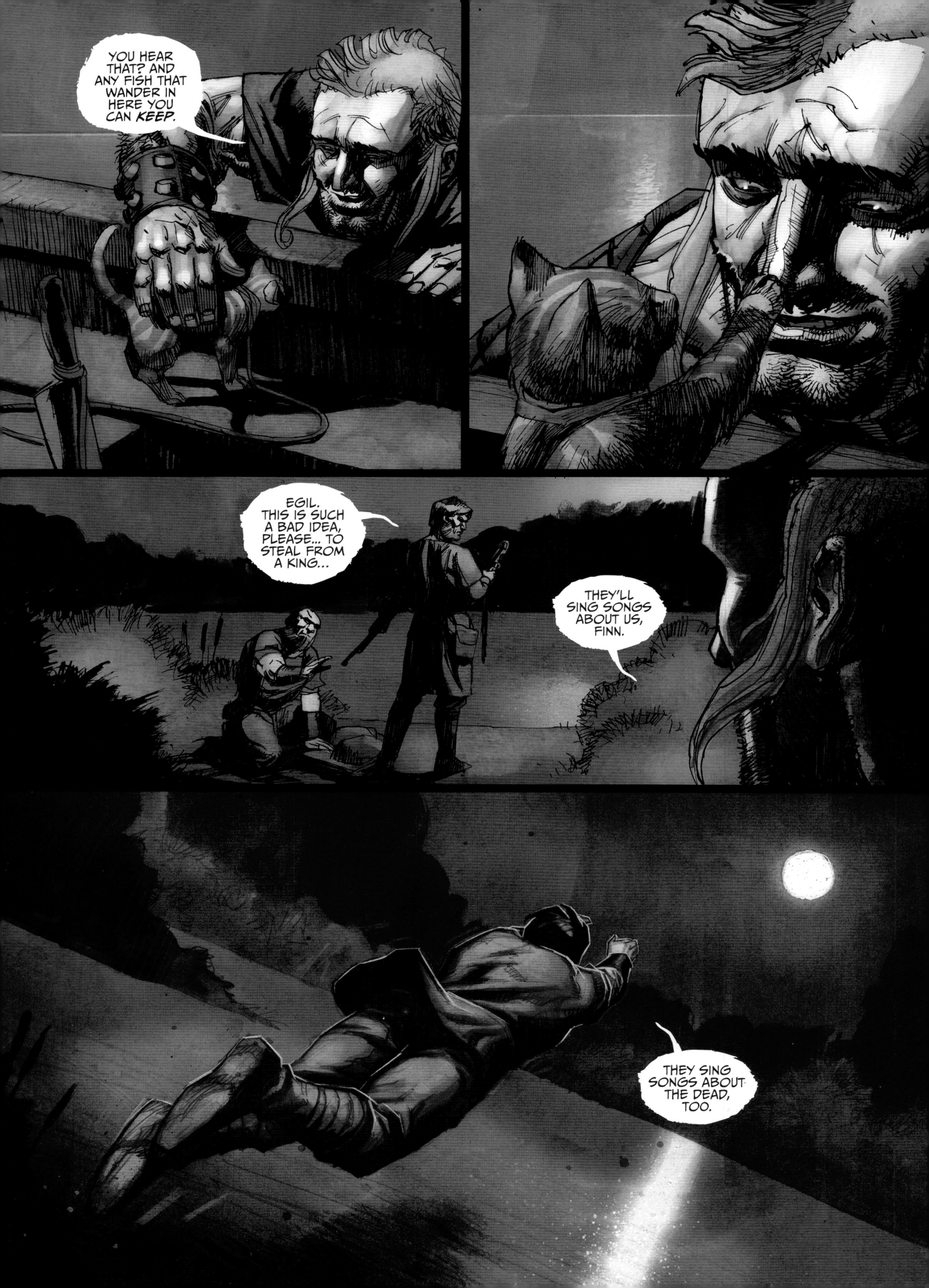

YOU HEAR THAT? AND ANY FISH THAT WANDER IN HERE YOU CAN **KEEP**.
EGIL. THIS IS SUCH A BAD IDEA, PLEASE... TO STEAL FROM A KING...
THEY'LL SING SONGS ABOUT US, FINN.
THEY SING SONGS ABOUT THE DEAD, TOO.

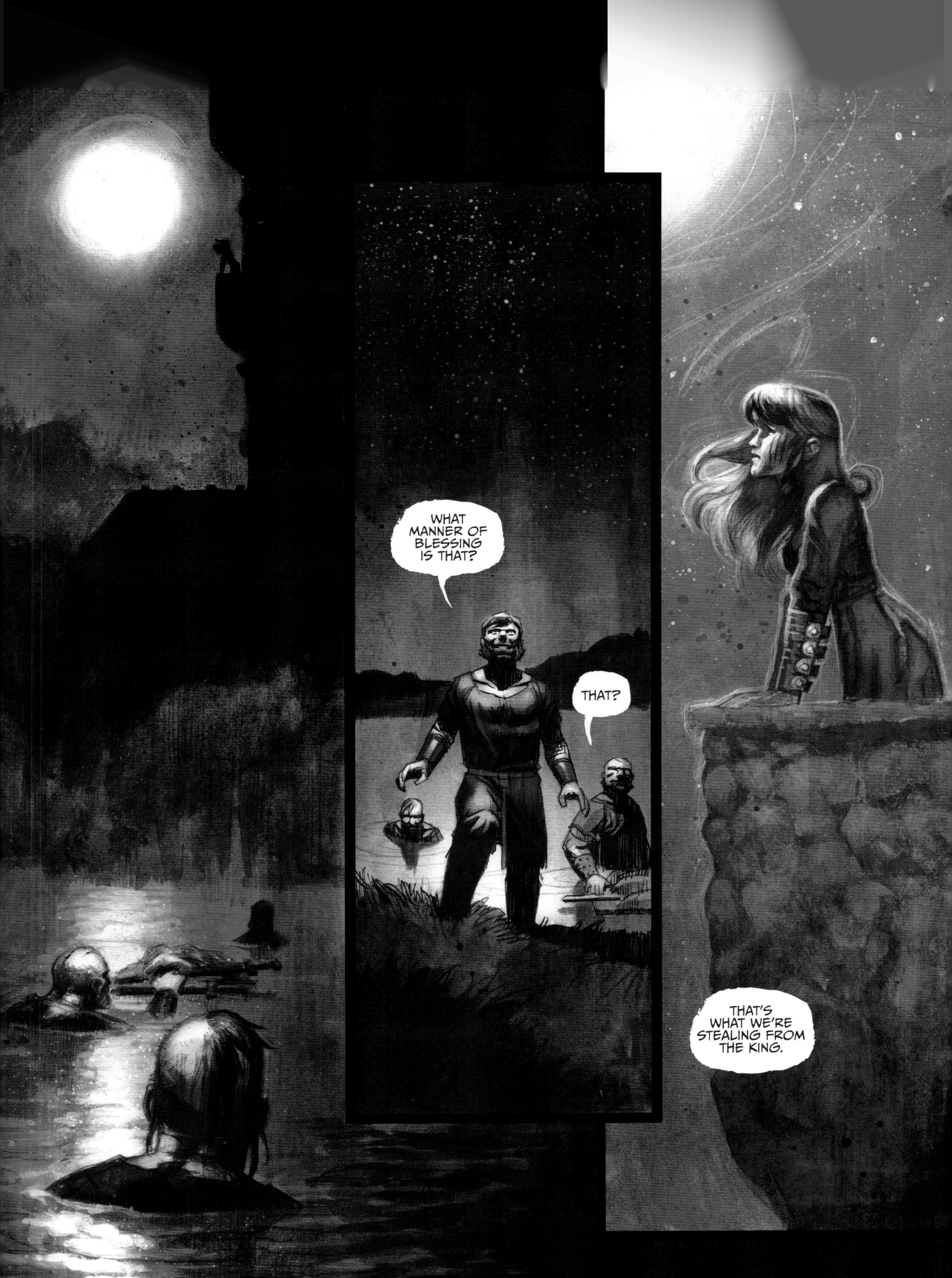
WHAT MANNER OF BLESSING IS THAT?
THAT?
THAT'S WHAT WE'RE STEALING FROM THE KING.

To Be Continued...

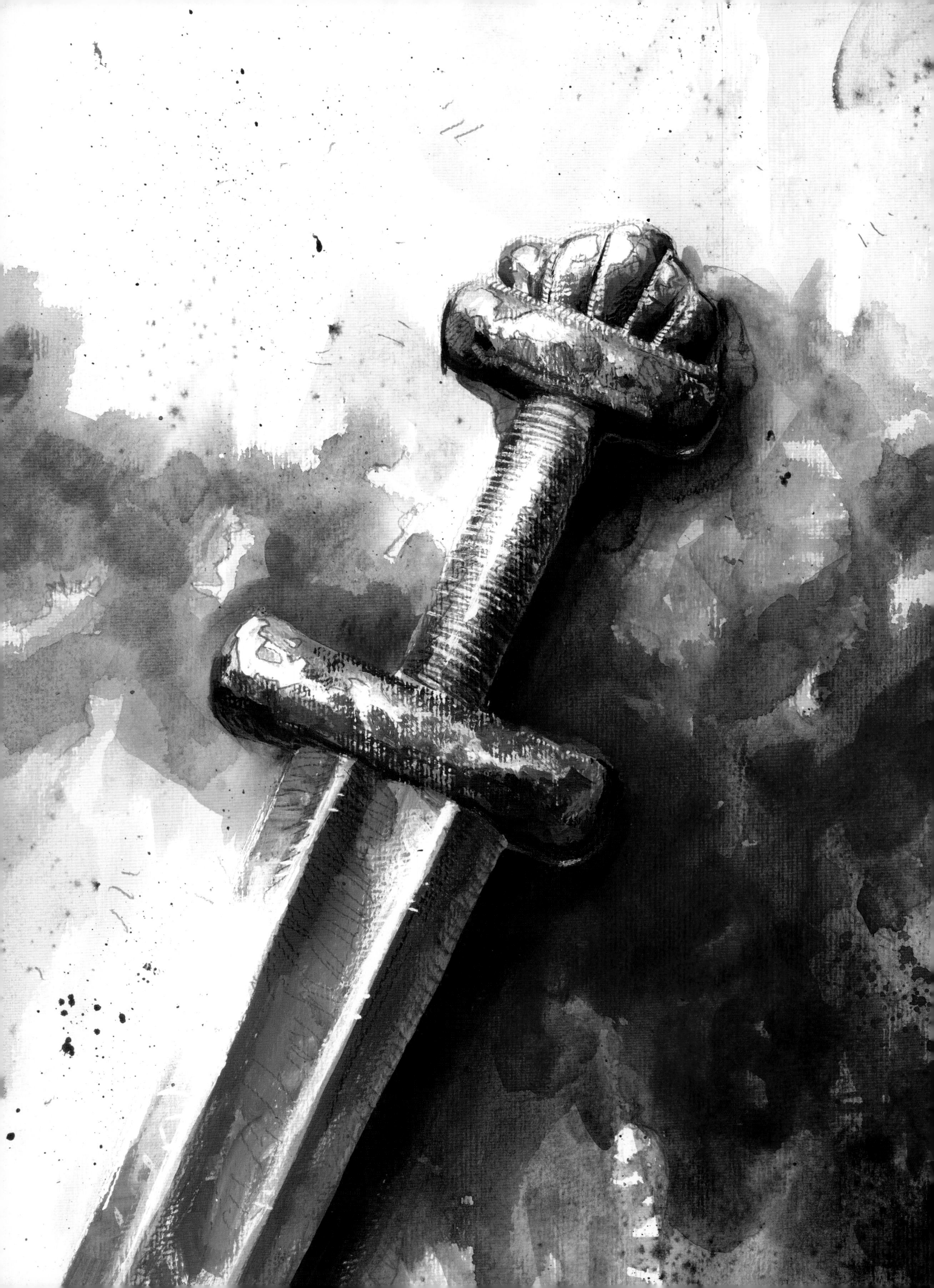

WHO'S THAT, LOOKING OVER YOUR SHOULDER?

EDGAR THE *GHOST.*

OH, NO... WHO'S *DEAD?*

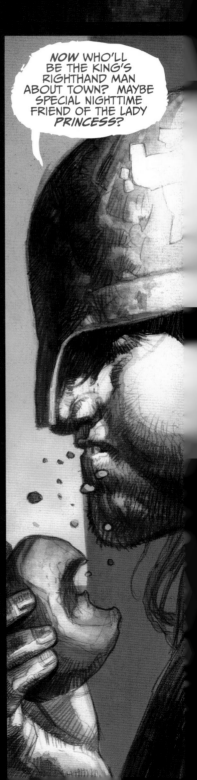

NOW WHO'LL BE THE KING'S RIGHTHAND MAN ABOUT TOWN? MAYBE SPECIAL NIGHTTIME FRIEND OF THE LADY *PRINCESS?*

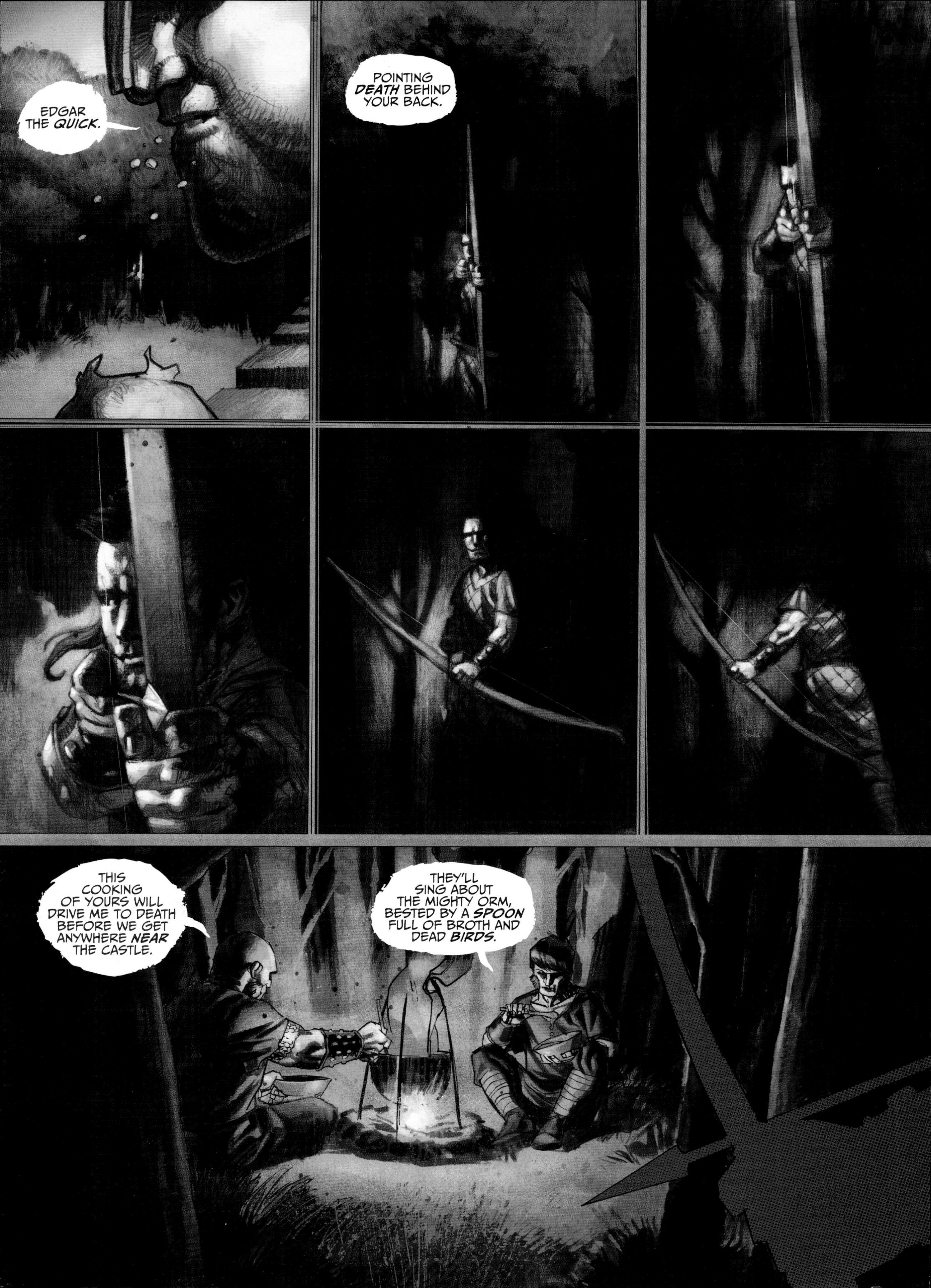
EDGAR THE QUICK.
POINTING DEATH BEHIND YOUR BACK.
THIS COOKING OF YOURS WILL DRIVE ME TO DEATH BEFORE WE GET ANYWHERE NEAR THE CASTLE.
THEY'LL SING ABOUT THE MIGHTY ORM, BESTED BY A SPOON FULL OF BROTH AND DEAD BIRDS.

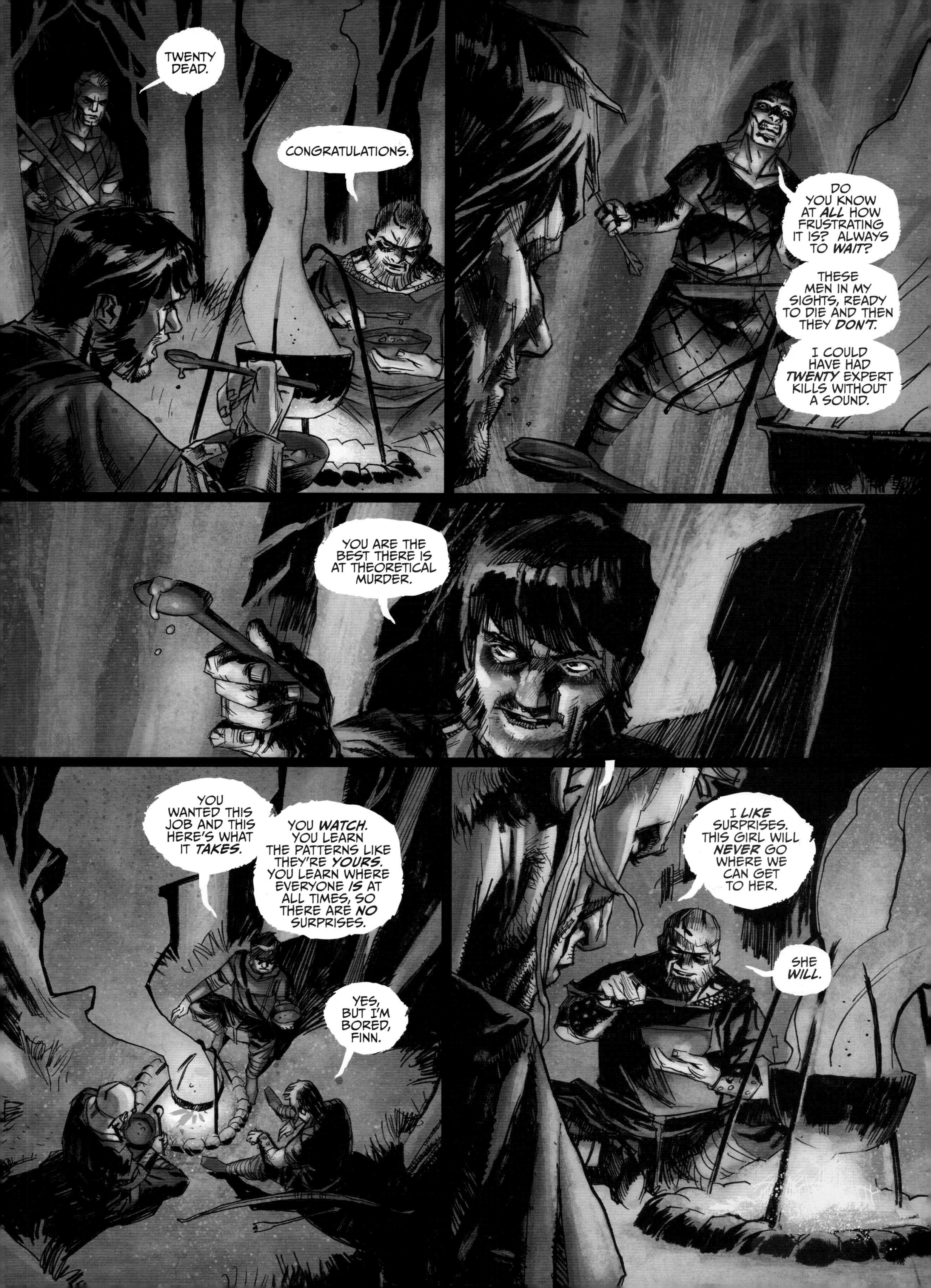
TWENTY DEAD.
CONGRATULATIONS.
DO YOU KNOW AT ALL HOW FRUSTRATING IT IS? ALWAYS TO WAIT?
THESE MEN IN MY SIGHTS, READY TO DIE AND THEN THEY DON'T.
I COULD HAVE HAD TWENTY EXPERT KILLS WITHOUT A SOUND.
YOU ARE THE BEST THERE IS AT THEORETICAL MURDER.
YOU WANTED THIS JOB AND THIS HERE'S WHAT IT TAKES.
YOU WATCH. YOU LEARN THE PATTERNS LIKE THEY'RE YOURS. YOU LEARN WHERE EVERYONE IS AT ALL TIMES, SO THERE ARE NO SURPRISES.
YES, BUT I'M BORED, FINN.
I LIKE SURPRISES. THIS GIRL WILL NEVER GO WHERE WE CAN GET TO HER.
SHE WILL.

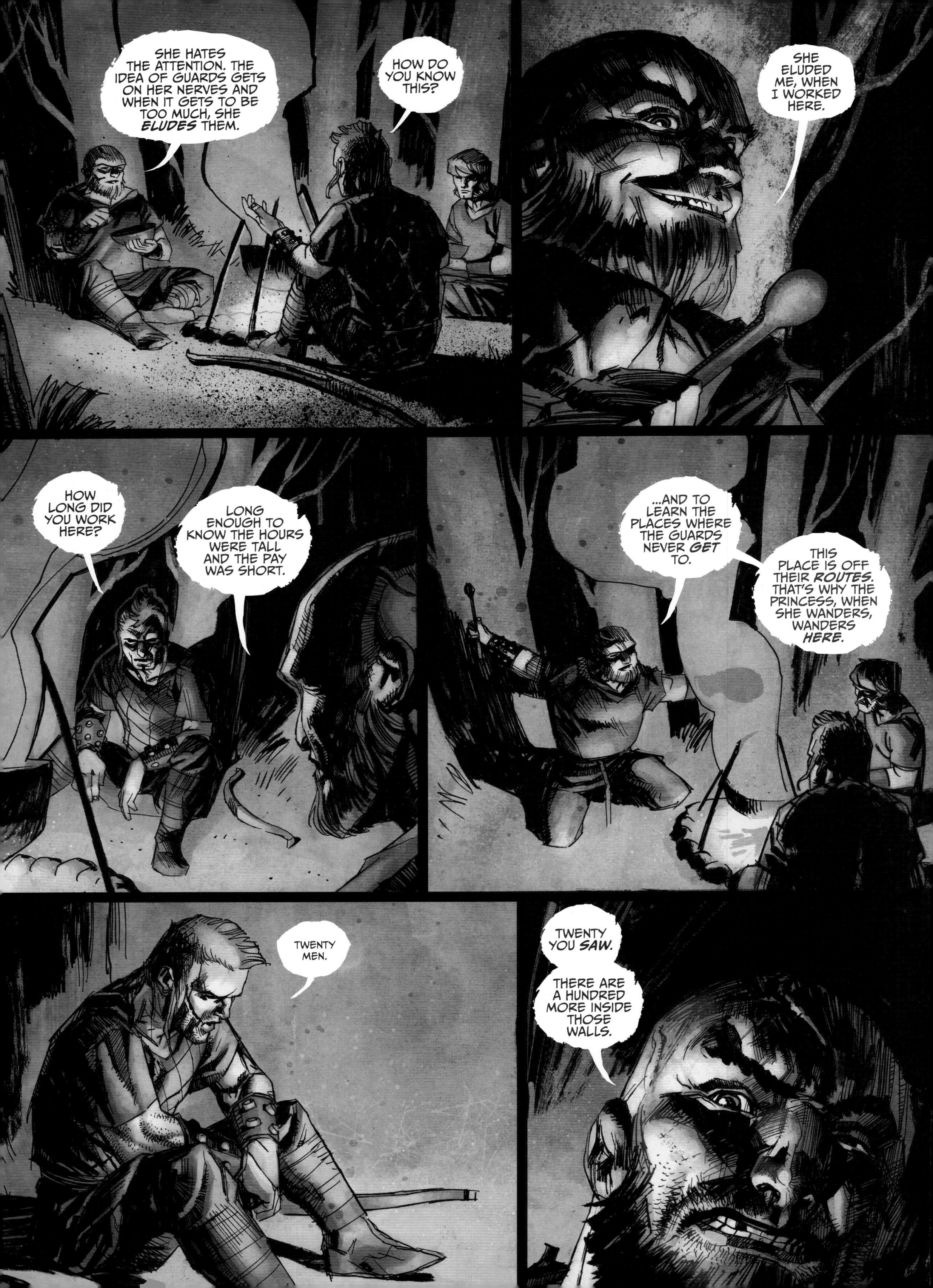
SHE HATES THE ATTENTION. THE IDEA OF GUARDS GETS ON HER NERVES AND WHEN IT GETS TO BE TOO MUCH, SHE ELUDES THEM.
HOW DO YOU KNOW THIS?
SHE ELUDED ME, WHEN I WORKED HERE.
HOW LONG DID YOU WORK HERE?
LONG ENOUGH TO KNOW THE HOURS WERE TALL AND THE PAY WAS SHORT.
...AND TO LEARN THE PLACES WHERE THE GUARDS NEVER GET TO.
THIS PLACE IS OFF THEIR ROUTES. THAT'S WHY THE PRINCESS, WHEN SHE WANDERS, WANDERS HERE.
TWENTY MEN.
TWENTY YOU SAW.
THERE ARE A HUNDRED MORE INSIDE THOSE WALLS.

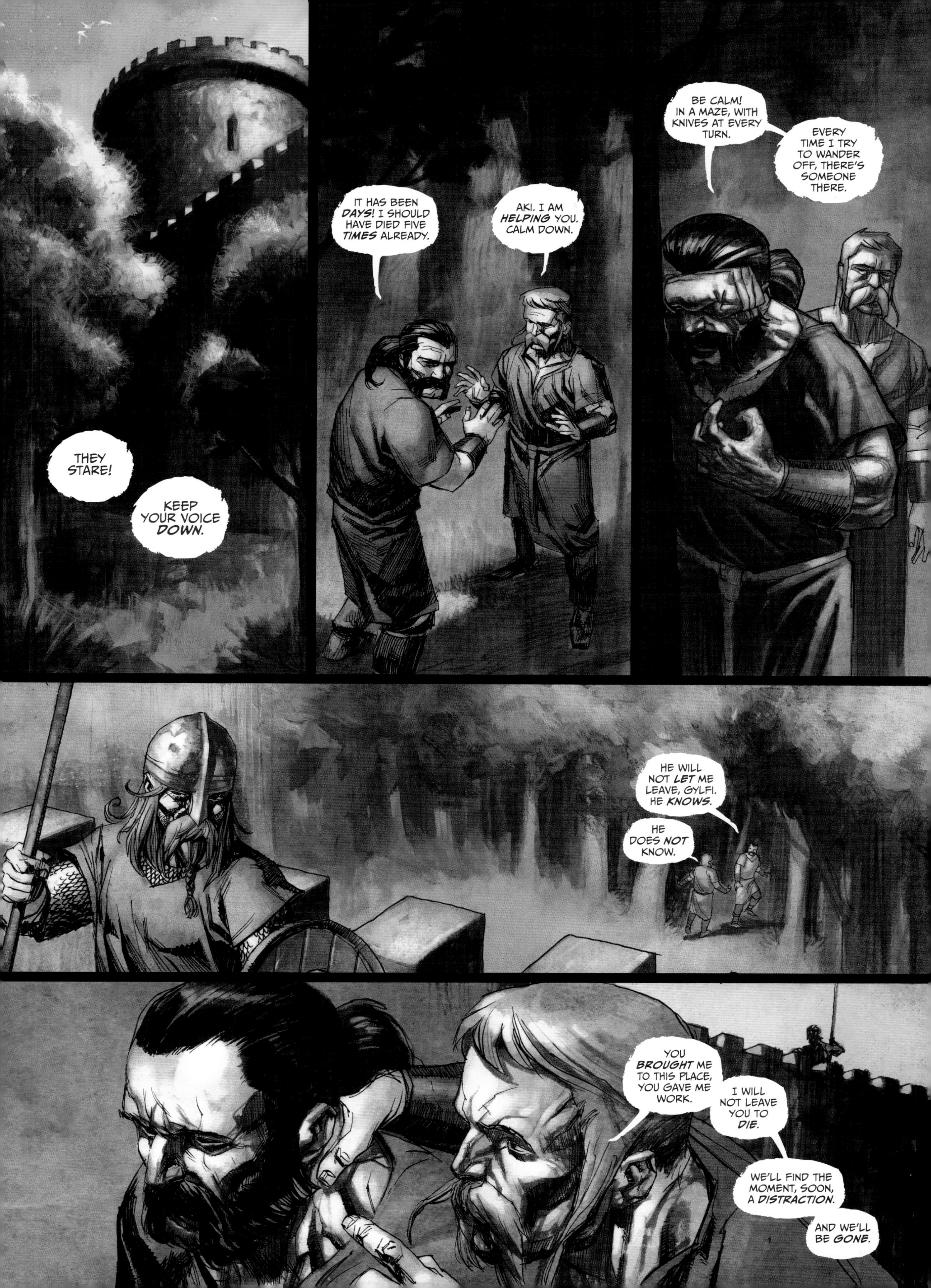
THEY STARE!
KEEP YOUR VOICE DOWN.
IT HAS BEEN DAYS! I SHOULD HAVE DIED FIVE TIMES ALREADY.
AKI. I AM HELPING YOU. CALM DOWN.
BE CALM! IN A MAZE, WITH KNIVES AT EVERY TURN.
EVERY TIME I TRY TO WANDER OFF, THERE'S SOMEONE THERE.
HE WILL NOT LET ME LEAVE, GYLFI. HE KNOWS.
HE DOES NOT KNOW.
YOU BROUGHT ME TO THIS PLACE, YOU GAVE ME WORK.
I WILL NOT LEAVE YOU TO DIE.
WE'LL FIND THE MOMENT, SOON, A DISTRACTION.
AND WE'LL BE GONE.

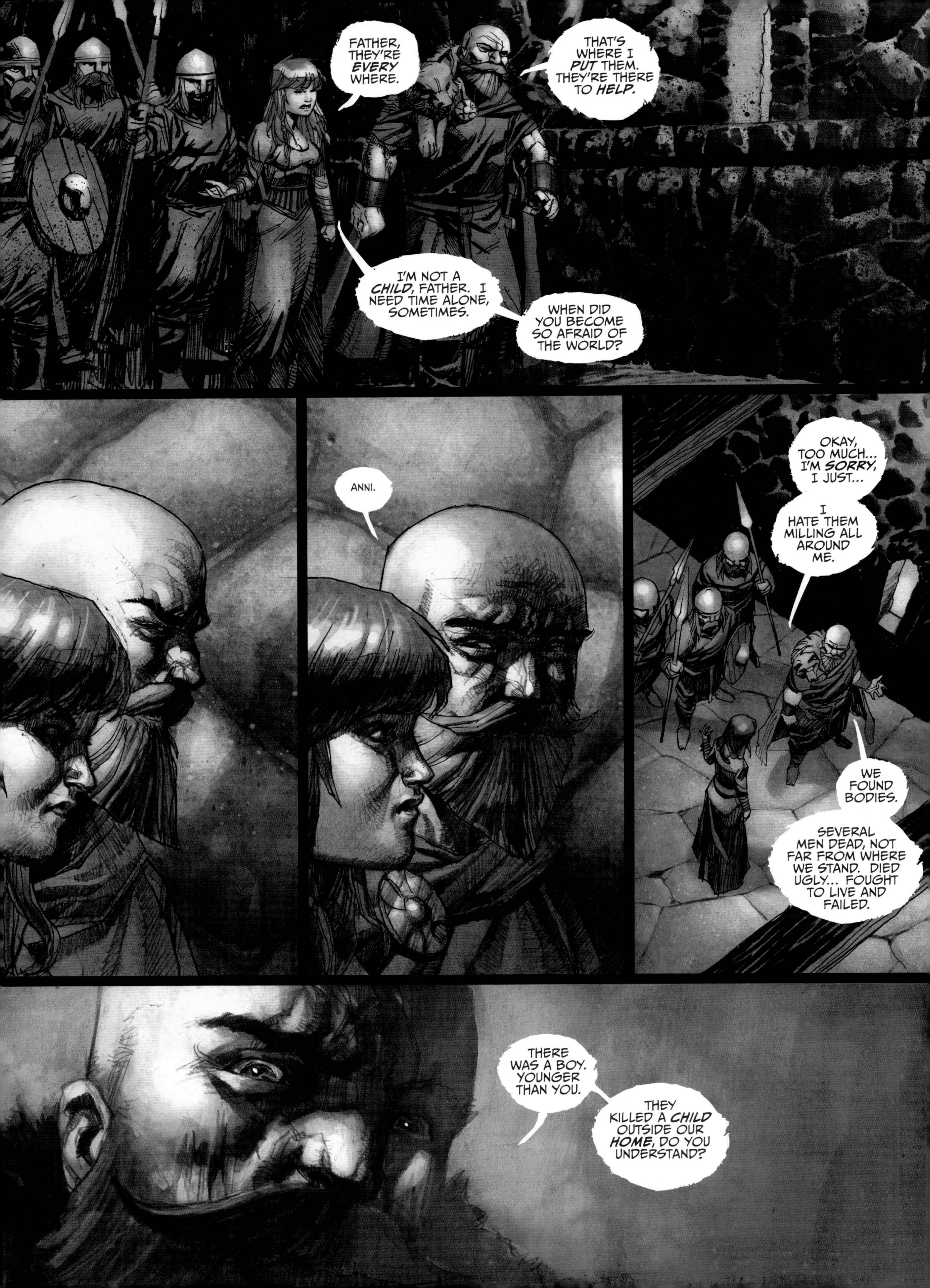
FATHER, THEY'RE EVERY WHERE.
THAT'S WHERE I PUT THEM. THEY'RE THERE TO HELP.
I'M NOT A CHILD, FATHER. I NEED TIME ALONE, SOMETIMES.
WHEN DID YOU BECOME SO AFRAID OF THE WORLD?
ANNI.
OKAY, TOO MUCH... I'M SORRY, I JUST...
I HATE THEM MILLING ALL AROUND ME.
WE FOUND BODIES.
SEVERAL MEN DEAD, NOT FAR FROM WHERE WE STAND. DIED UGLY... FOUGHT TO LIVE AND FAILED.
THERE WAS A BOY. YOUNGER THAN YOU.
THEY KILLED A CHILD OUTSIDE OUR HOME, DO YOU UNDERSTAND?

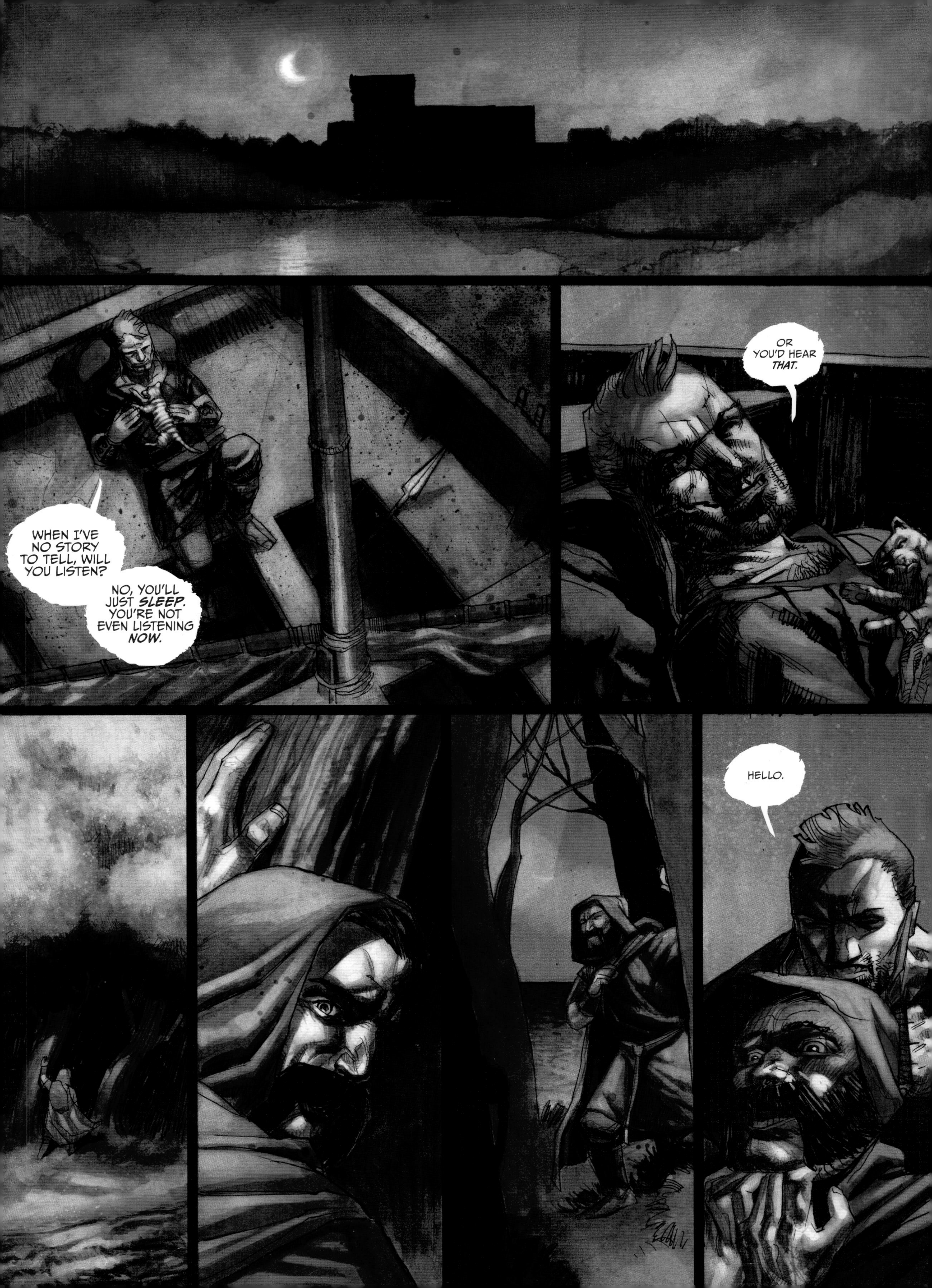
WHEN I'VE NO STORY TO TELL, WILL YOU LISTEN?
NO, YOU'LL JUST *SLEEP*. YOU'RE NOT EVEN LISTENING *NOW*.
OR YOU'D HEAR *THAT*.
HELLO.

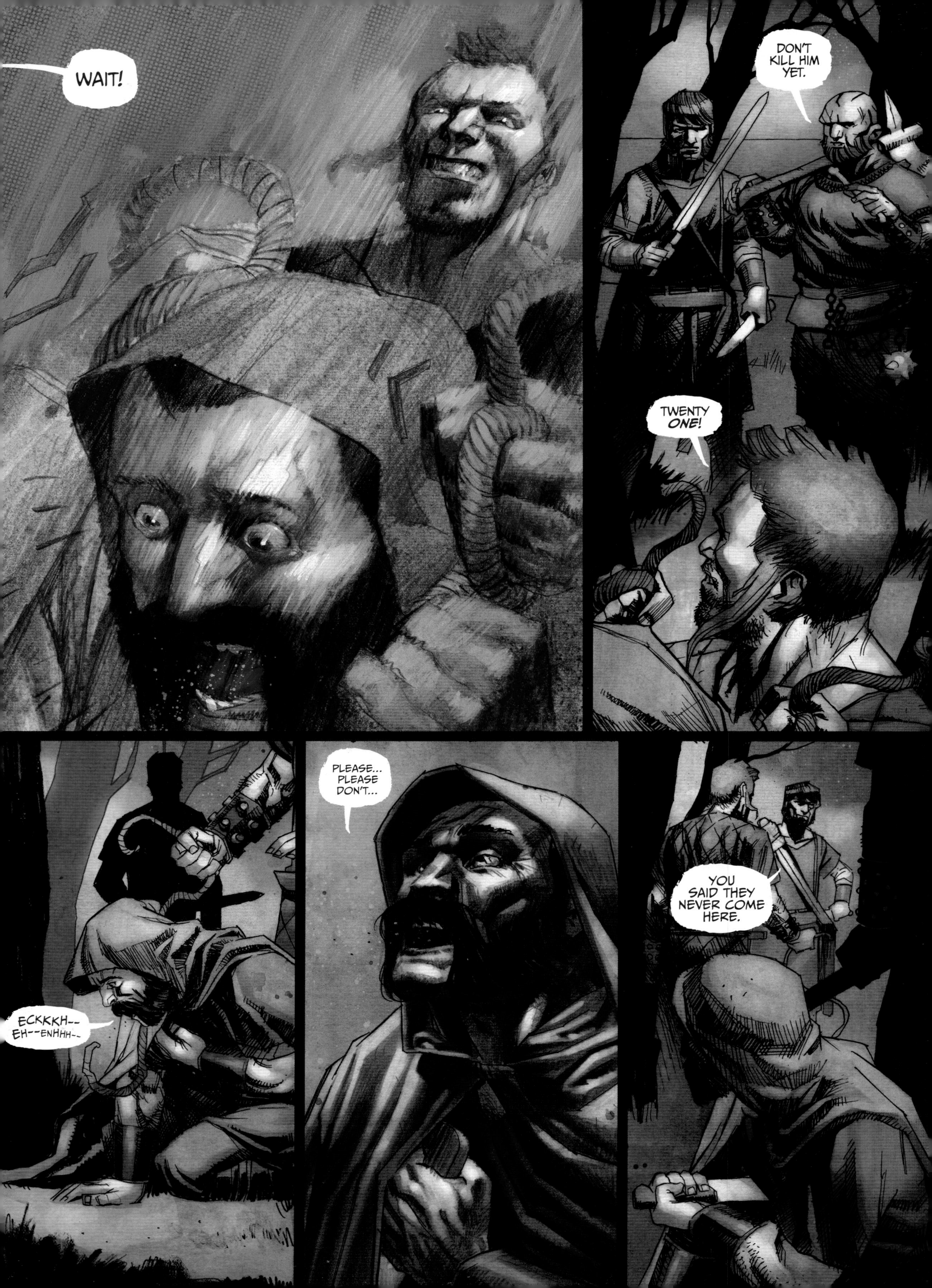
WAIT!
DON'T KILL HIM YET.
TWENTY ONE!
ECKKKH-- EH--ENHHH--
PLEASE... PLEASE DON'T...
YOU SAID THEY NEVER COME HERE.

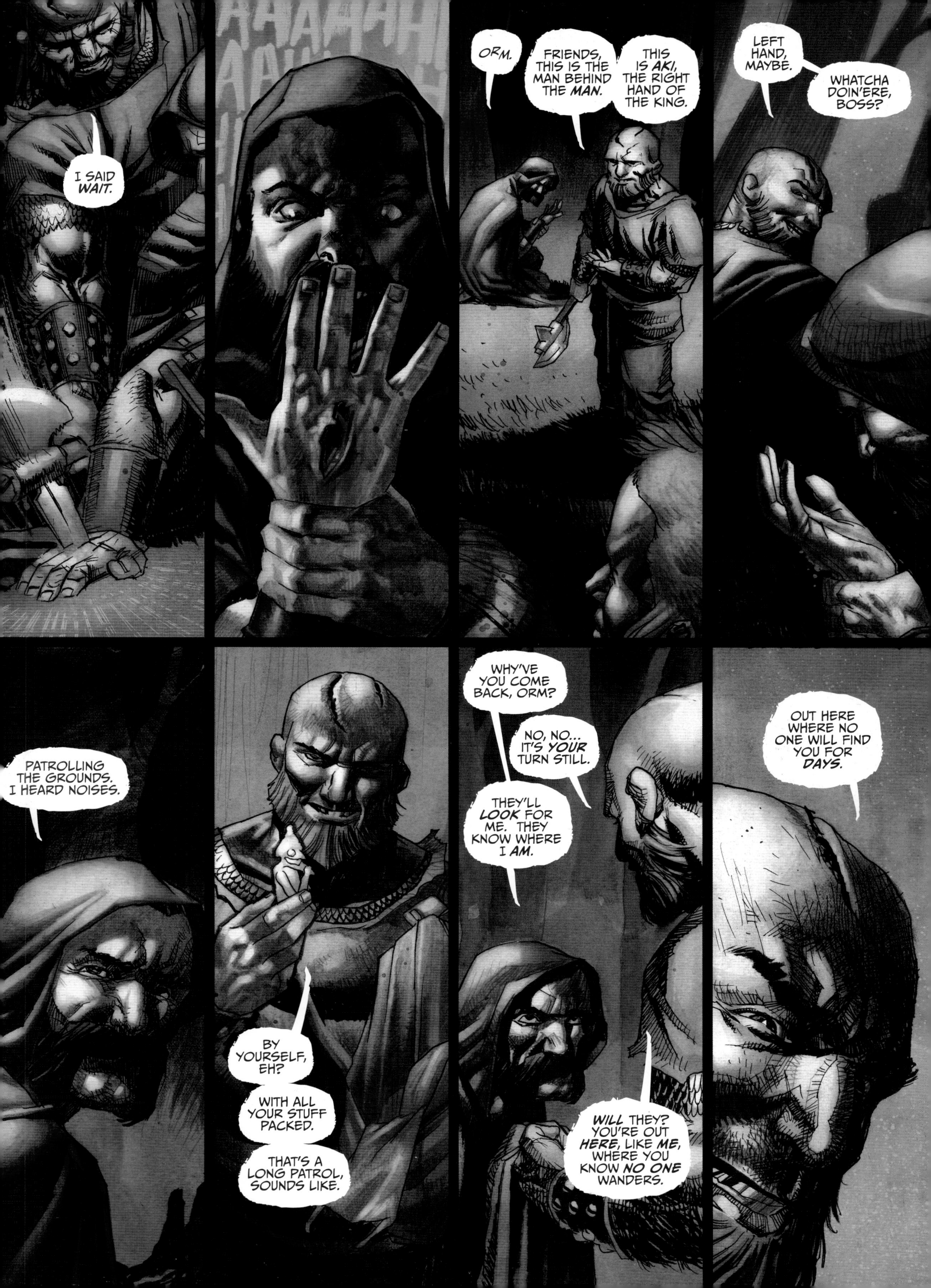
I SAID WAIT.
AAAHHH! AAAHHH!
ORM.
FRIENDS, THIS IS THE MAN BEHIND THE MAN.
THIS IS AKI, THE RIGHT HAND OF THE KING.
LEFT HAND, MAYBE.
WHATCHA DOIN'ERE, BOSS?
PATROLLING THE GROUNDS. I HEARD NOISES.
BY YOURSELF, EH?
WITH ALL YOUR STUFF PACKED.
THAT'S A LONG PATROL, SOUNDS LIKE.
WHY'VE YOU COME BACK, ORM?
NO, NO... IT'S YOUR TURN STILL.
THEY'LL LOOK FOR ME. THEY KNOW WHERE I AM.
WILL THEY? YOU'RE OUT HERE, LIKE ME, WHERE YOU KNOW NO ONE WANDERS.
OUT HERE WHERE NO ONE WILL FIND YOU FOR DAYS.

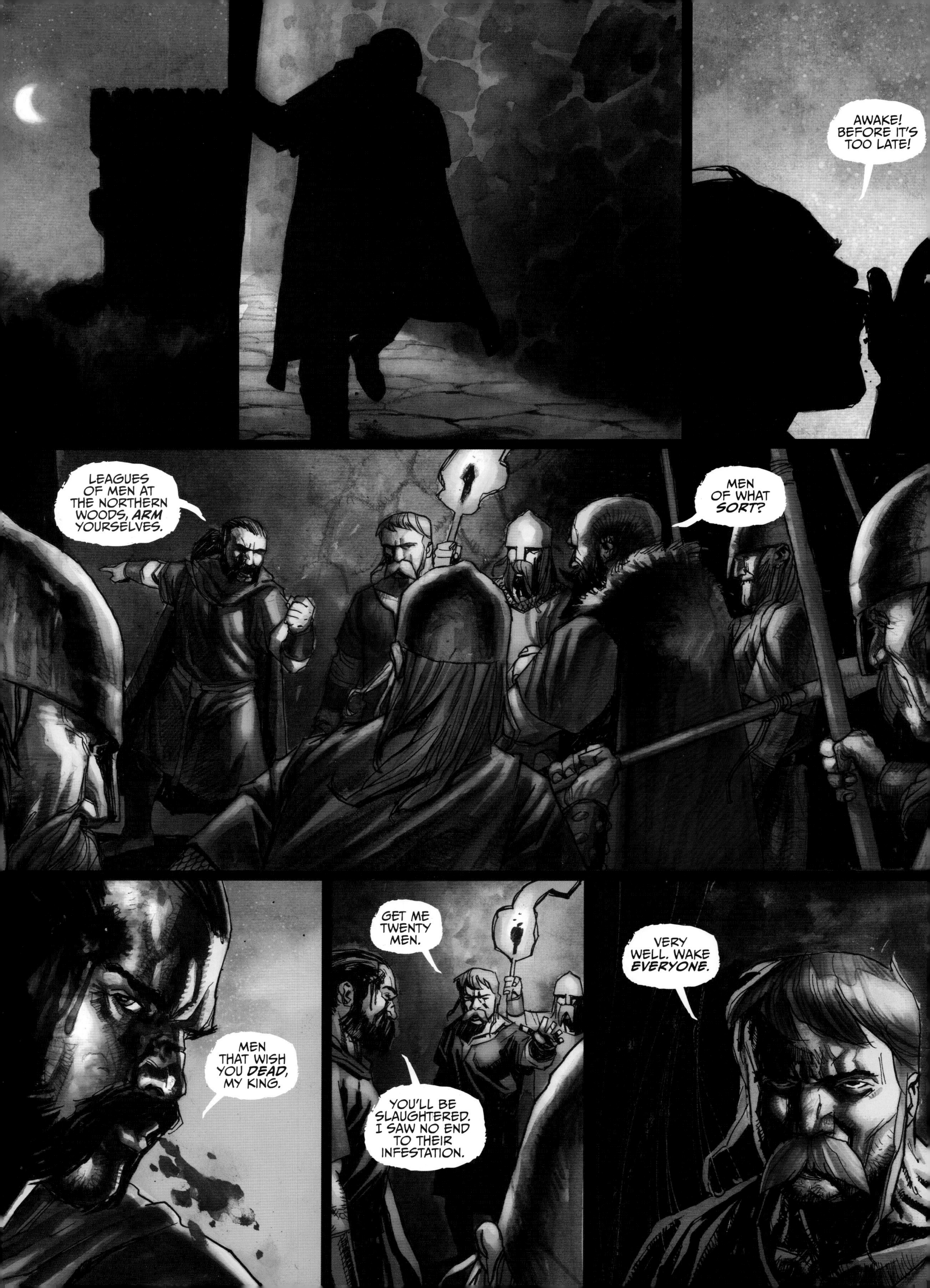
AWAKE! BEFORE IT'S TOO LATE!
LEAGUES OF MEN AT THE NORTHERN WOODS, ARM YOURSELVES.
MEN OF WHAT SORT?
MEN THAT WISH YOU DEAD, MY KING.
GET ME TWENTY MEN.
YOU'LL BE SLAUGHTERED. I SAW NO END TO THEIR INFESTATION.
VERY WELL. WAKE EVERYONE.

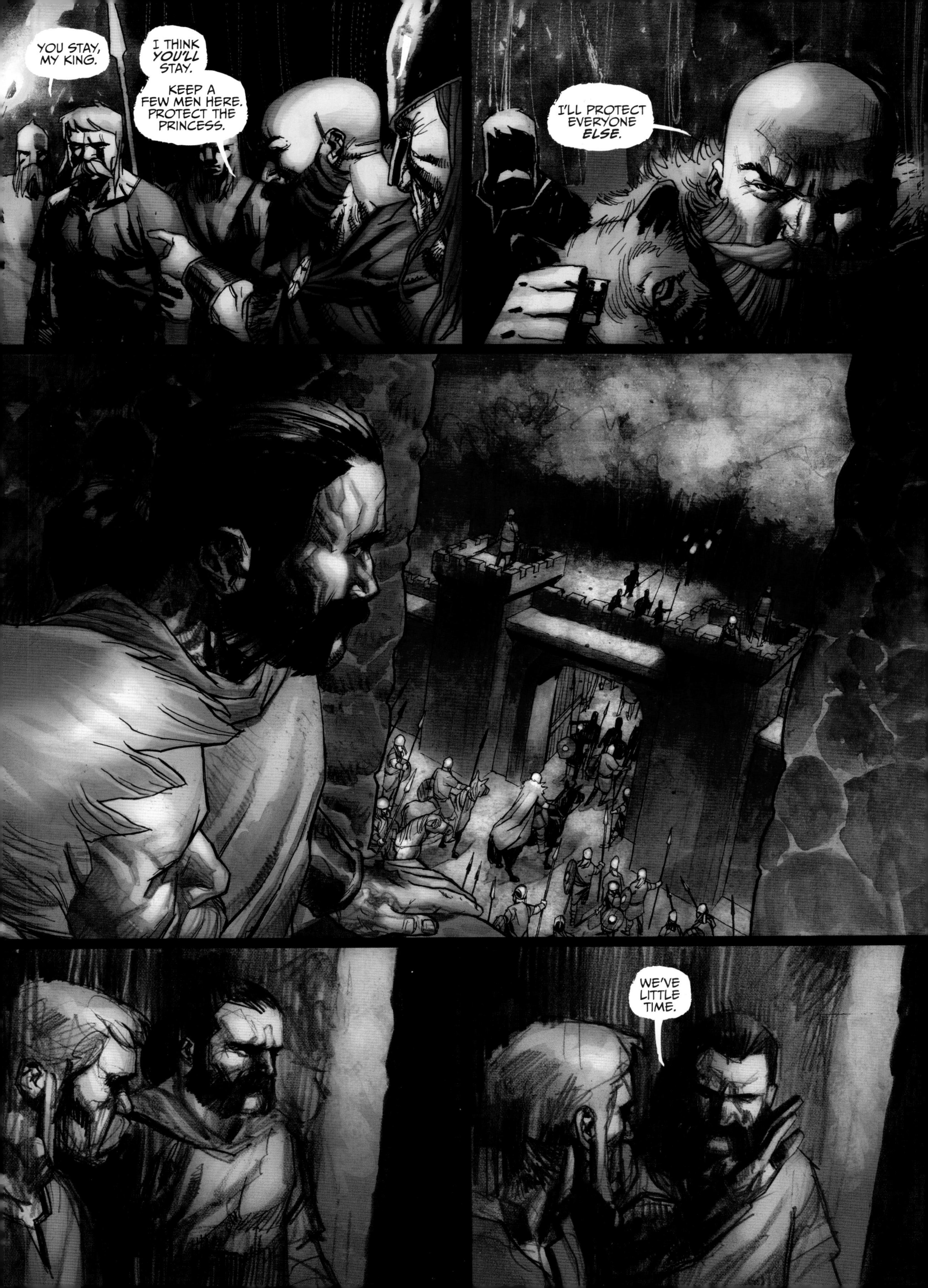
YOU STAY, MY KING.
I THINK *YOU'LL* STAY.
KEEP A FEW MEN HERE. PROTECT THE PRINCESS.
I'LL PROTECT EVERYONE *ELSE*.
WE'VE LITTLE TIME.

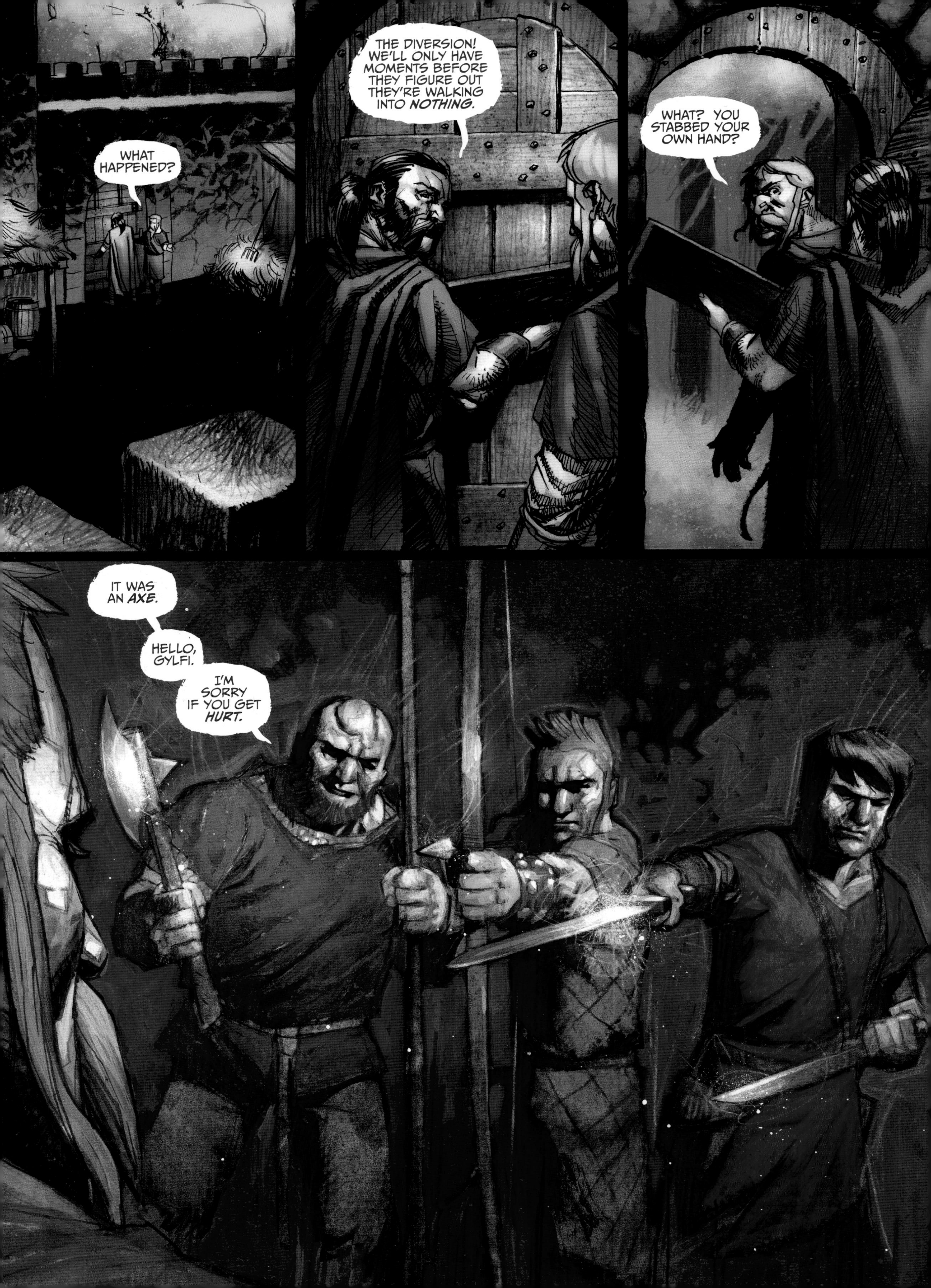
WHAT HAPPENED?
THE DIVERSION! WE'LL ONLY HAVE MOMENTS BEFORE THEY FIGURE OUT THEY'RE WALKING INTO NOTHING.
WHAT? YOU STABBED YOUR OWN HAND?
IT WAS AN AXE.
HELLO, GYLFI.
I'M SORRY IF YOU GET HURT.

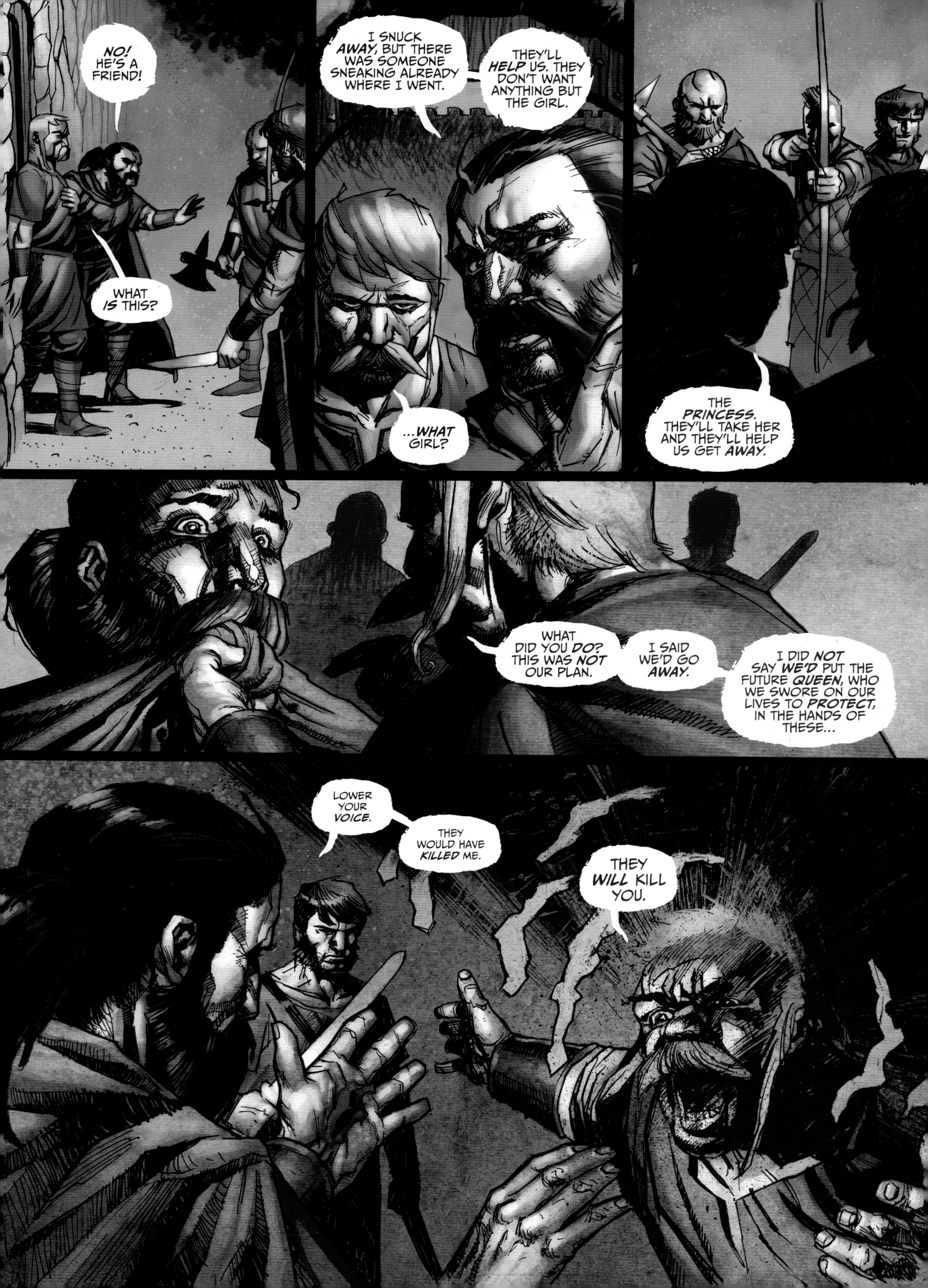
NO! HE'S A FRIEND!
WHAT IS THIS?
I SNUCK AWAY, BUT THERE WAS SOMEONE SNEAKING ALREADY WHERE I WENT.
THEY'LL HELP US. THEY DON'T WANT ANYTHING BUT THE GIRL.
...WHAT GIRL?
THE PRINCESS. THEY'LL TAKE HER AND THEY'LL HELP US GET AWAY.
WHAT DID YOU DO? THIS WAS NOT OUR PLAN.
I SAID WE'D GO AWAY.
I DID NOT SAY WE'D PUT THE FUTURE QUEEN, WHO WE SWORE ON OUR LIVES TO PROTECT, IN THE HANDS OF THESE...
LOWER YOUR VOICE.
THEY WOULD HAVE KILLED ME.
THEY WILL KILL YOU.

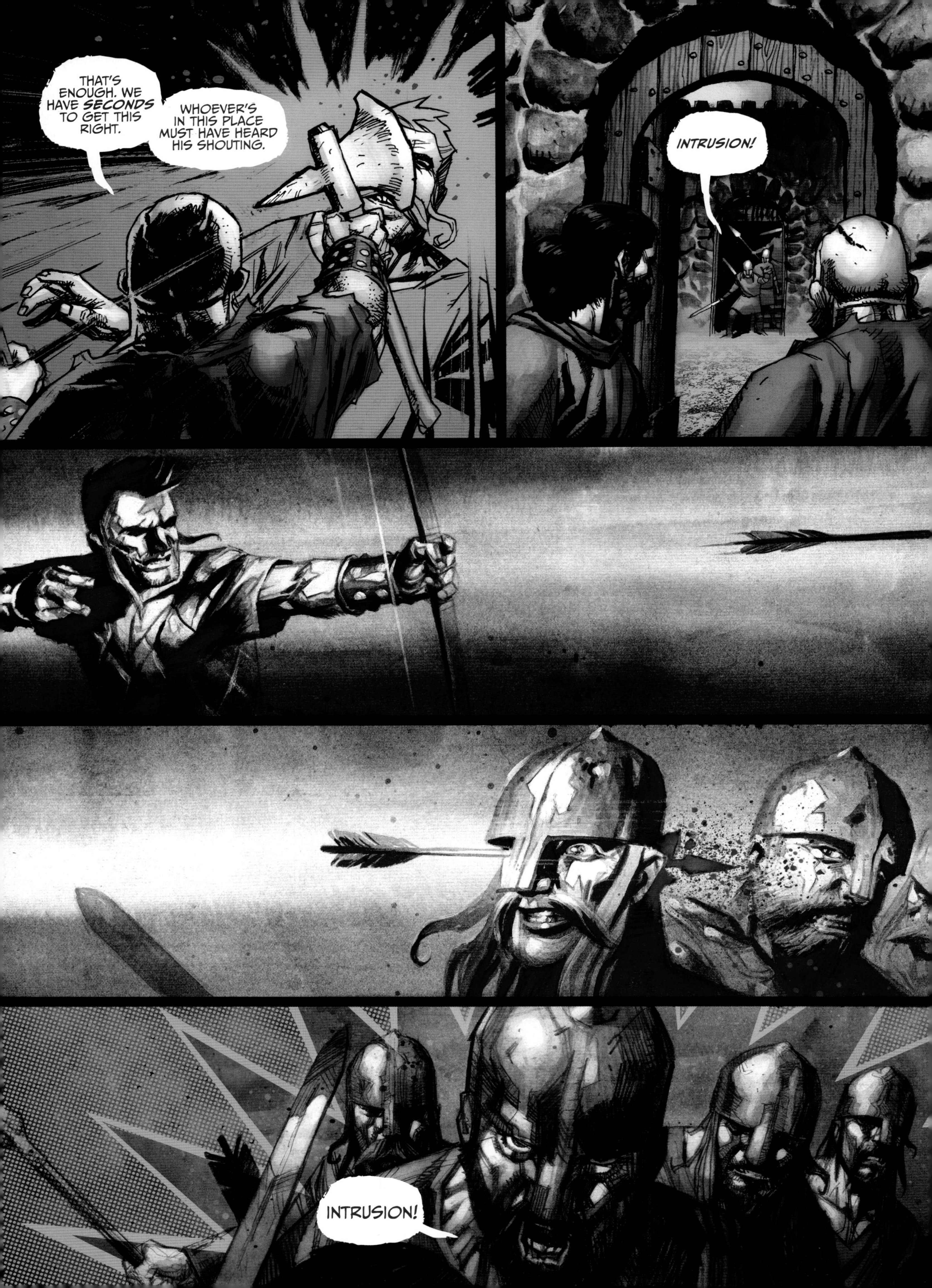
THAT'S ENOUGH. WE HAVE SECONDS TO GET THIS RIGHT.
WHOEVER'S IN THIS PLACE MUST HAVE HEARD HIS SHOUTING.
INTRUSION!
INTRUSION!

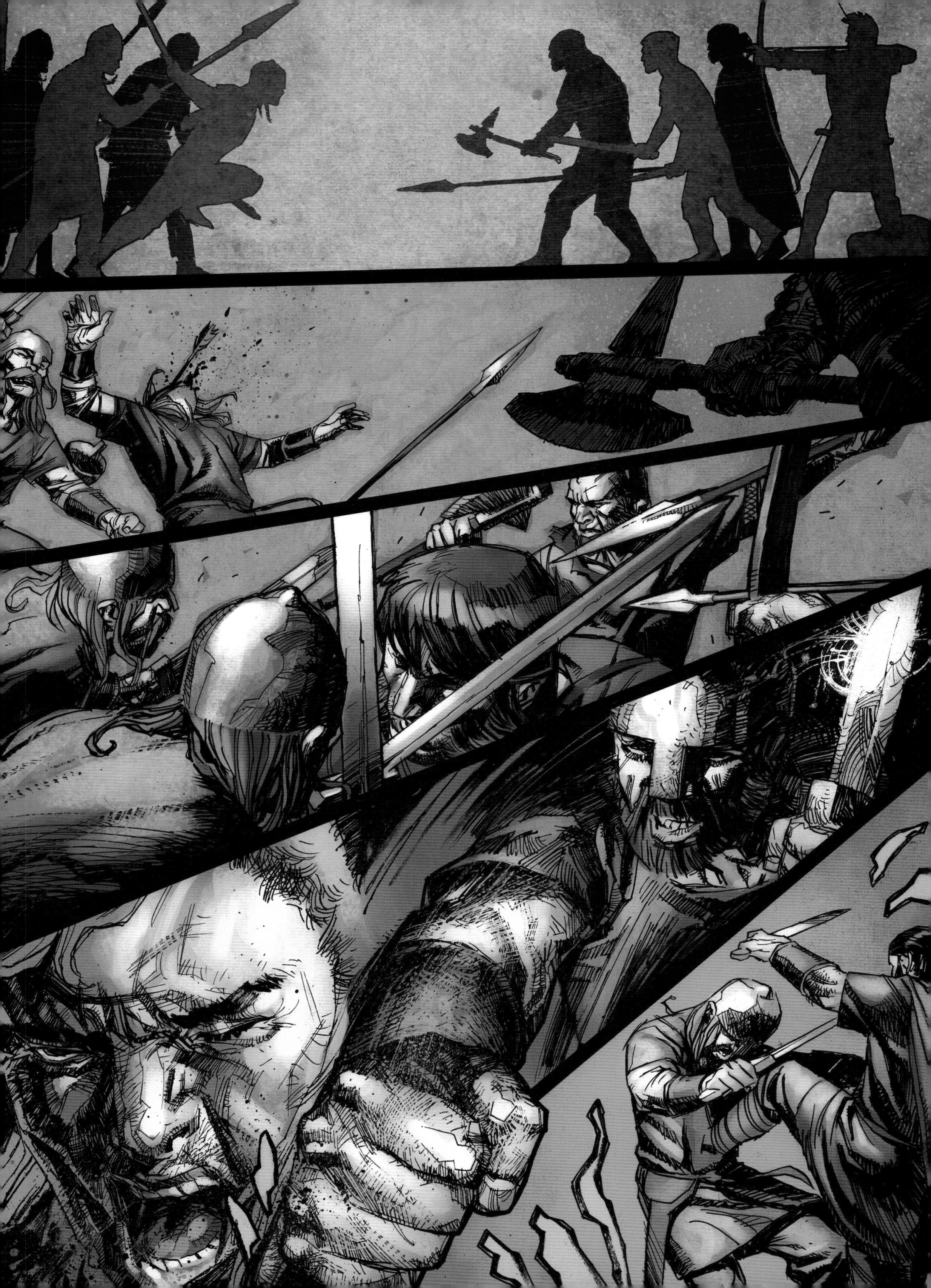

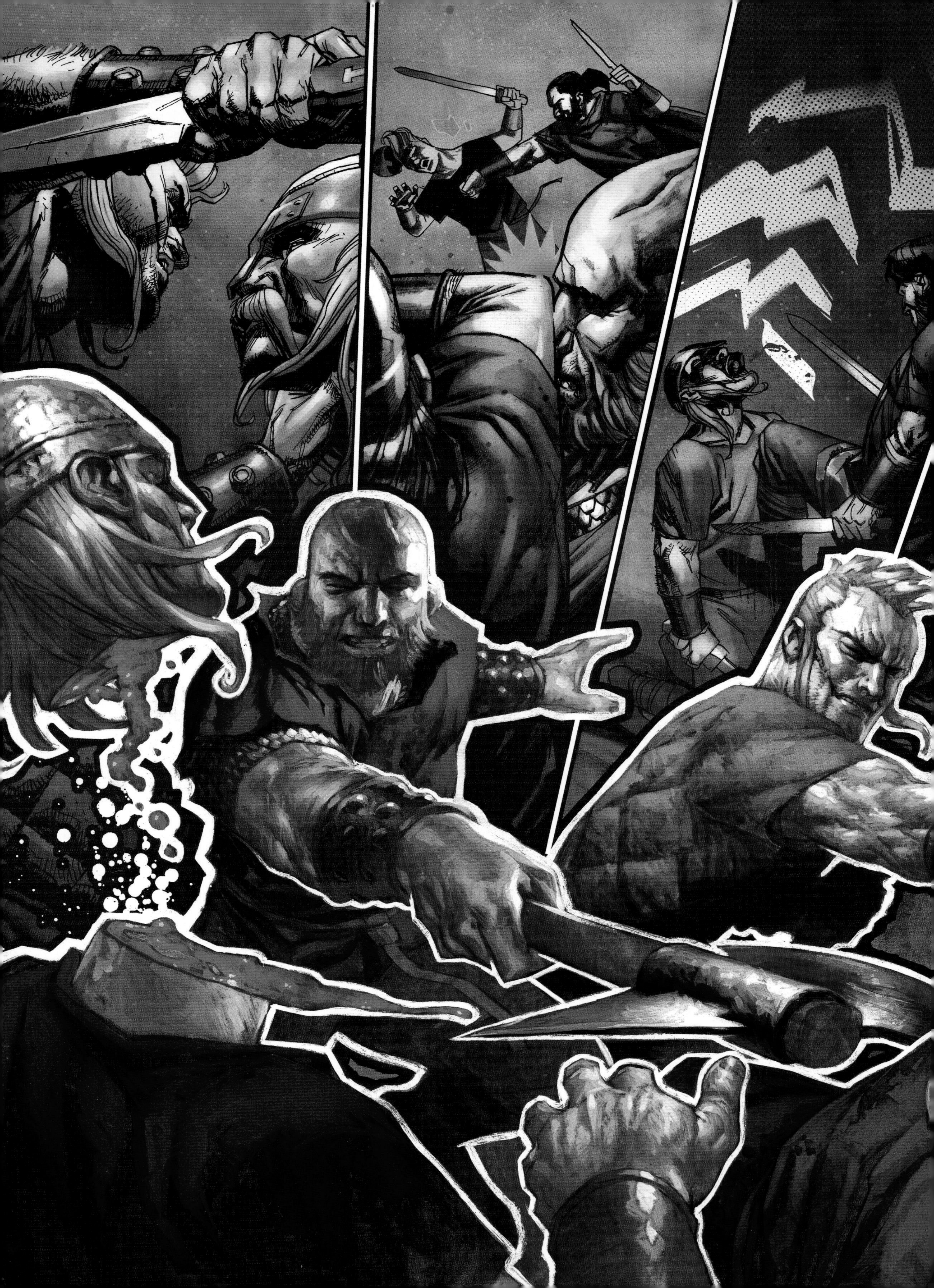

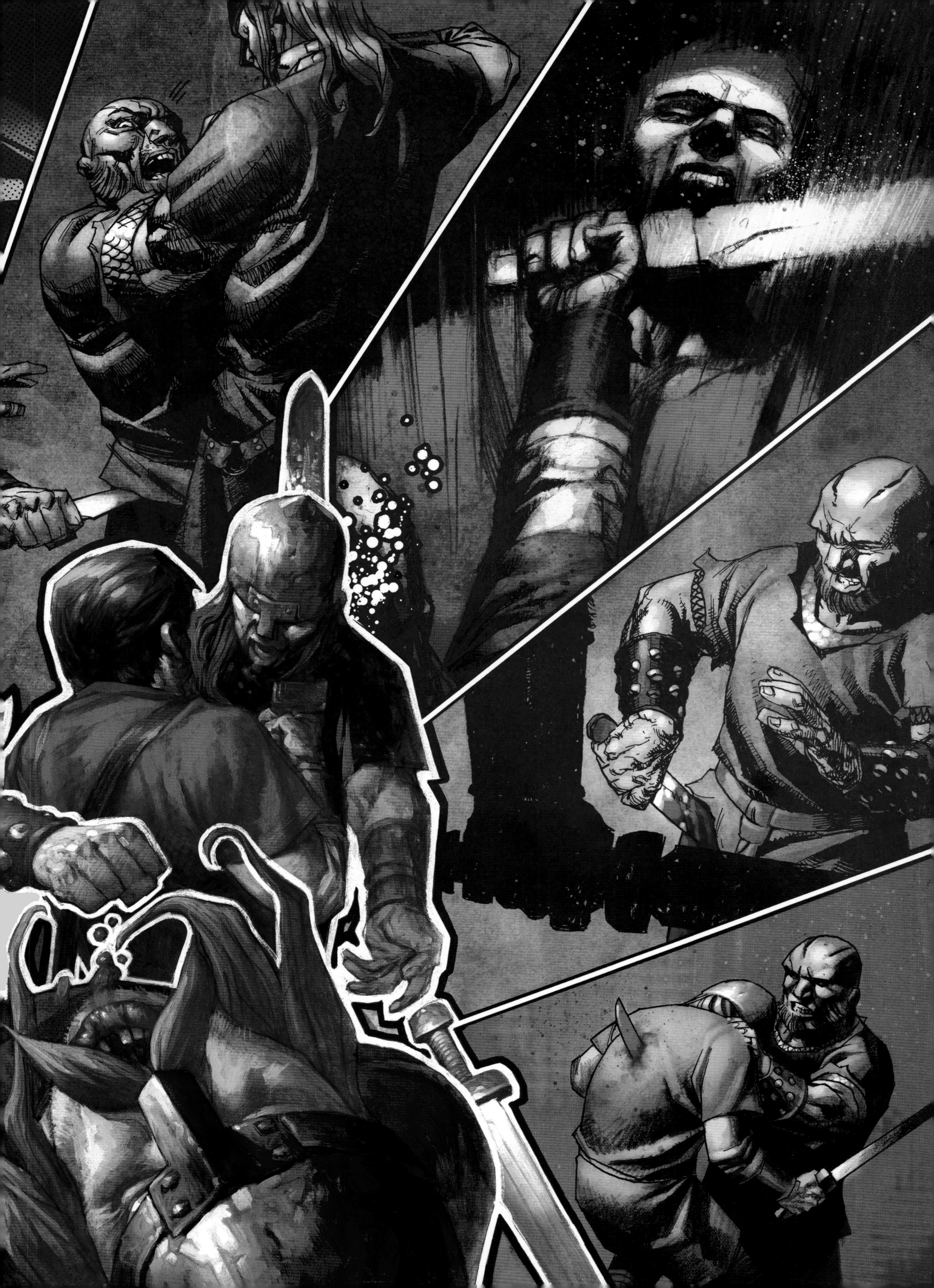

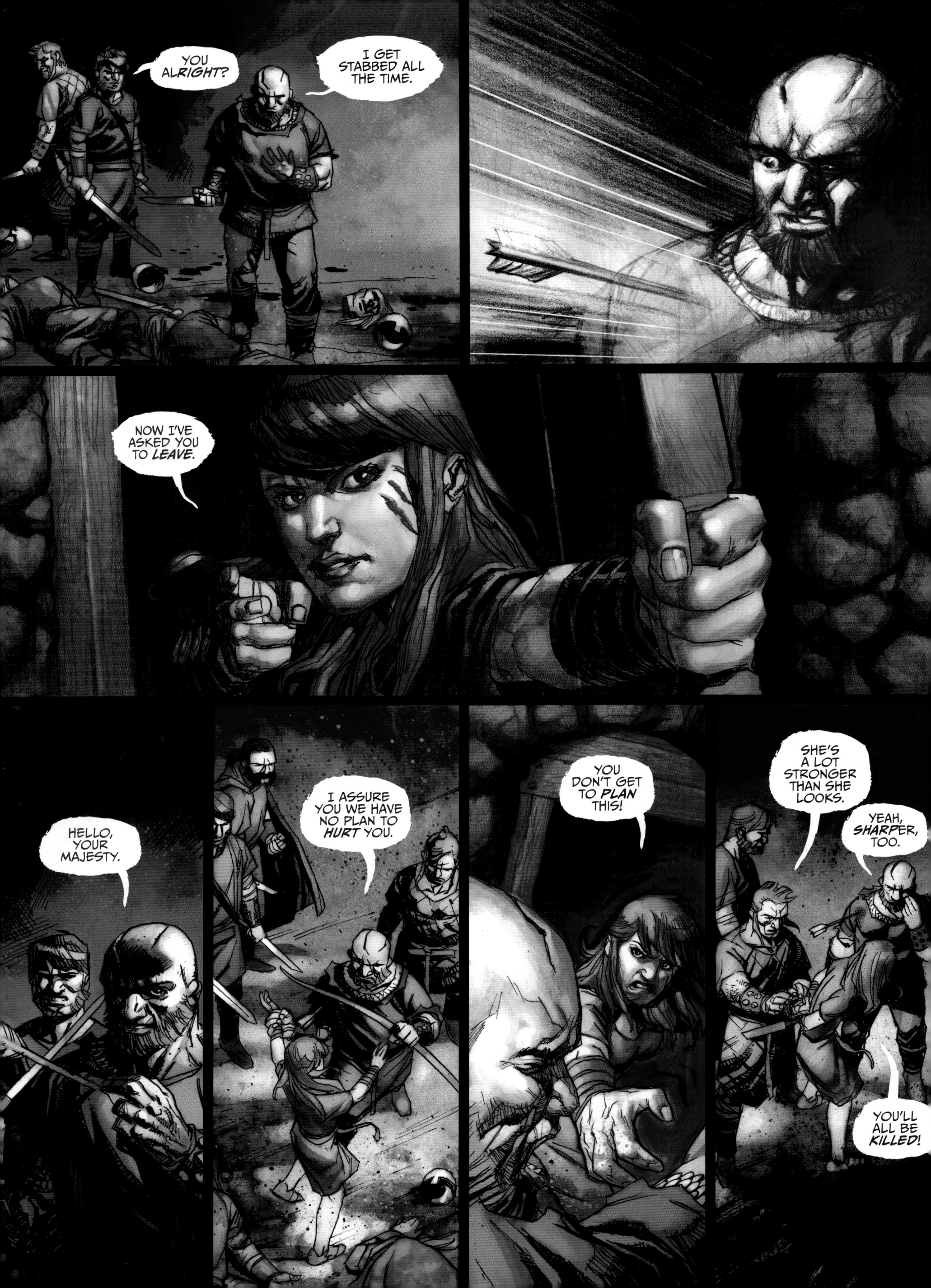
YOU ALRIGHT?
I GET STABBED ALL THE TIME.
NOW I'VE ASKED YOU TO LEAVE.
HELLO, YOUR MAJESTY.
I ASSURE YOU WE HAVE NO PLAN TO HURT YOU.
YOU DON'T GET TO PLAN THIS!
SHE'S A LOT STRONGER THAN SHE LOOKS.
YEAH, SHARPER, TOO.
YOU'LL ALL BE KILLED!

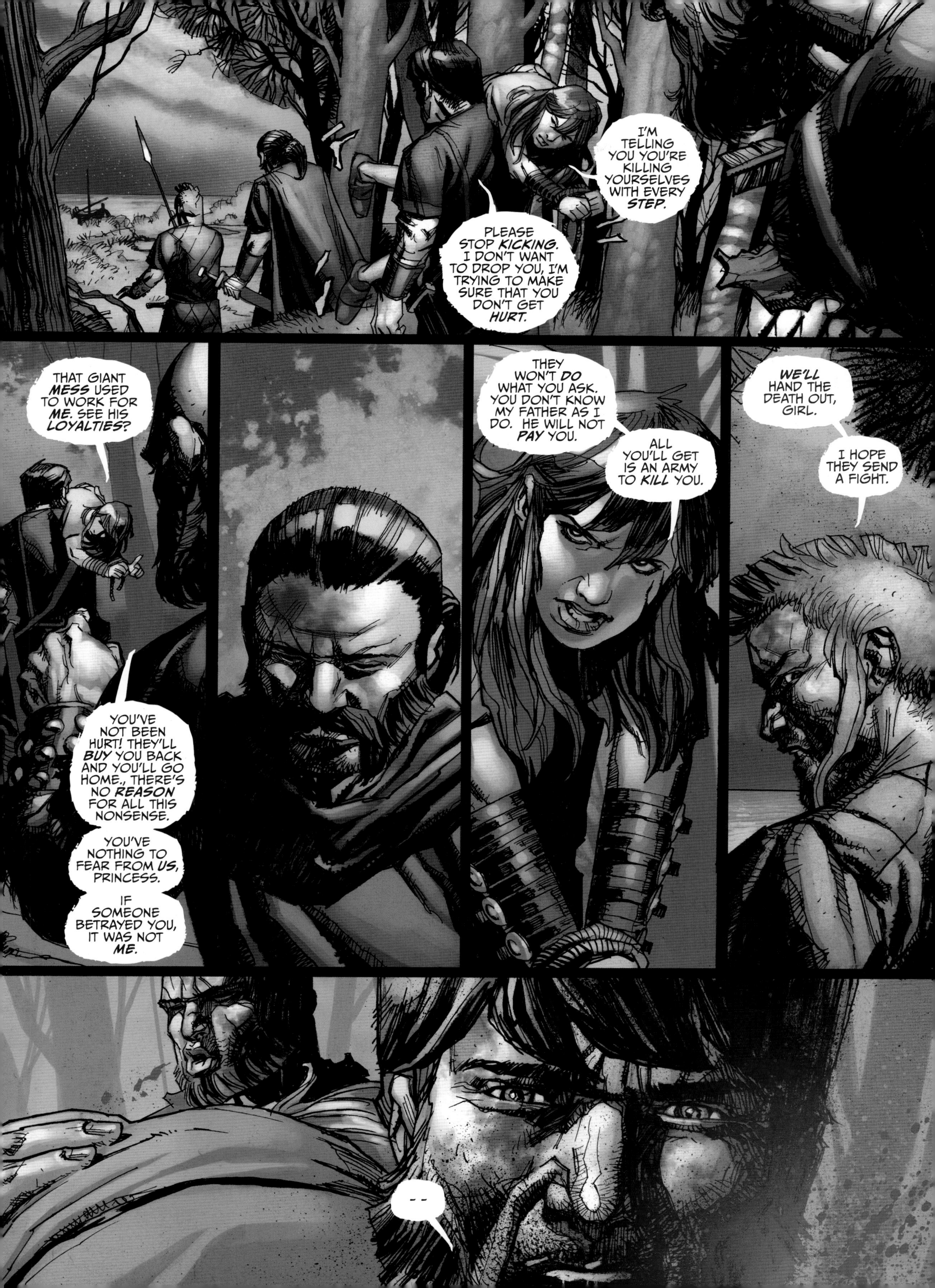
I'M TELLING YOU YOU'RE KILLING YOURSELVES WITH EVERY STEP.
PLEASE STOP KICKING. I DON'T WANT TO DROP YOU, I'M TRYING TO MAKE SURE THAT YOU DON'T GET HURT.
THAT GIANT MESS USED TO WORK FOR ME. SEE HIS LOYALTIES?
YOU'VE NOT BEEN HURT! THEY'LL BUY YOU BACK AND YOU'LL GO HOME., THERE'S NO REASON FOR ALL THIS NONSENSE.
YOU'VE NOTHING TO FEAR FROM US, PRINCESS.
IF SOMEONE BETRAYED YOU, IT WAS NOT ME.
THEY WON'T DO WHAT YOU ASK. YOU DON'T KNOW MY FATHER AS I DO. HE WILL NOT PAY YOU.
ALL YOU'LL GET IS AN ARMY TO KILL YOU.
WE'LL HAND THE DEATH OUT, GIRL.
I HOPE THEY SEND A FIGHT.
--

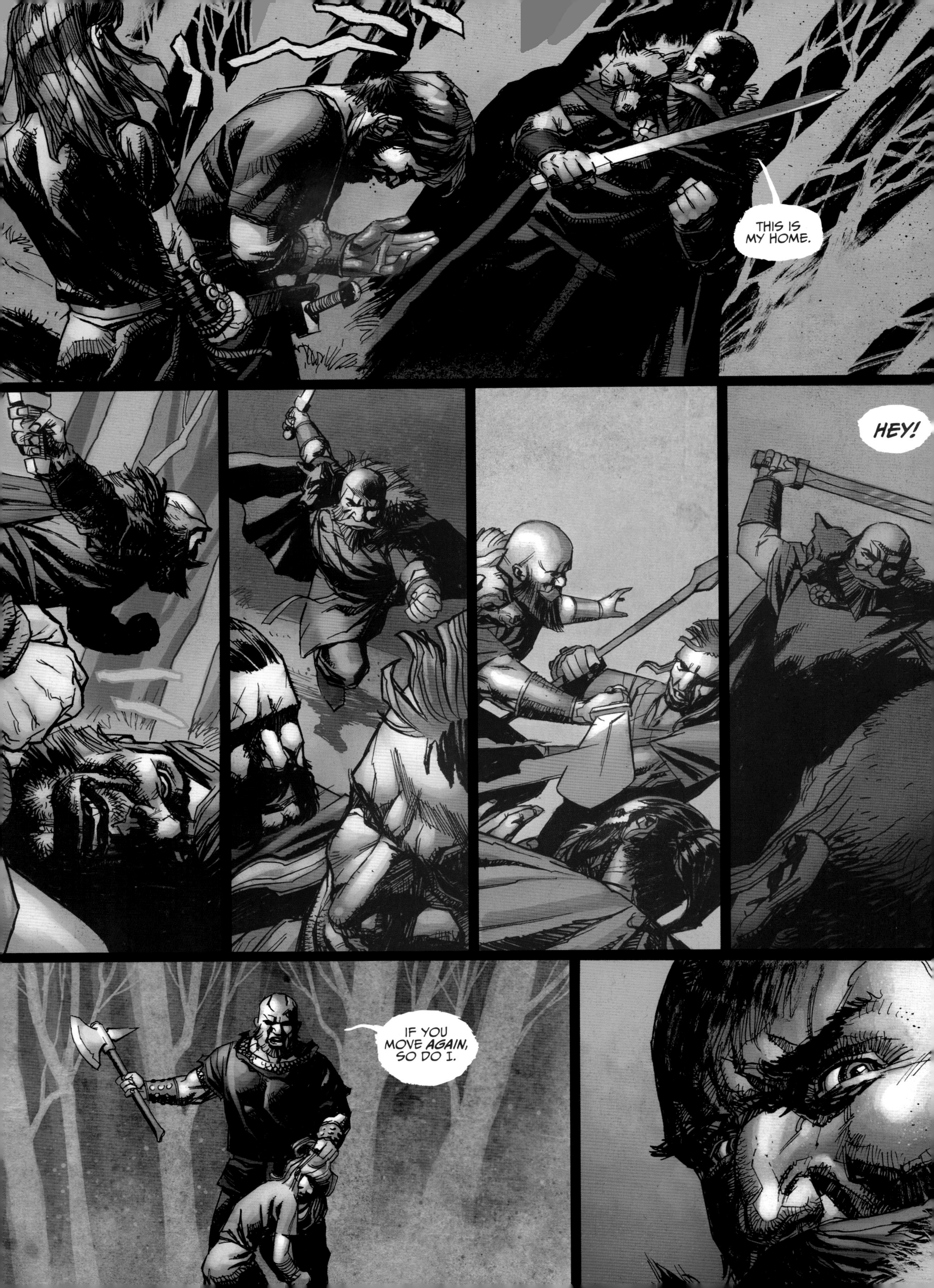
THIS IS MY HOME.
HEY!
IF YOU MOVE AGAIN, SO DO I.

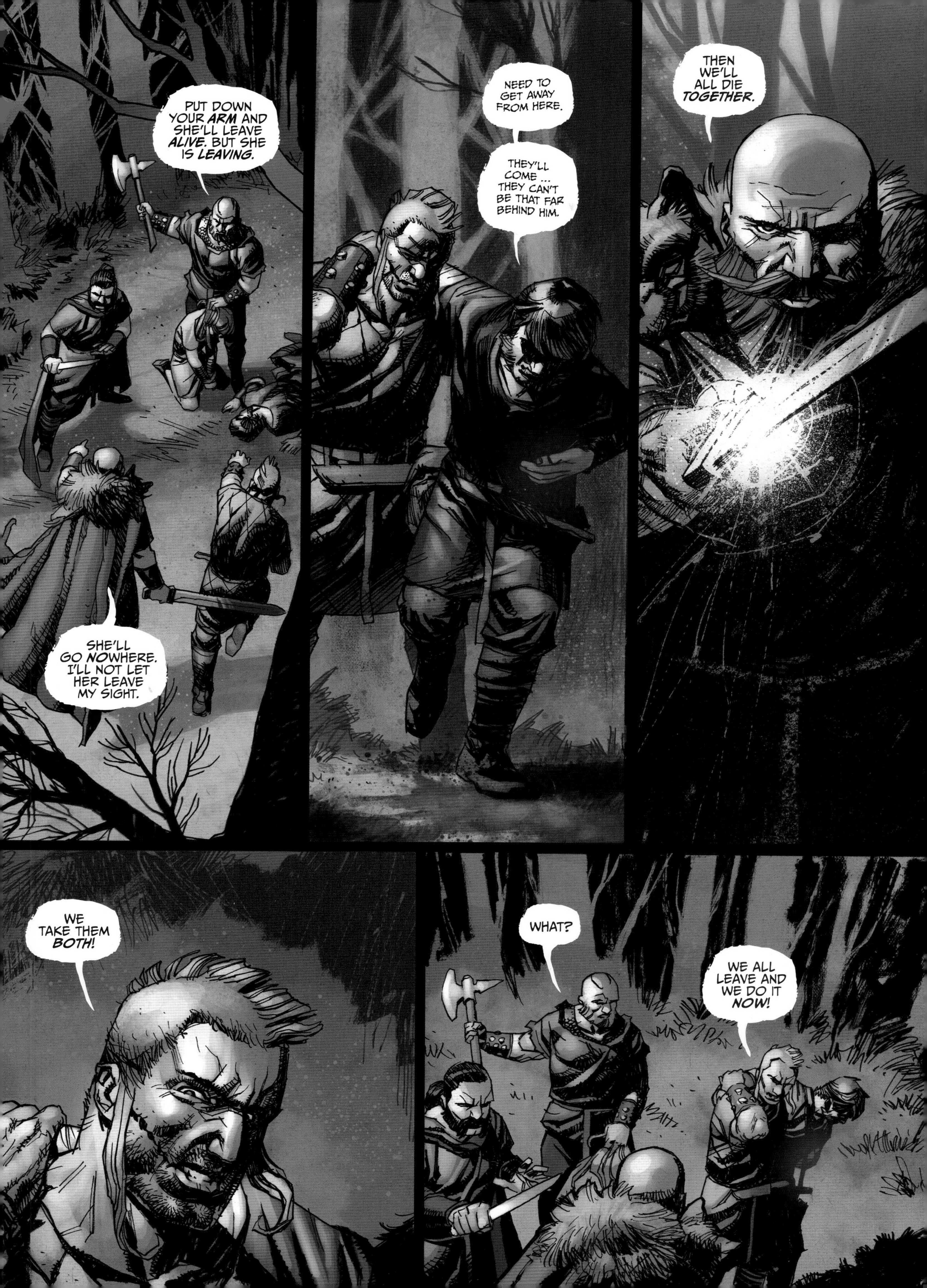
PUT DOWN YOUR ARM AND SHE'LL LEAVE ALIVE. BUT SHE IS LEAVING.
SHE'LL GO NOWHERE. I'LL NOT LET HER LEAVE MY SIGHT.
NEED TO GET AWAY FROM HERE.
THEY'LL COME ... THEY CAN'T BE THAT FAR BEHIND HIM.
THEN WE'LL ALL DIE TOGETHER.
WE TAKE THEM BOTH!
WHAT?
WE ALL LEAVE AND WE DO IT NOW!

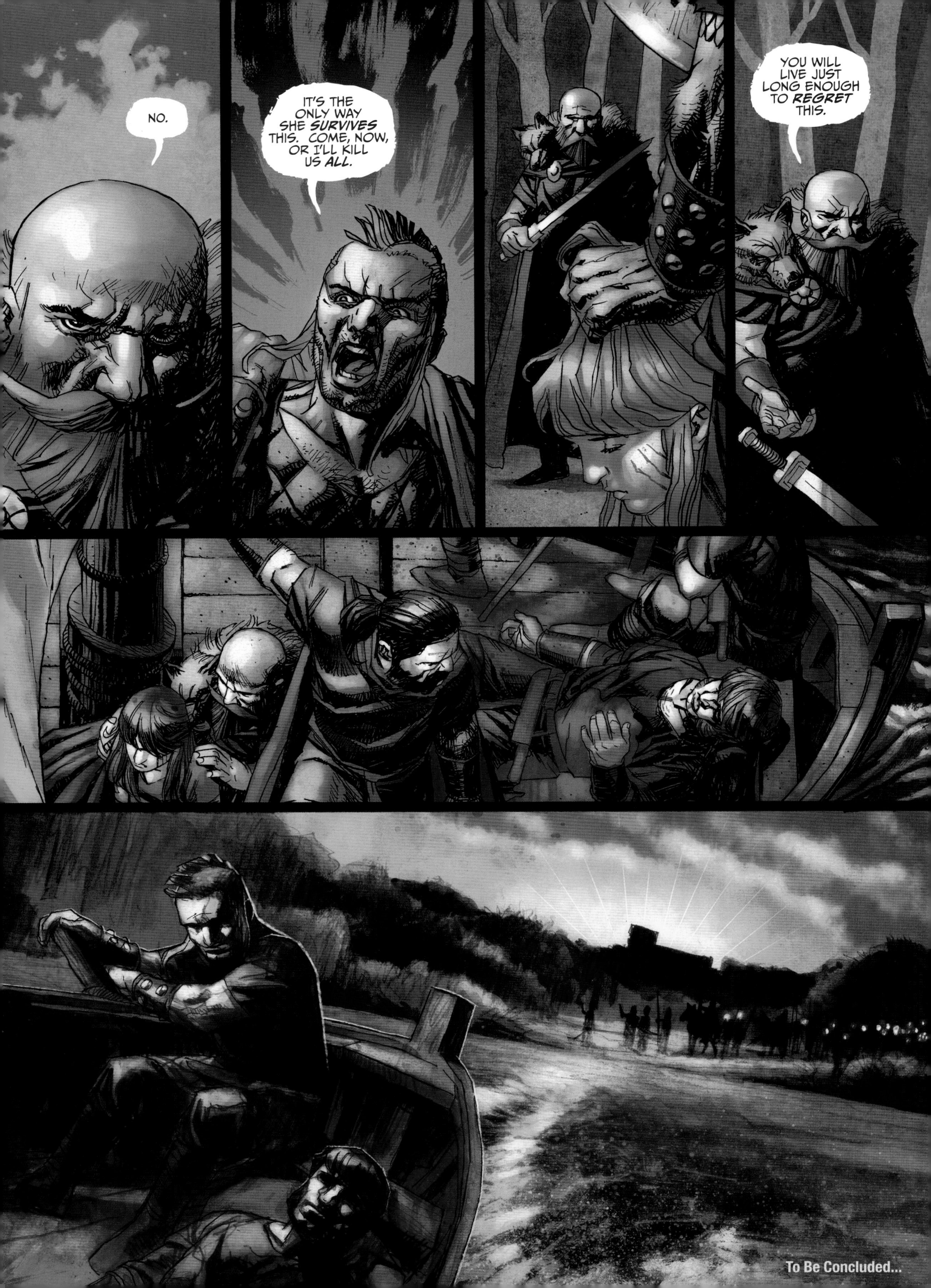
NO.
IT'S THE ONLY WAY SHE SURVIVES THIS. COME, NOW, OR I'LL KILL US ALL.
YOU WILL LIVE JUST LONG ENOUGH TO REGRET THIS.
To Be Concluded...

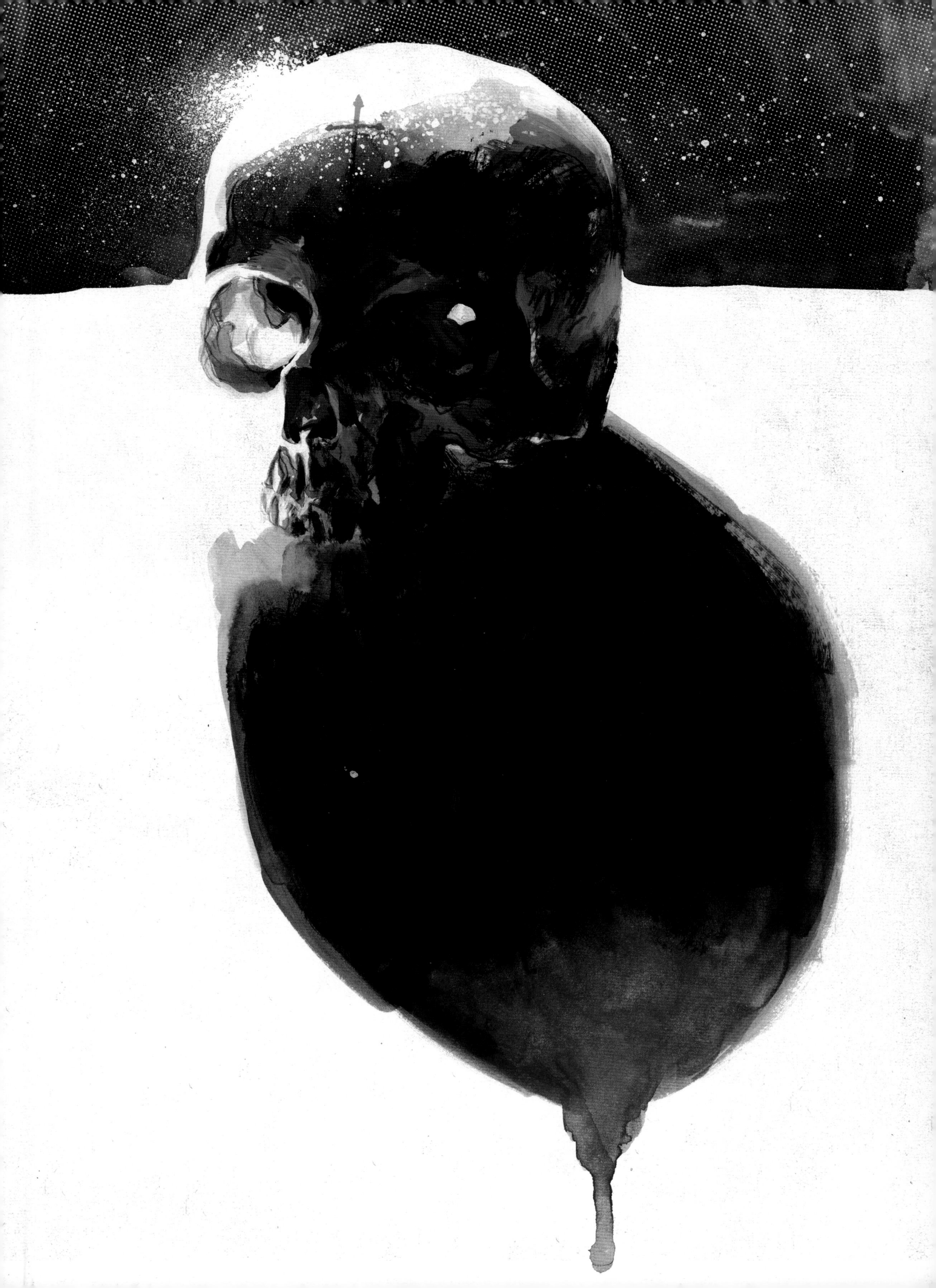

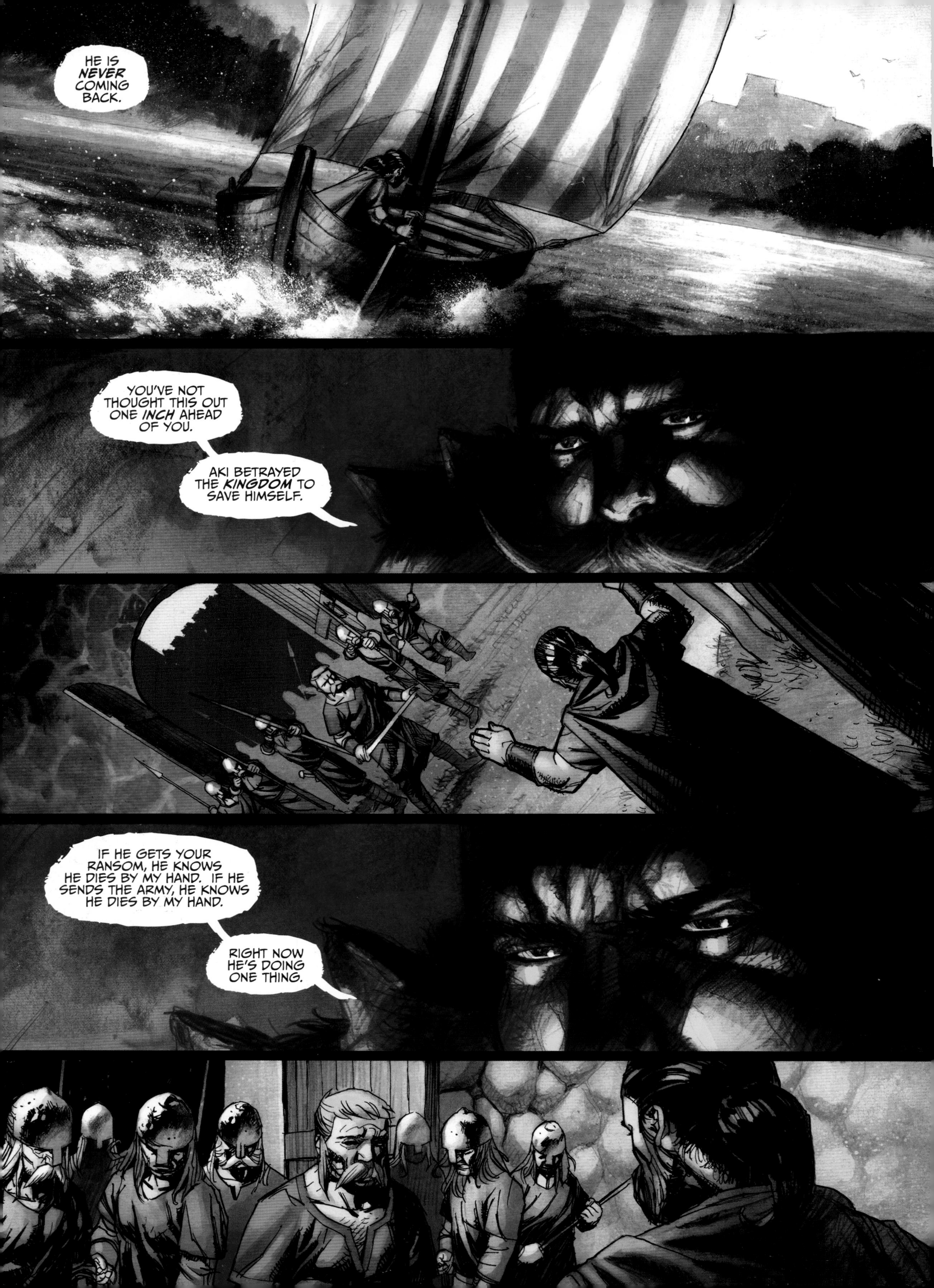
HE IS NEVER COMING BACK.
YOU'VE NOT THOUGHT THIS OUT ONE INCH AHEAD OF YOU.
AKI BETRAYED THE KINGDOM TO SAVE HIMSELF.
IF HE GETS YOUR RANSOM, HE KNOWS HE DIES BY MY HAND. IF HE SENDS THE ARMY, HE KNOWS HE DIES BY MY HAND.
RIGHT NOW HE'S DOING ONE THING.

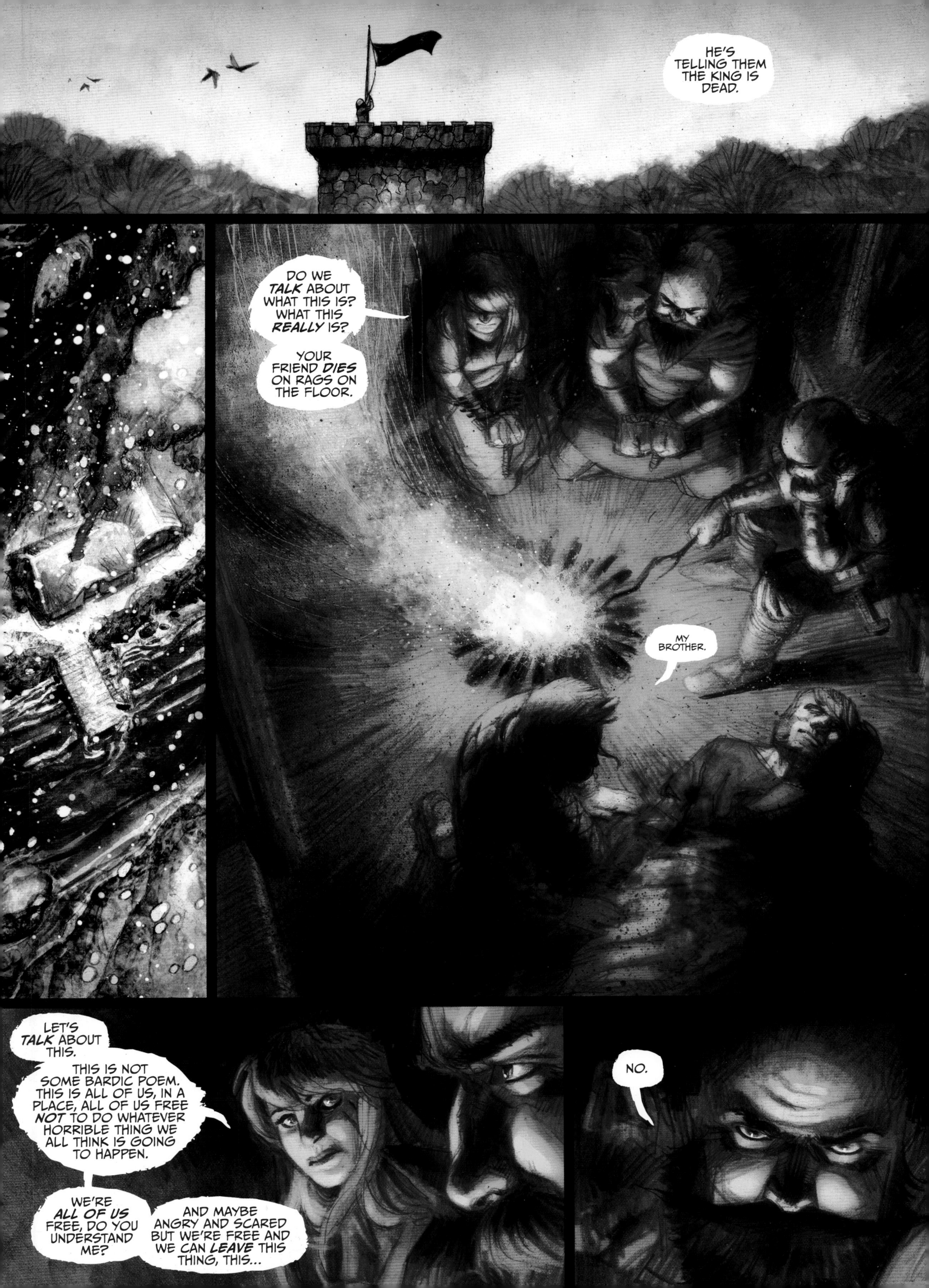
HE'S TELLING THEM THE KING IS DEAD.
DO WE TALK ABOUT WHAT THIS IS? WHAT THIS REALLY IS?
YOUR FRIEND DIES ON RAGS ON THE FLOOR.
MY BROTHER.
LET'S TALK ABOUT THIS.
THIS IS NOT SOME BARDIC POEM. THIS IS ALL OF US, IN A PLACE, ALL OF US FREE NOT TO DO WHATEVER HORRIBLE THING WE ALL THINK IS GOING TO HAPPEN.
WE'RE ALL OF US FREE, DO YOU UNDERSTAND ME?
AND MAYBE ANGRY AND SCARED BUT WE'RE FREE AND WE CAN LEAVE THIS THING, THIS...
NO.

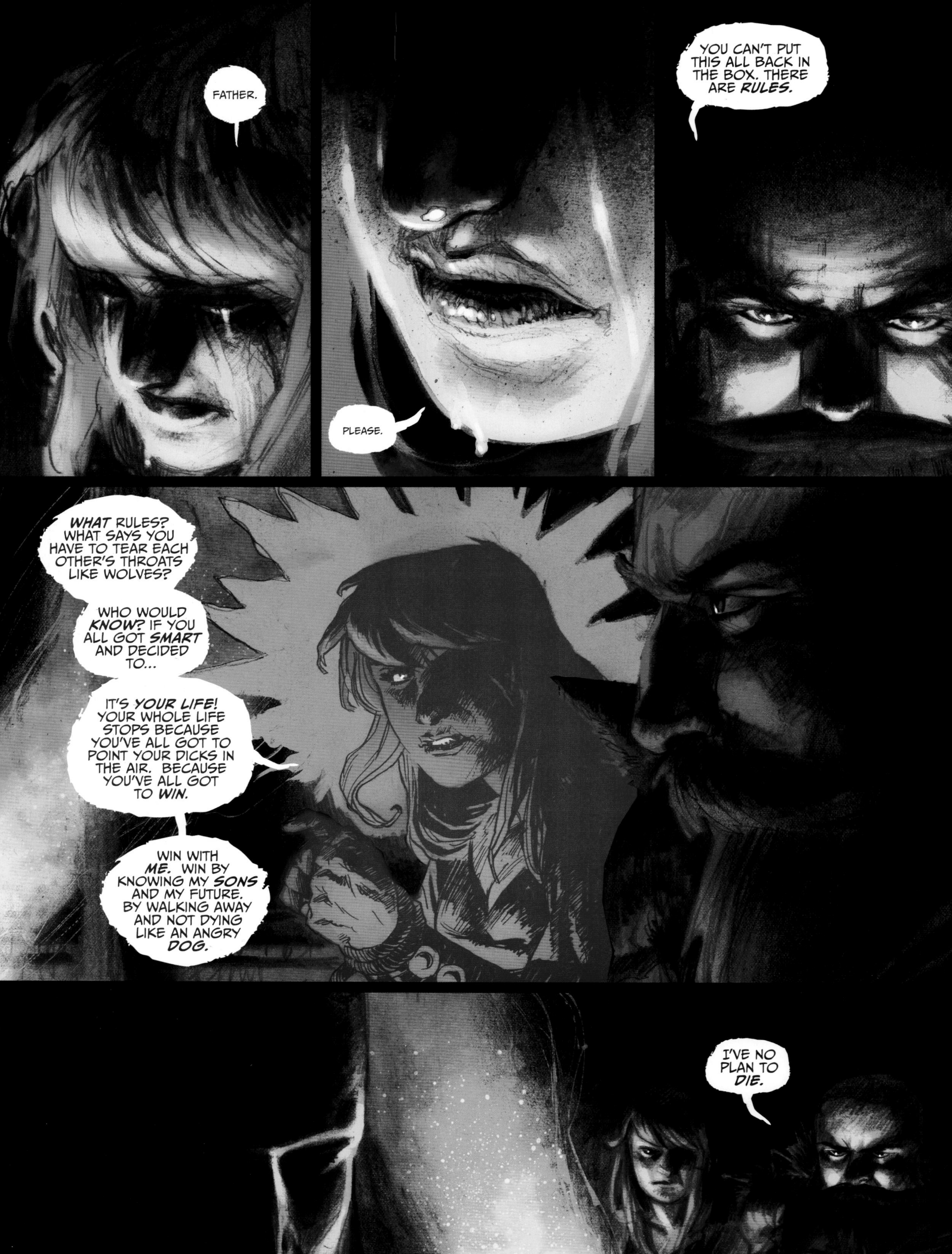
FATHER.
PLEASE.
YOU CAN'T PUT THIS ALL BACK IN THE BOX. THERE ARE RULES.
WHAT RULES? WHAT SAYS YOU HAVE TO TEAR EACH OTHER'S THROATS LIKE WOLVES?
WHO WOULD KNOW? IF YOU ALL GOT SMART AND DECIDED TO...
IT'S YOUR LIFE! YOUR WHOLE LIFE STOPS BECAUSE YOU'VE ALL GOT TO POINT YOUR DICKS IN THE AIR. BECAUSE YOU'VE ALL GOT TO WIN.
WIN WITH ME. WIN BY KNOWING MY SONS AND MY FUTURE. BY WALKING AWAY AND NOT DYING LIKE AN ANGRY DOG.
I'VE NO PLAN TO DIE.

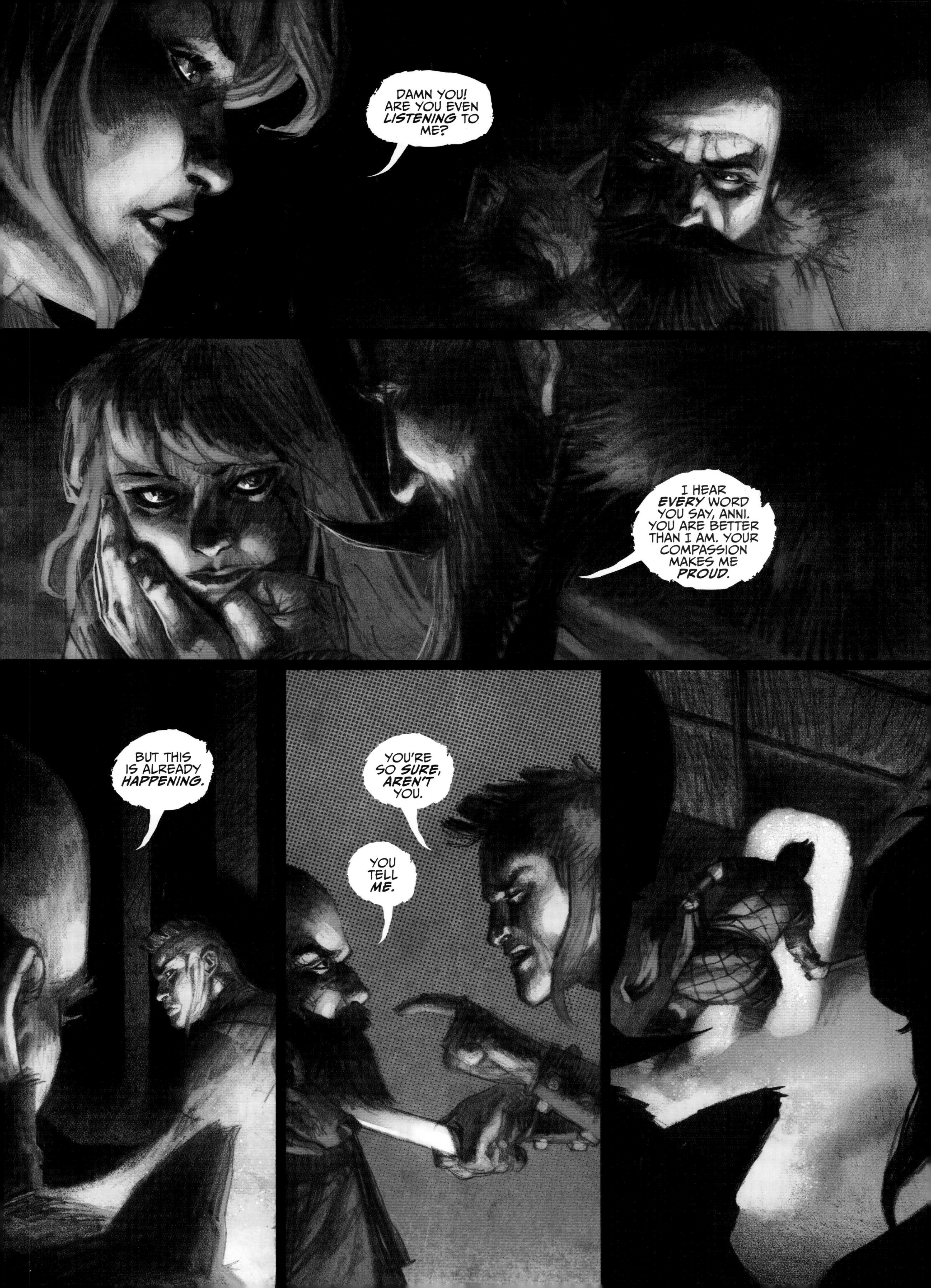
DAMN YOU! ARE YOU EVEN LISTENING TO ME?
I HEAR EVERY WORD YOU SAY, ANNI. YOU ARE BETTER THAN I AM. YOUR COMPASSION MAKES ME PROUD.
BUT THIS IS ALREADY HAPPENING.
YOU'RE SO SURE, AREN'T YOU.
YOU TELL ME.

MRRRR?

HAHAAHAA
AHAHHAA
HAHAHHAA
HAHAHAA

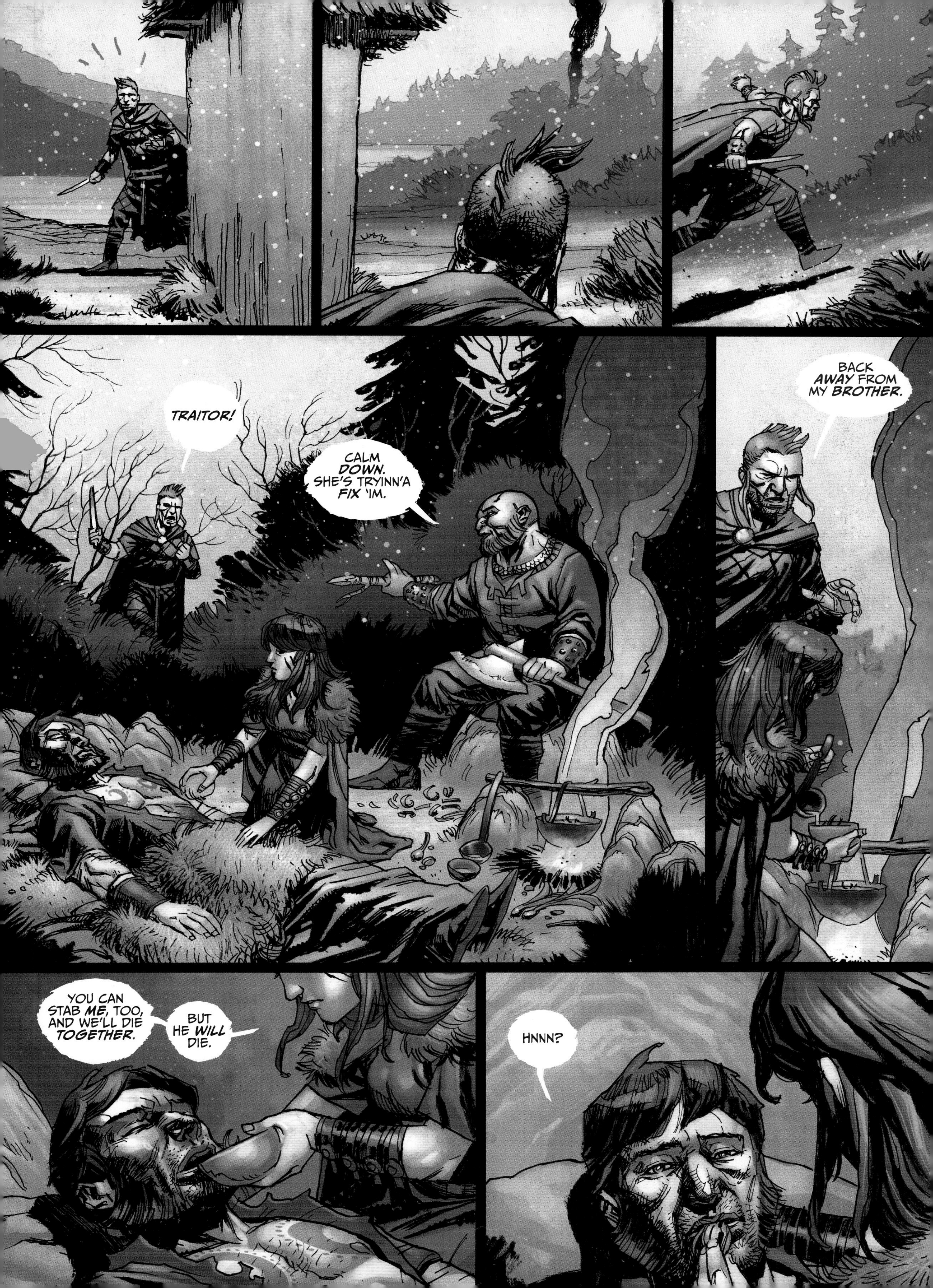
TRAITOR!
CALM DOWN. SHE'S TRYINN'A FIX 'IM.
BACK AWAY FROM MY BROTHER.
YOU CAN STAB ME, TOO, AND WE'LL DIE TOGETHER.
BUT HE WILL DIE.
HNNN?

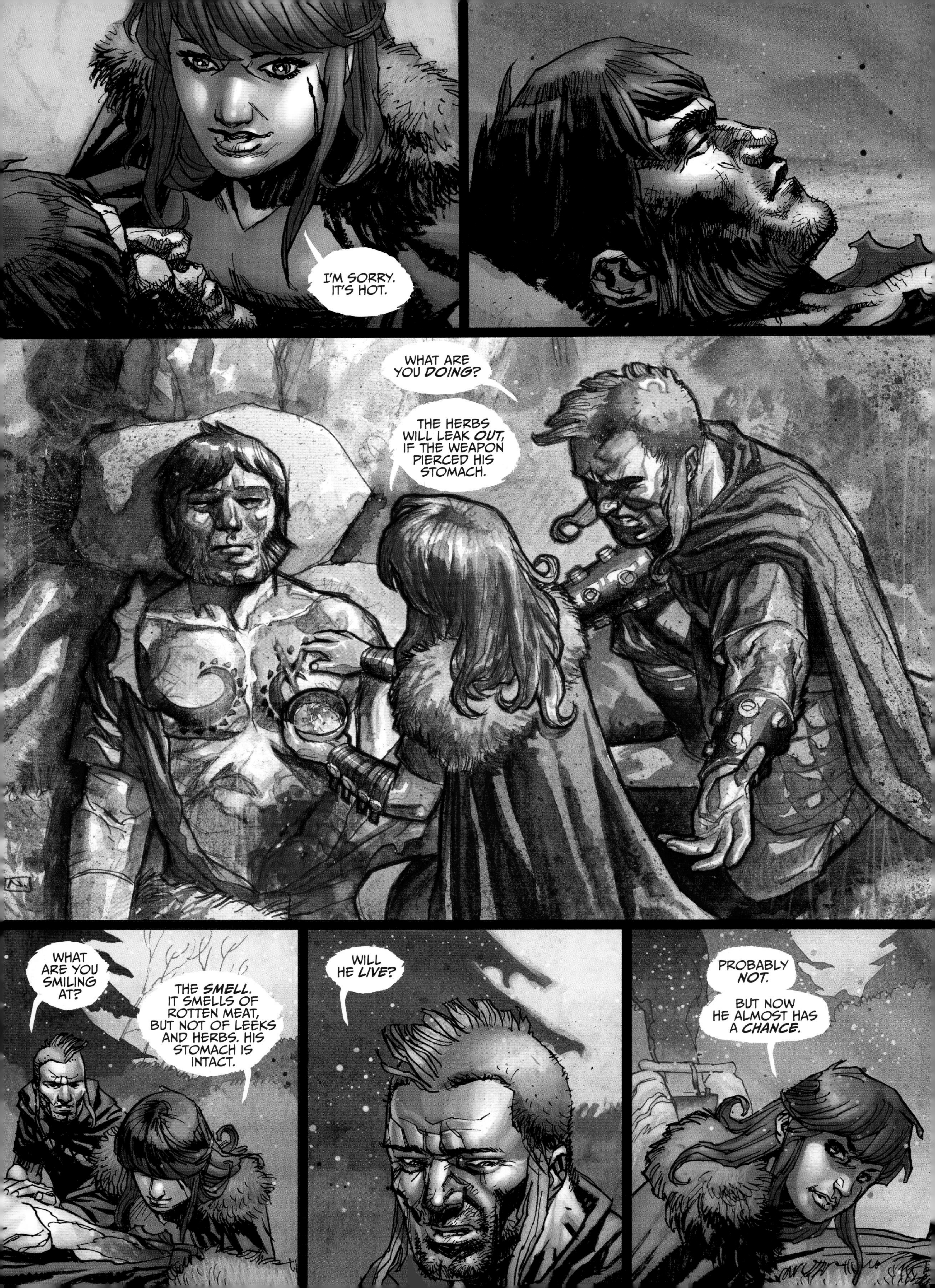
I'M SORRY. IT'S HOT.
WHAT ARE YOU DOING?
THE HERBS WILL LEAK OUT, IF THE WEAPON PIERCED HIS STOMACH.
WHAT ARE YOU SMILING AT?
THE SMELL. IT SMELLS OF ROTTEN MEAT, BUT NOT OF LEEKS AND HERBS. HIS STOMACH IS INTACT.
WILL HE LIVE?
PROBABLY NOT.
BUT NOW HE ALMOST HAS A CHANCE.

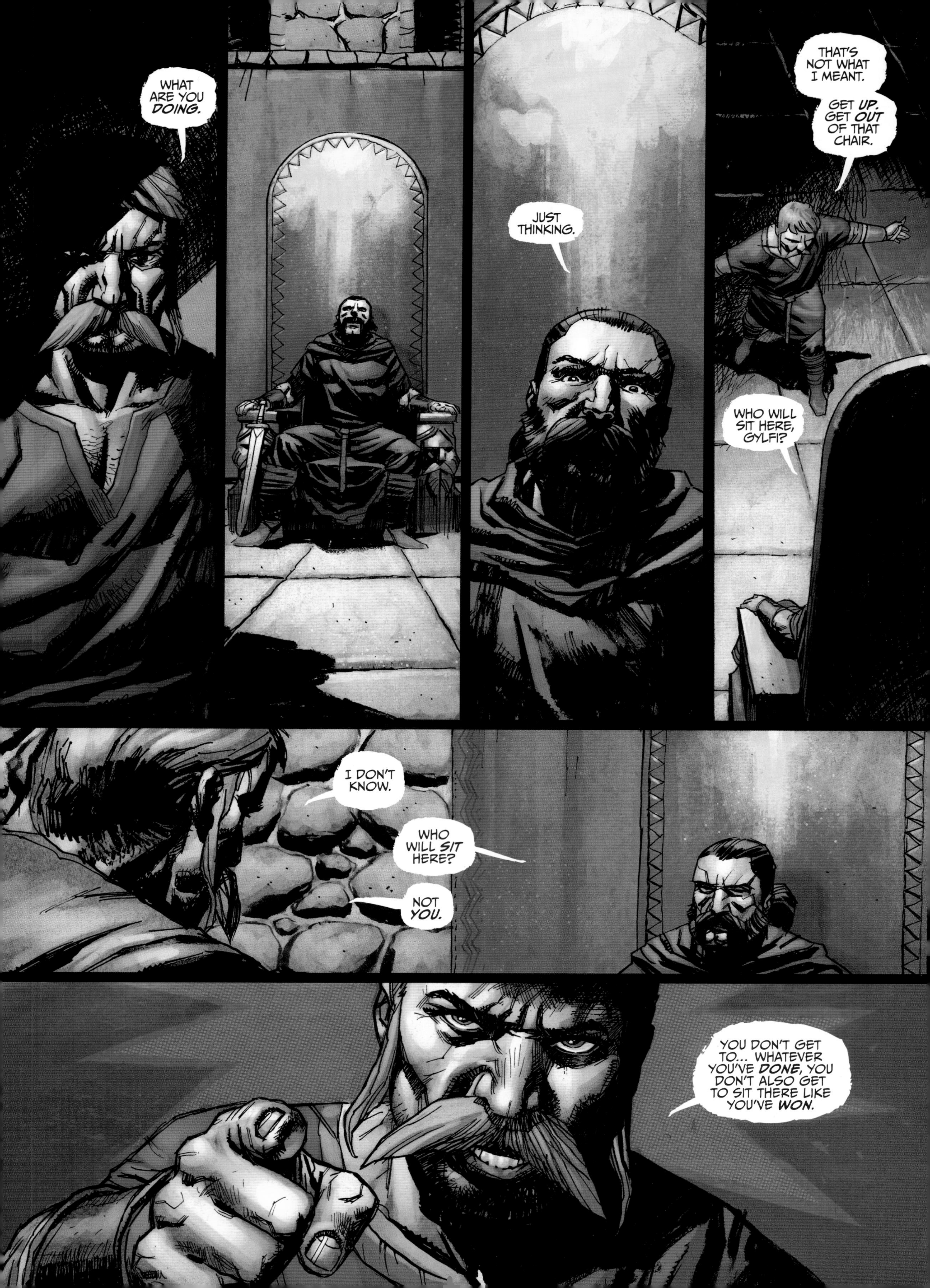
WHAT ARE YOU DOING.
JUST THINKING.
THAT'S NOT WHAT I MEANT.
GET UP. GET OUT OF THAT CHAIR.
WHO WILL SIT HERE, GYLFI?
I DON'T KNOW.
WHO WILL SIT HERE?
NOT YOU.
YOU DON'T GET TO... WHATEVER YOU'VE DONE, YOU DON'T ALSO GET TO SIT THERE LIKE YOU'VE WON.

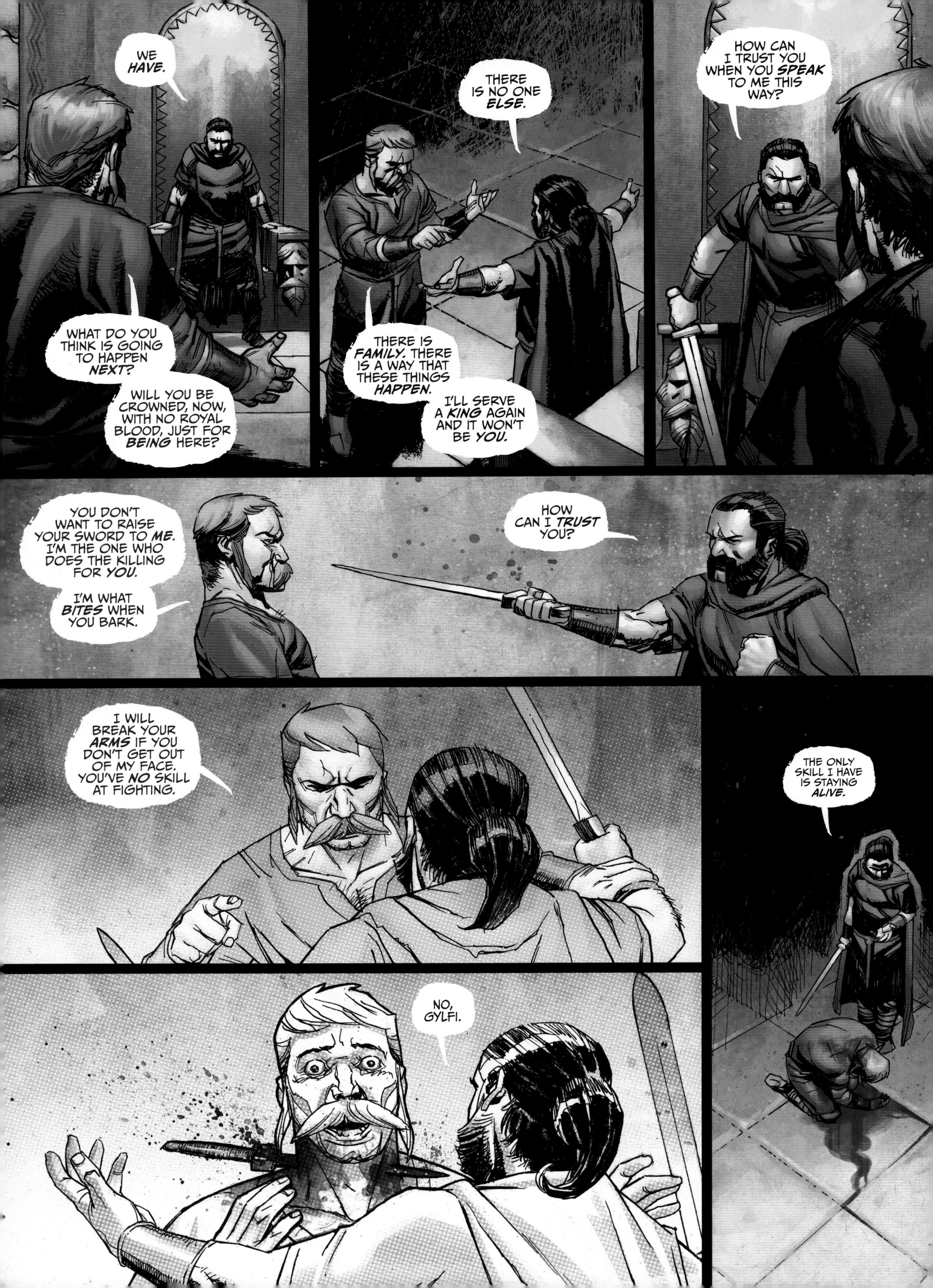
WE HAVE.
WHAT DO YOU THINK IS GOING TO HAPPEN NEXT?
WILL YOU BE CROWNED, NOW, WITH NO ROYAL BLOOD, JUST FOR BEING HERE?
THERE IS NO ONE ELSE.
THERE IS FAMILY. THERE IS A WAY THAT THESE THINGS HAPPEN.
I'LL SERVE A KING AGAIN AND IT WON'T BE YOU.
HOW CAN I TRUST YOU WHEN YOU SPEAK TO ME THIS WAY?
YOU DON'T WANT TO RAISE YOUR SWORD TO ME. I'M THE ONE WHO DOES THE KILLING FOR YOU.
I'M WHAT BITES WHEN YOU BARK.
HOW CAN I TRUST YOU?
I WILL BREAK YOUR ARMS IF YOU DON'T GET OUT OF MY FACE. YOU'VE NO SKILL AT FIGHTING.
NO, GYLFI.
THE ONLY SKILL I HAVE IS STAYING ALIVE.

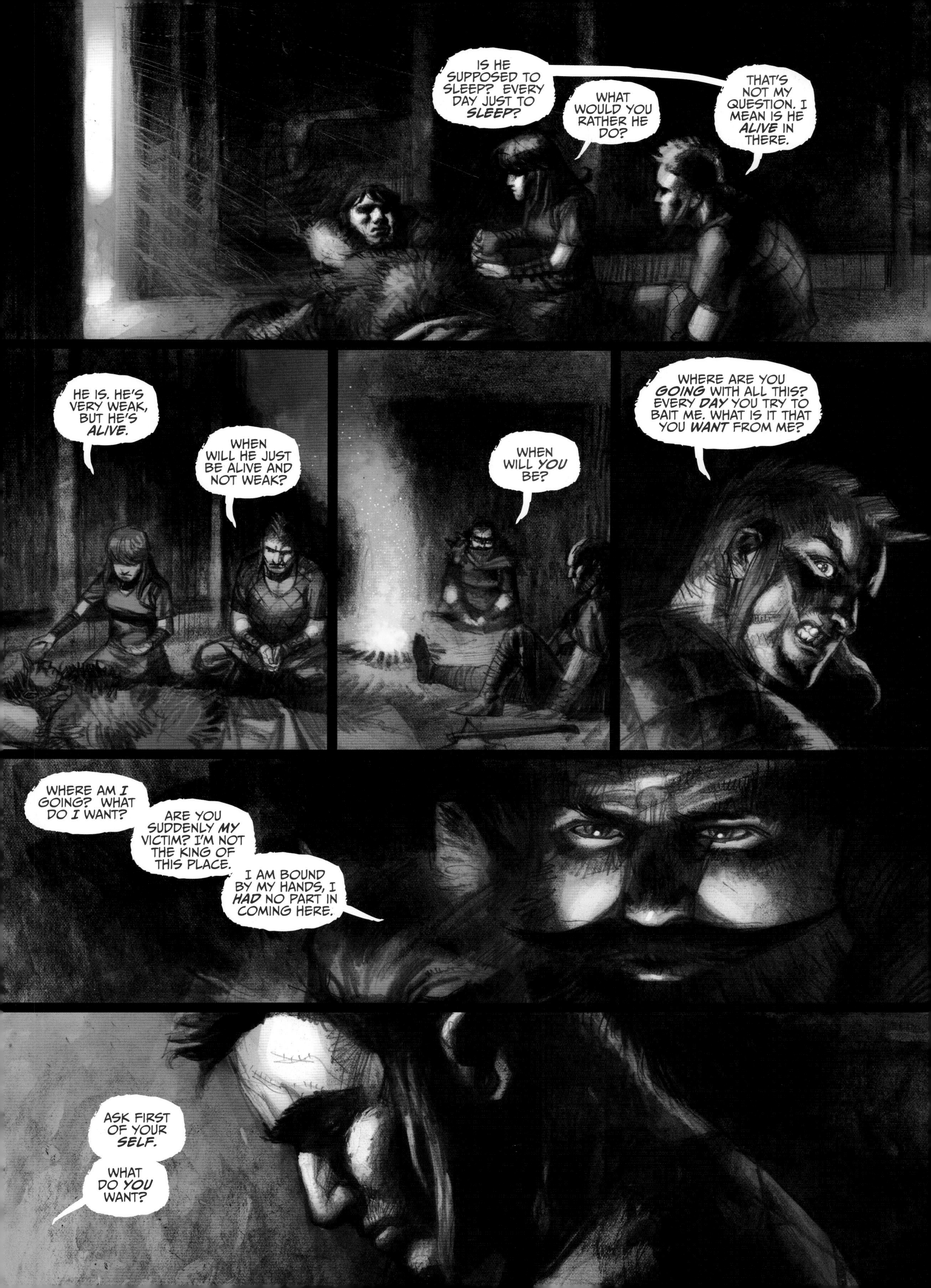
IS HE SUPPOSED TO SLEEP? EVERY DAY JUST TO *SLEEP?*
WHAT WOULD YOU RATHER HE DO?
THAT'S NOT MY QUESTION. I MEAN IS HE *ALIVE* IN THERE.
HE IS. HE'S VERY WEAK, BUT HE'S *ALIVE*.
WHEN WILL HE JUST BE ALIVE AND NOT WEAK?
WHEN WILL *YOU* BE?
WHERE ARE YOU *GOING* WITH ALL THIS? EVERY *DAY* YOU TRY TO BAIT ME. WHAT IS IT THAT YOU *WANT* FROM ME?
WHERE AM *I* GOING? WHAT DO *I* WANT?
ARE YOU SUDDENLY *MY* VICTIM? I'M NOT THE KING OF THIS PLACE.
I AM BOUND BY MY HANDS, I *HAD* NO PART IN COMING HERE.
ASK FIRST OF YOUR *SELF*.
WHAT DO *YOU* WANT?

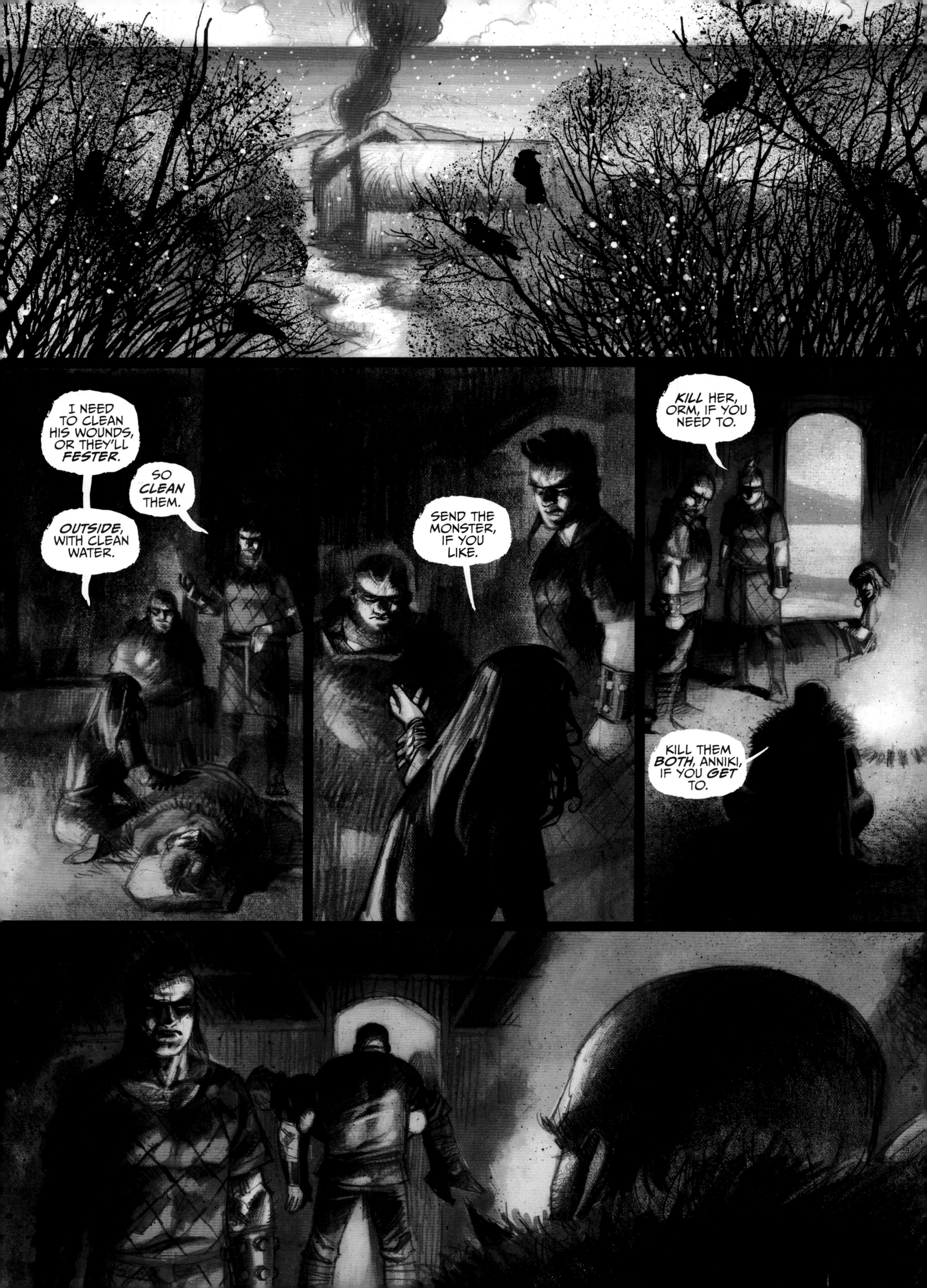
I NEED TO CLEAN HIS WOUNDS, OR THEY'LL FESTER.
SO CLEAN THEM.
OUTSIDE, WITH CLEAN WATER.
SEND THE MONSTER, IF YOU LIKE.
KILL HER, ORM, IF YOU NEED TO.
KILL THEM BOTH, ANNIKI, IF YOU GET TO.

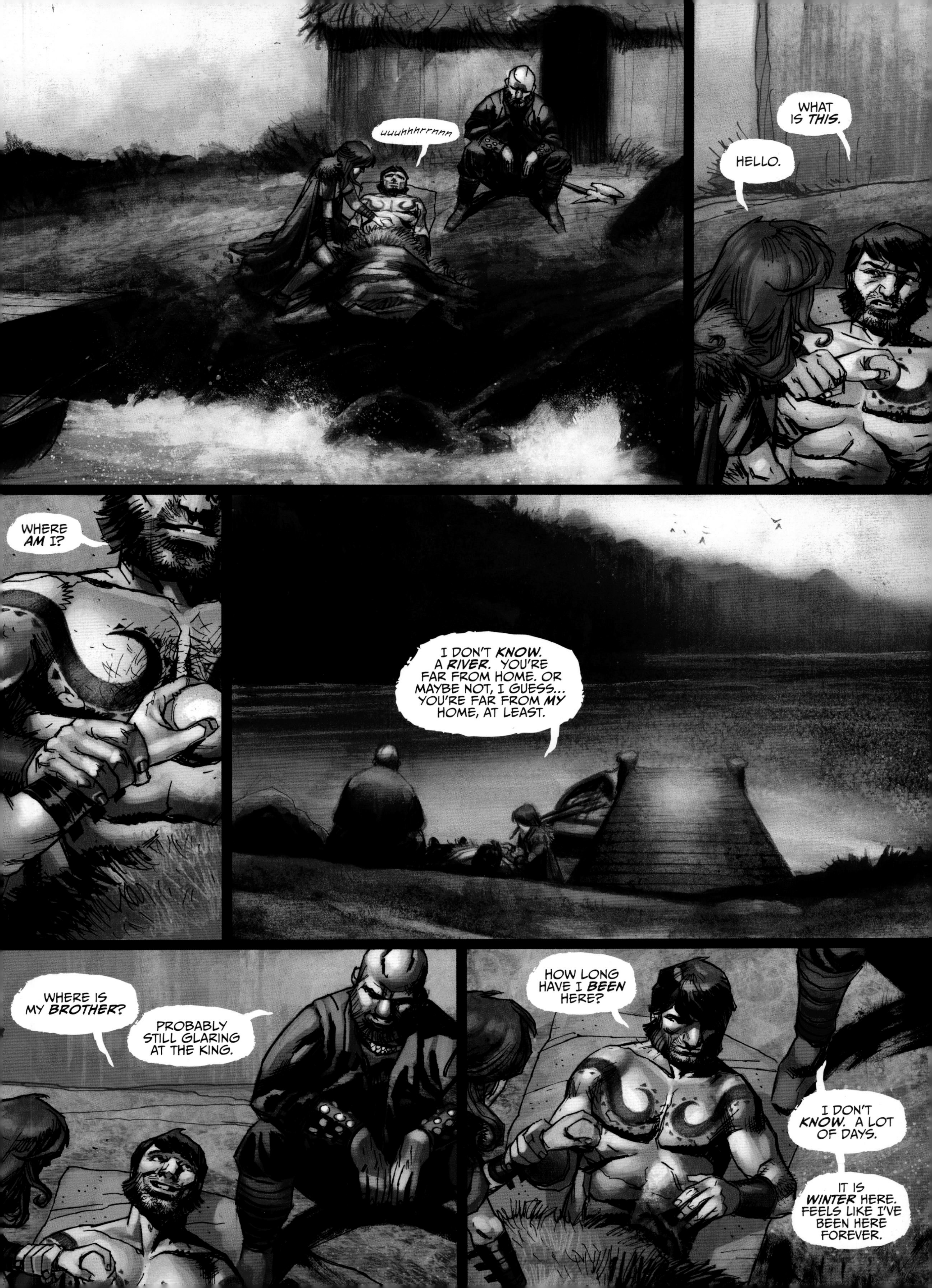
uuuhhhrrnnn
WHAT IS THIS.
HELLO.
WHERE AM I?
I DON'T KNOW. A RIVER. YOU'RE FAR FROM HOME. OR MAYBE NOT, I GUESS... YOU'RE FAR FROM MY HOME, AT LEAST.
WHERE IS MY BROTHER?
PROBABLY STILL GLARING AT THE KING.
HOW LONG HAVE I BEEN HERE?
I DON'T KNOW. A LOT OF DAYS.
IT IS WINTER HERE. FEELS LIKE I'VE BEEN HERE FOREVER.

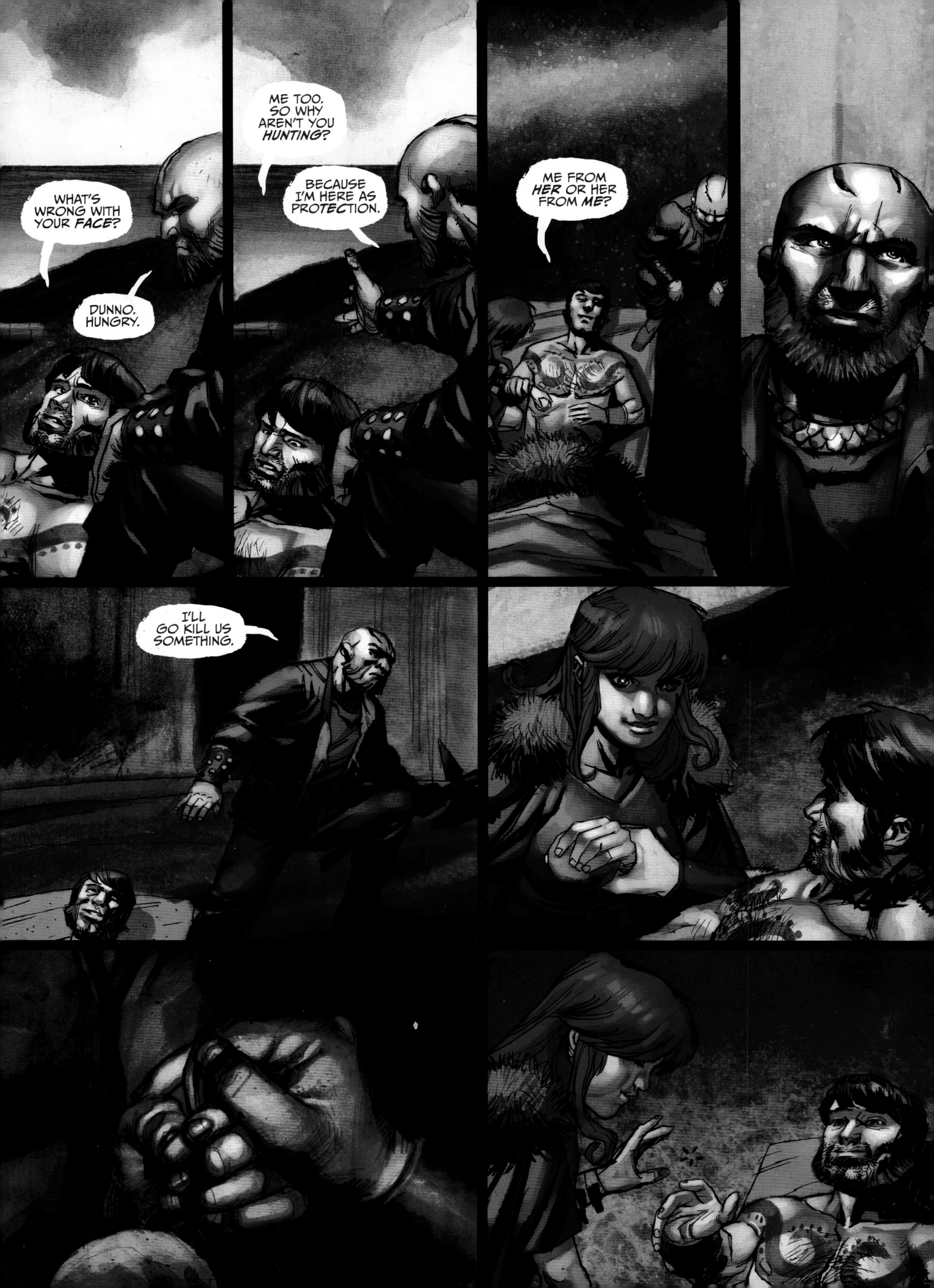
WHAT'S WRONG WITH YOUR FACE?
DUNNO. HUNGRY.
ME TOO. SO WHY AREN'T YOU HUNTING?
BECAUSE I'M HERE AS PROTECTION.
ME FROM HER OR HER FROM ME?
I'LL GO KILL US SOMETHING.

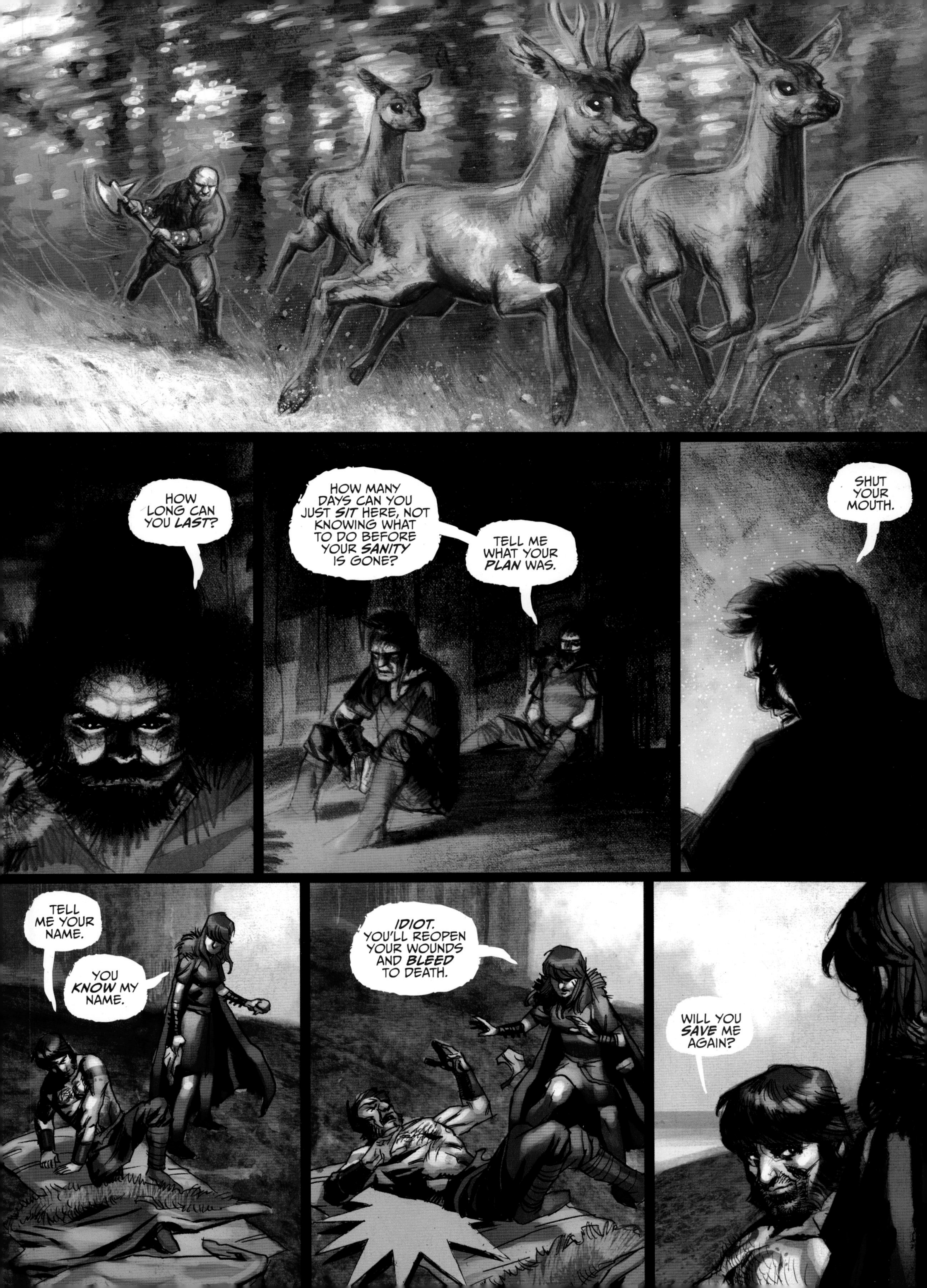

HOW LONG CAN YOU LAST?
HOW MANY DAYS CAN YOU JUST SIT HERE, NOT KNOWING WHAT TO DO BEFORE YOUR SANITY IS GONE?
TELL ME WHAT YOUR PLAN WAS.
SHUT YOUR MOUTH.
TELL ME YOUR NAME.
YOU KNOW MY NAME.
IDIOT. YOU'LL REOPEN YOUR WOUNDS AND BLEED TO DEATH.
WILL YOU SAVE ME AGAIN?

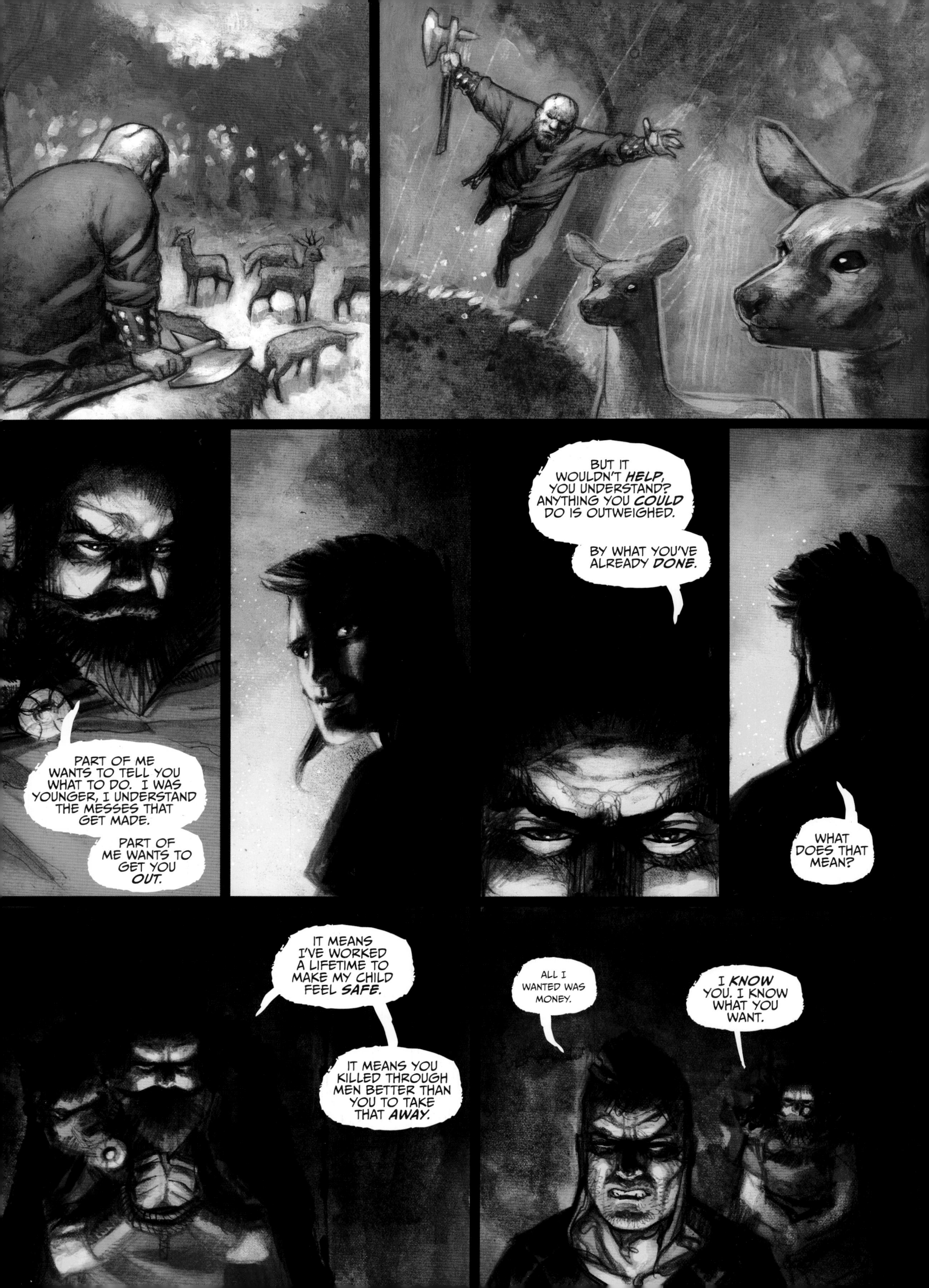
PART OF ME WANTS TO TELL YOU WHAT TO DO. I WAS YOUNGER, I UNDERSTAND THE MESSES THAT GET MADE.
PART OF ME WANTS TO GET YOU OUT.
BUT IT WOULDN'T HELP, YOU UNDERSTAND? ANYTHING YOU COULD DO IS OUTWEIGHED.
BY WHAT YOU'VE ALREADY DONE.
WHAT DOES THAT MEAN?
IT MEANS I'VE WORKED A LIFETIME TO MAKE MY CHILD FEEL SAFE.
IT MEANS YOU KILLED THROUGH MEN BETTER THAN YOU TO TAKE THAT AWAY.
ALL I WANTED WAS MONEY.
I KNOW YOU. I KNOW WHAT YOU WANT.

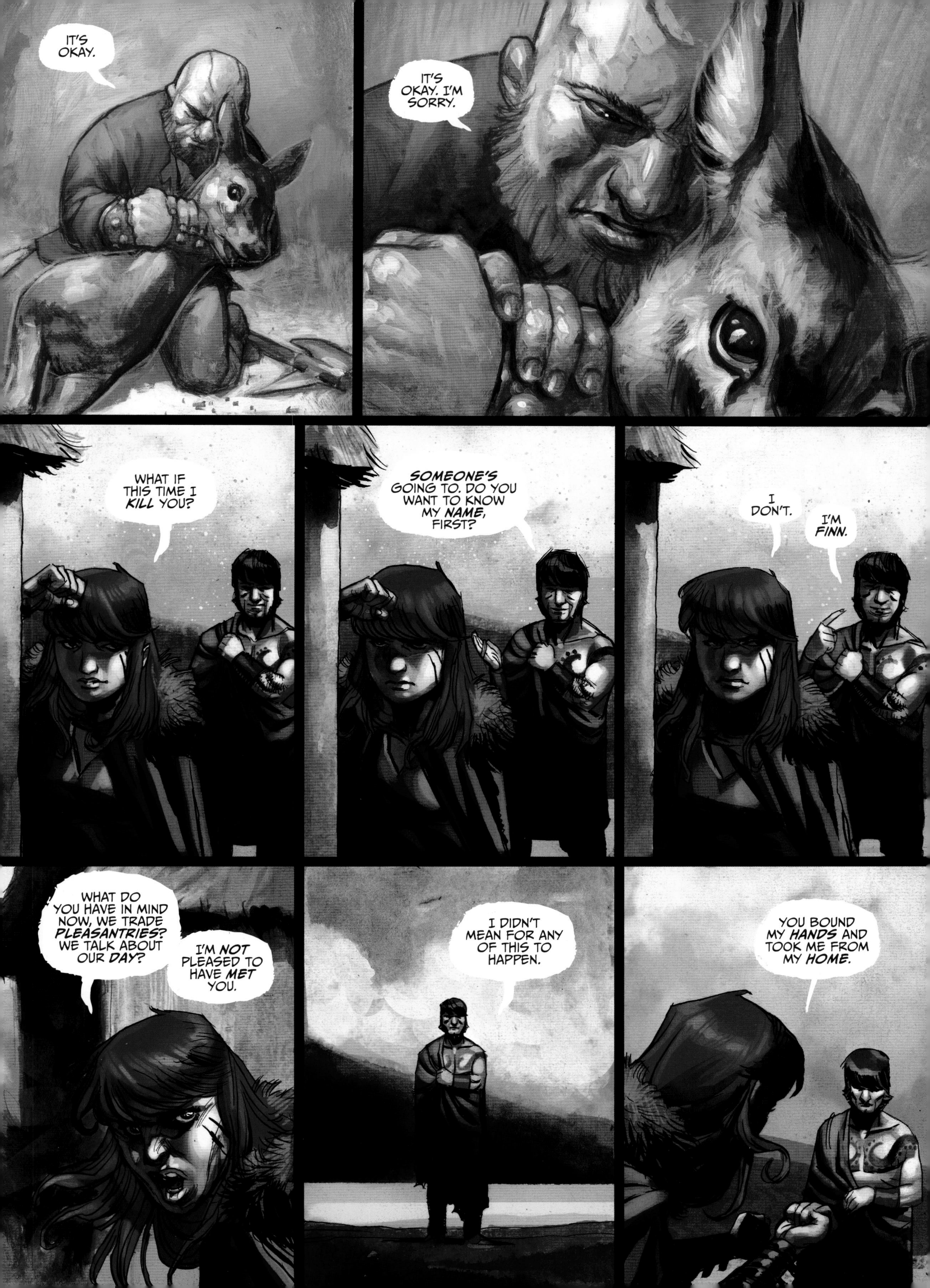
IT'S OKAY.
IT'S OKAY. I'M SORRY.
WHAT IF THIS TIME I KILL YOU?
SOMEONE'S GOING TO. DO YOU WANT TO KNOW MY NAME, FIRST?
I DON'T.
I'M FINN.
WHAT DO YOU HAVE IN MIND NOW, WE TRADE PLEASANTRIES? WE TALK ABOUT OUR DAY?
I'M NOT PLEASED TO HAVE MET YOU.
I DIDN'T MEAN FOR ANY OF THIS TO HAPPEN.
YOU BOUND MY HANDS AND TOOK ME FROM MY HOME.

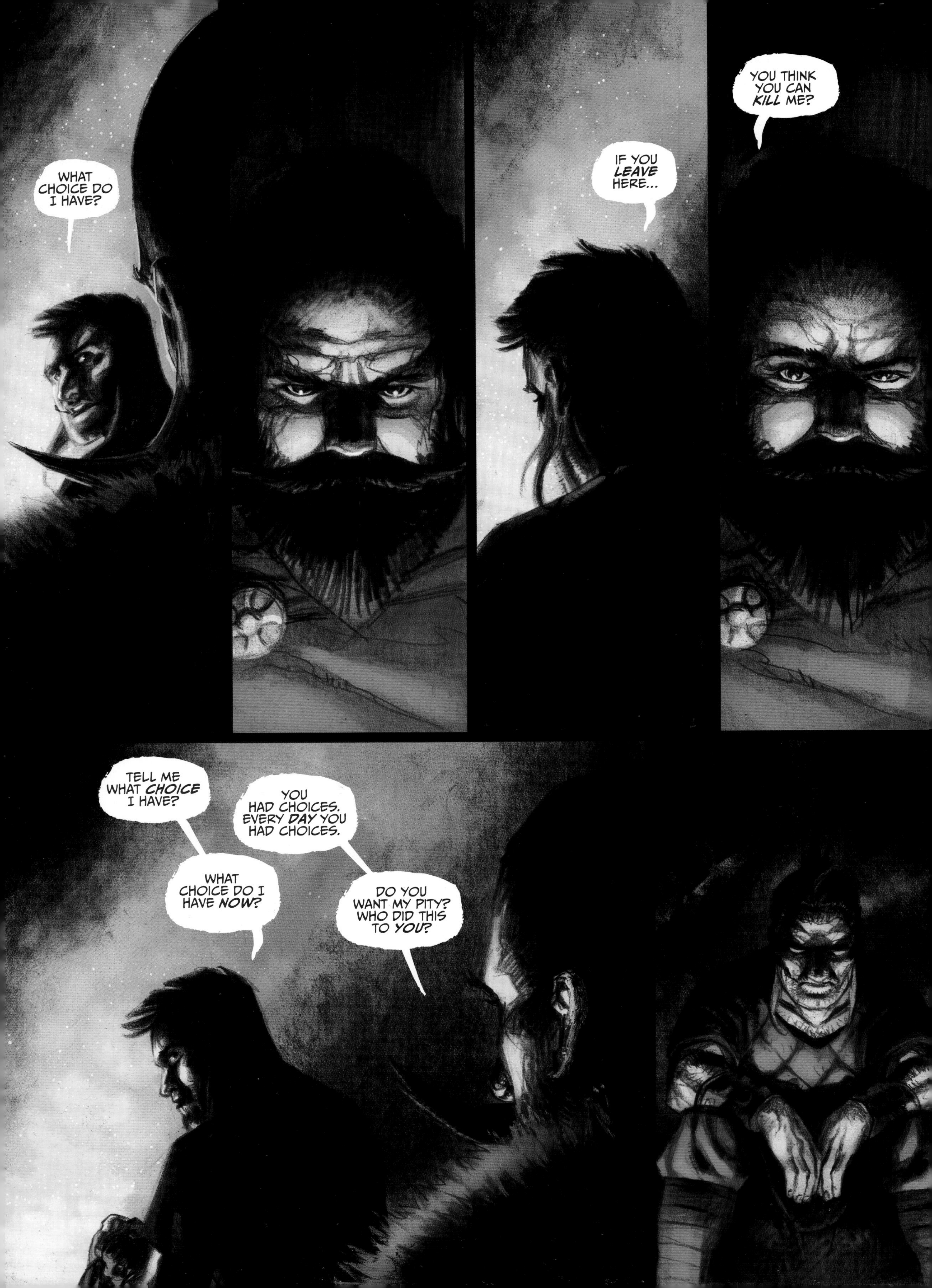
WHAT CHOICE DO I HAVE?
IF YOU LEAVE HERE...
YOU THINK YOU CAN KILL ME?
TELL ME WHAT CHOICE I HAVE?
YOU HAD CHOICES. EVERY DAY YOU HAD CHOICES.
WHAT CHOICE DO I HAVE NOW?
DO YOU WANT MY PITY? WHO DID THIS TO YOU?

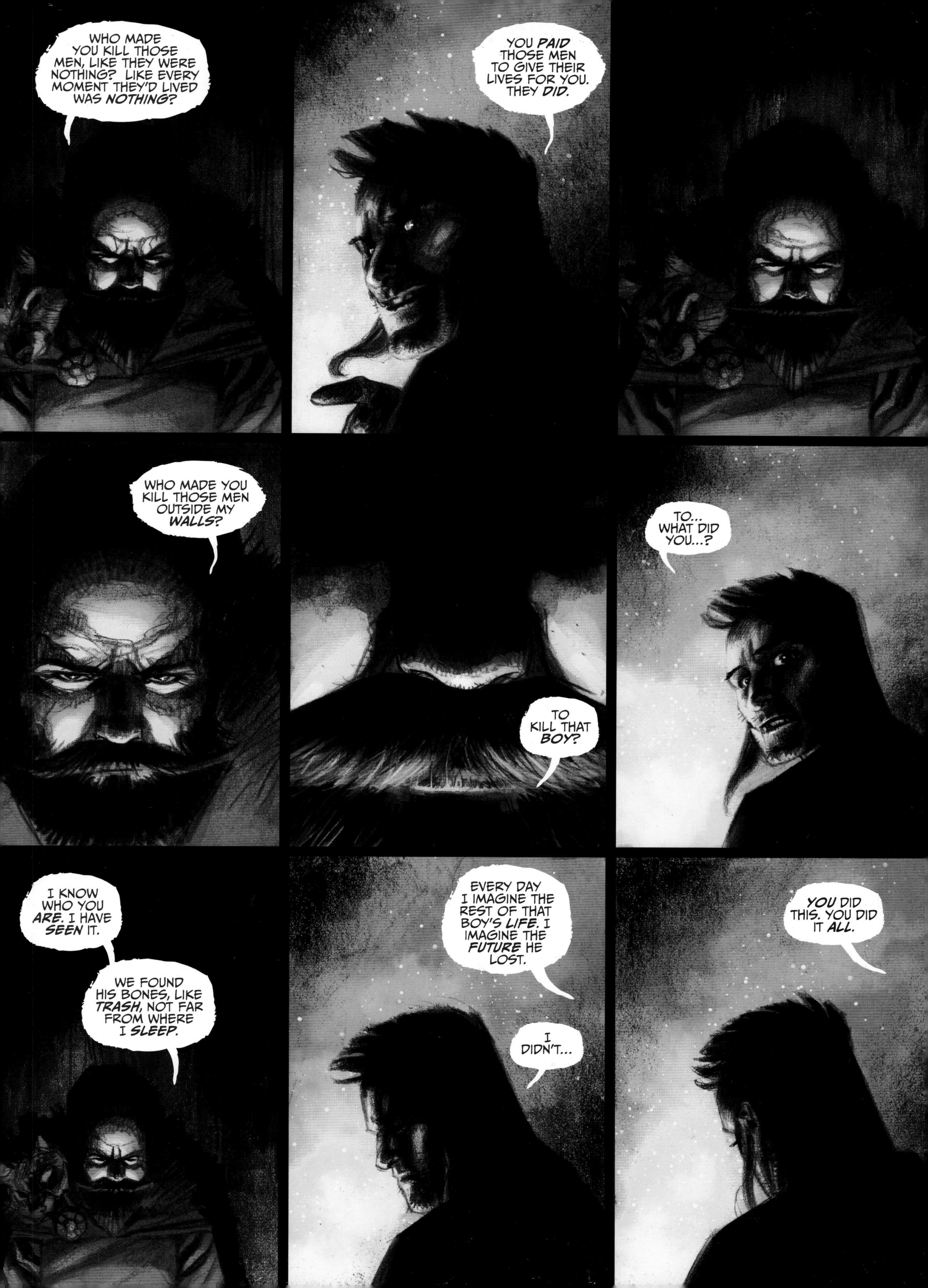
WHO MADE YOU KILL THOSE MEN, LIKE THEY WERE NOTHING? LIKE EVERY MOMENT THEY'D LIVED WAS NOTHING?
YOU PAID THOSE MEN TO GIVE THEIR LIVES FOR YOU. THEY DID.
WHO MADE YOU KILL THOSE MEN OUTSIDE MY WALLS?
TO KILL THAT BOY?
TO... WHAT DID YOU...?
I KNOW WHO YOU ARE. I HAVE SEEN IT.
WE FOUND HIS BONES, LIKE TRASH, NOT FAR FROM WHERE I SLEEP.
EVERY DAY I IMAGINE THE REST OF THAT BOY'S LIFE. I IMAGINE THE FUTURE HE LOST.
I DIDN'T...
YOU DID THIS. YOU DID IT ALL.

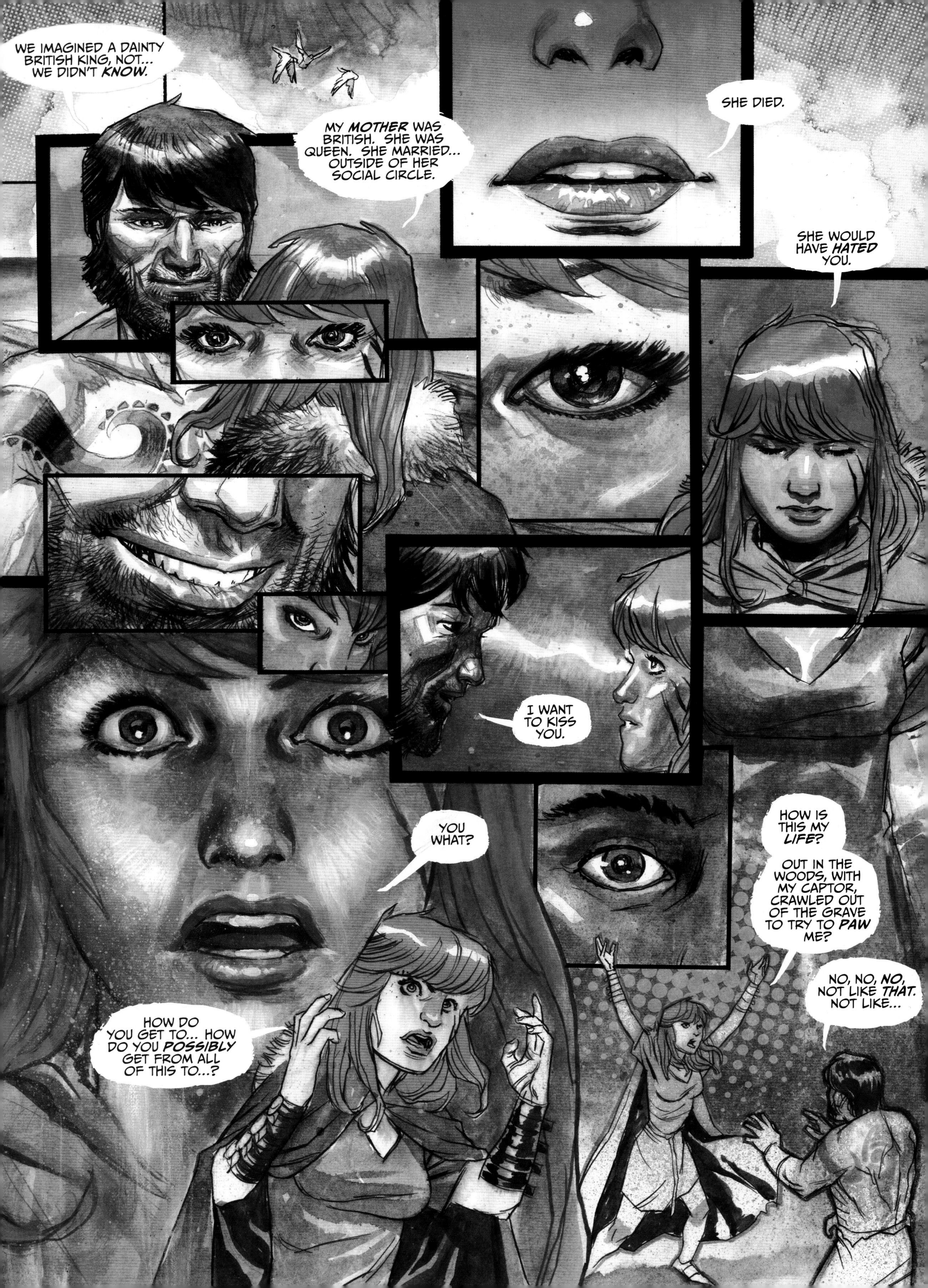
WE IMAGINED A DAINTY BRITISH KING, NOT... WE DIDN'T KNOW.
MY MOTHER WAS BRITISH. SHE WAS QUEEN. SHE MARRIED... OUTSIDE OF HER SOCIAL CIRCLE.
SHE DIED.
SHE WOULD HAVE HATED YOU.
I WANT TO KISS YOU.
YOU WHAT?
HOW DO YOU GET TO... HOW DO YOU POSSIBLY GET FROM ALL OF THIS TO...?
HOW IS THIS MY LIFE?
OUT IN THE WOODS, WITH MY CAPTOR, CRAWLED OUT OF THE GRAVE TO TRY TO PAW ME?
NO, NO, NO, NOT LIKE THAT. NOT LIKE...

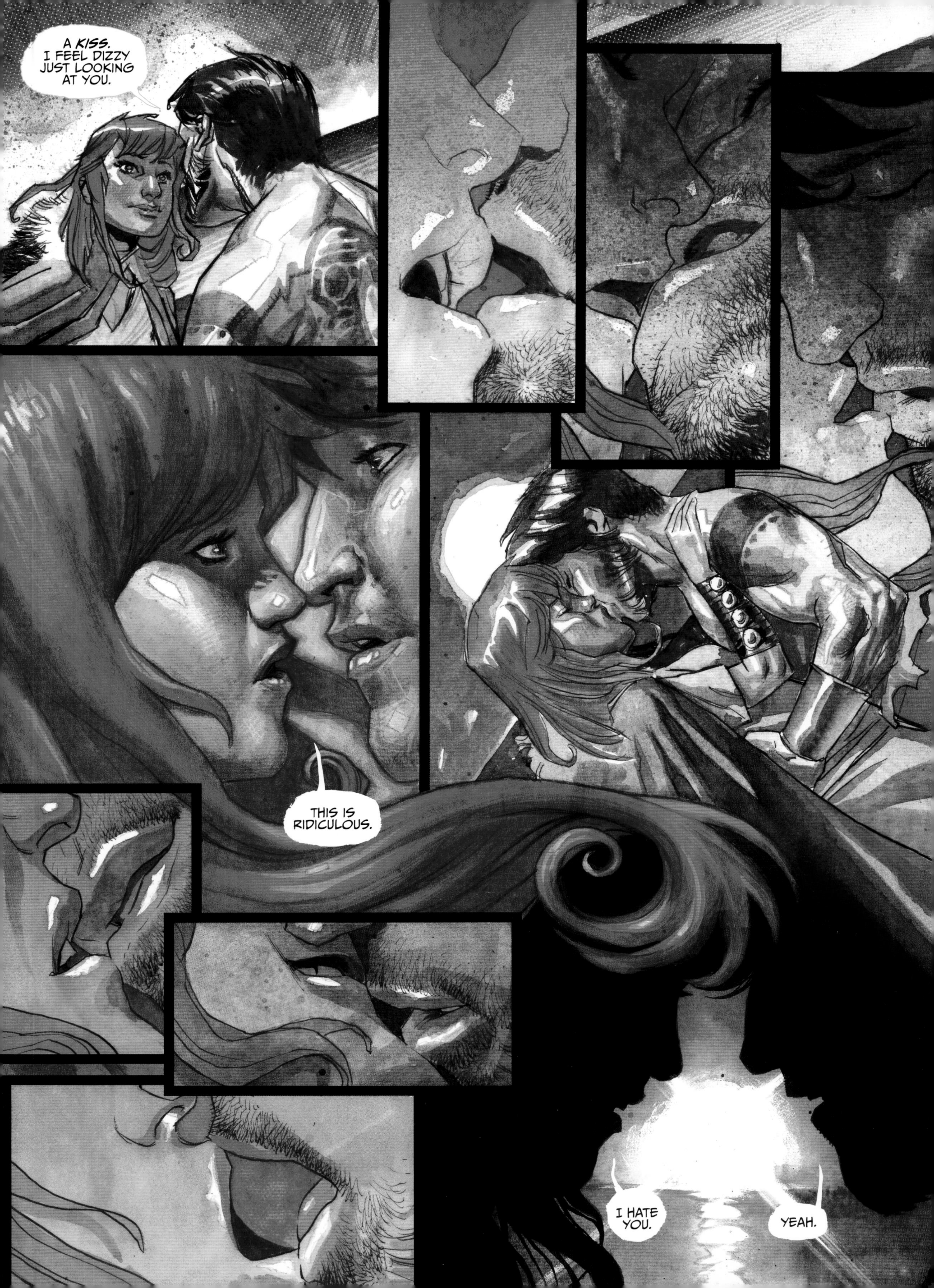
A KISS. I FEEL DIZZY JUST LOOKING AT YOU.
THIS IS RIDICULOUS.
I HATE YOU.
YEAH.

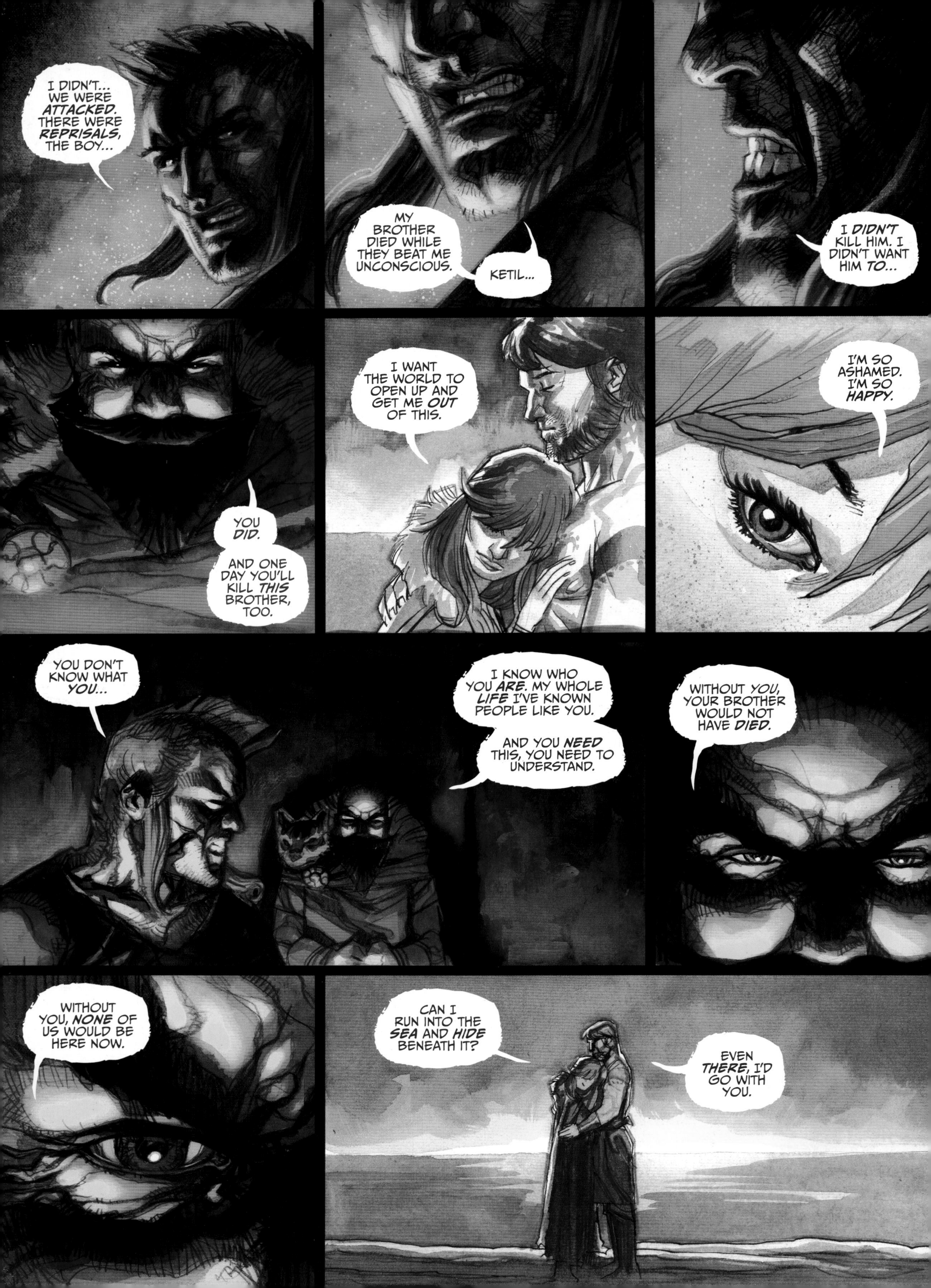
I DIDN'T... WE WERE ATTACKED. THERE WERE REPRISALS, THE BOY...
MY BROTHER DIED WHILE THEY BEAT ME UNCONSCIOUS.
KETIL...
I DIDN'T KILL HIM. I DIDN'T WANT HIM TO...
YOU DID.
AND ONE DAY YOU'LL KILL THIS BROTHER, TOO.
I WANT THE WORLD TO OPEN UP AND GET ME OUT OF THIS.
I'M SO ASHAMED. I'M SO HAPPY.
YOU DON'T KNOW WHAT YOU...
I KNOW WHO YOU ARE. MY WHOLE LIFE I'VE KNOWN PEOPLE LIKE YOU.
AND YOU NEED THIS, YOU NEED TO UNDERSTAND.
WITHOUT YOU, YOUR BROTHER WOULD NOT HAVE DIED.
WITHOUT YOU, NONE OF US WOULD BE HERE NOW.
CAN I RUN INTO THE SEA AND HIDE BENEATH IT?
EVEN THERE, I'D GO WITH YOU.

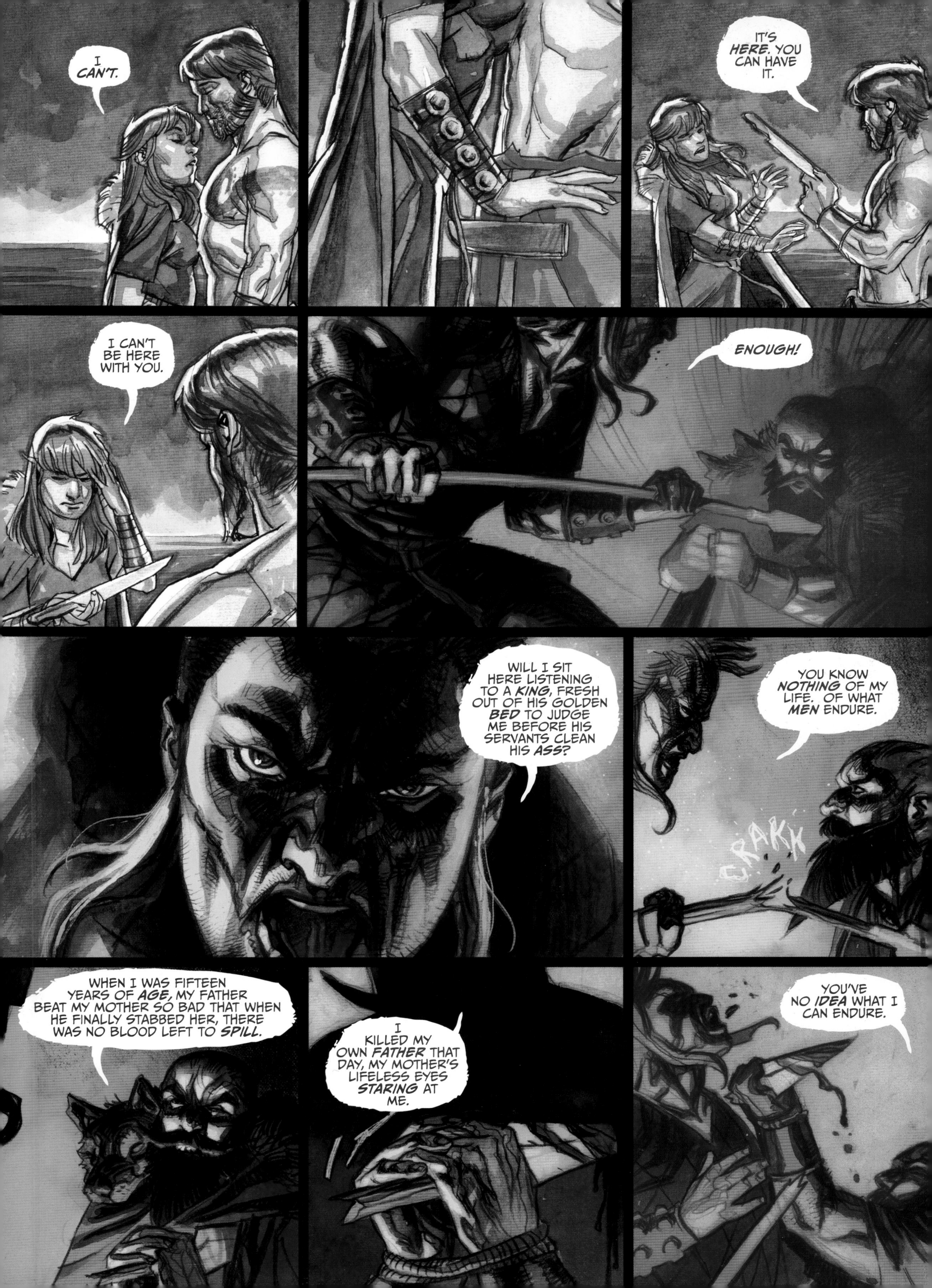
I CAN'T.
IT'S HERE. YOU CAN HAVE IT.
I CAN'T BE HERE WITH YOU.
ENOUGH!
WILL I SIT HERE LISTENING TO A KING, FRESH OUT OF HIS GOLDEN BED TO JUDGE ME BEFORE HIS SERVANTS CLEAN HIS ASS?
YOU KNOW NOTHING OF MY LIFE. OF WHAT MEN ENDURE.
CRAKK
WHEN I WAS FIFTEEN YEARS OF AGE, MY FATHER BEAT MY MOTHER SO BAD THAT WHEN HE FINALLY STABBED HER, THERE WAS NO BLOOD LEFT TO SPILL.
I KILLED MY OWN FATHER THAT DAY, MY MOTHER'S LIFELESS EYES STARING AT ME.
YOU'VE NO IDEA WHAT I CAN ENDURE.

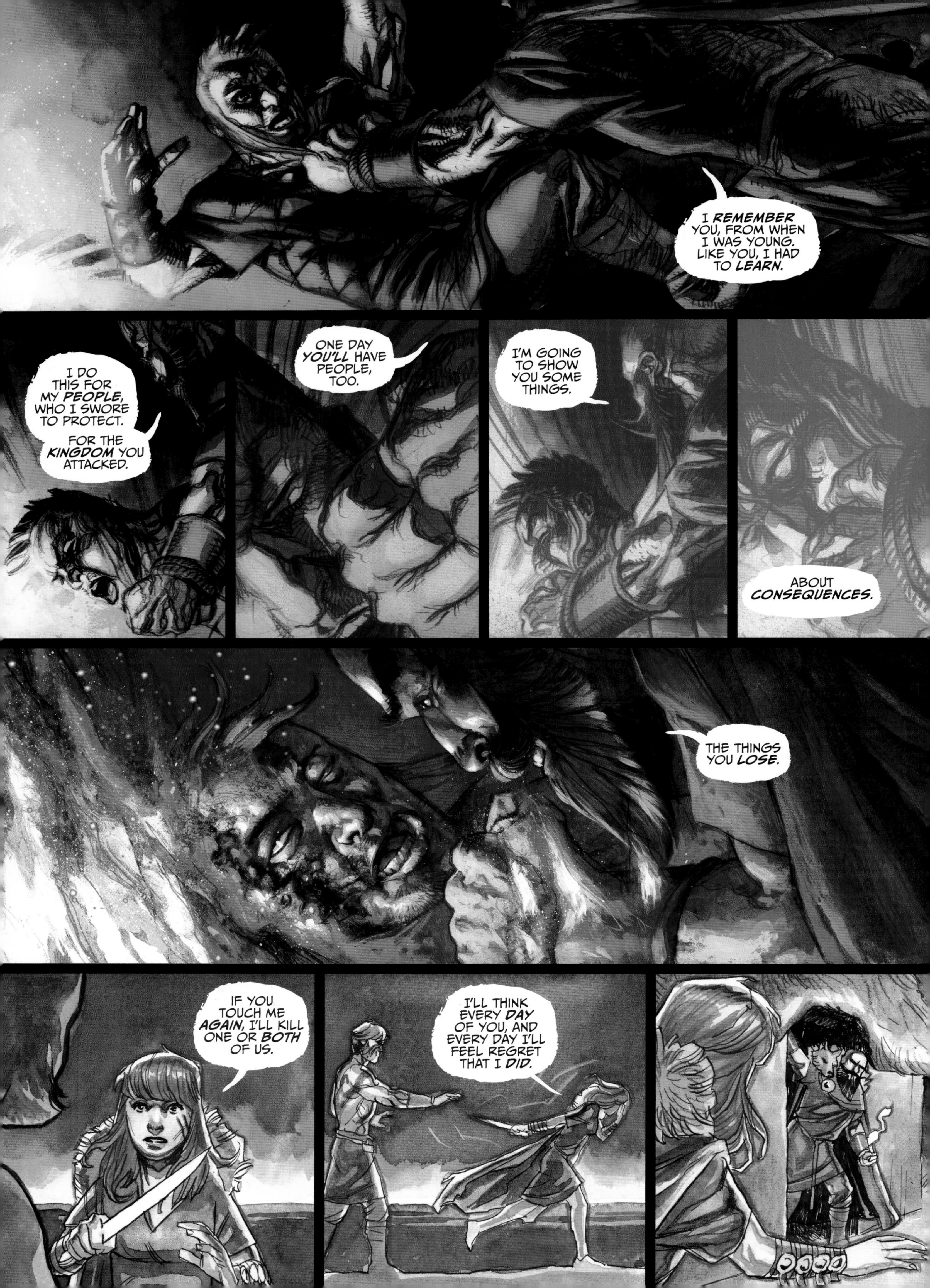
I REMEMBER YOU, FROM WHEN I WAS YOUNG. LIKE YOU, I HAD TO LEARN.
I DO THIS FOR MY PEOPLE, WHO I SWORE TO PROTECT.
FOR THE KINGDOM YOU ATTACKED.
ONE DAY YOU'LL HAVE PEOPLE, TOO.
I'M GOING TO SHOW YOU SOME THINGS.
ABOUT CONSEQUENCES.
THE THINGS YOU LOSE.
IF YOU TOUCH ME AGAIN, I'LL KILL ONE OR BOTH OF US.
I'LL THINK EVERY DAY OF YOU, AND EVERY DAY I'LL FEEL REGRET THAT I DID.

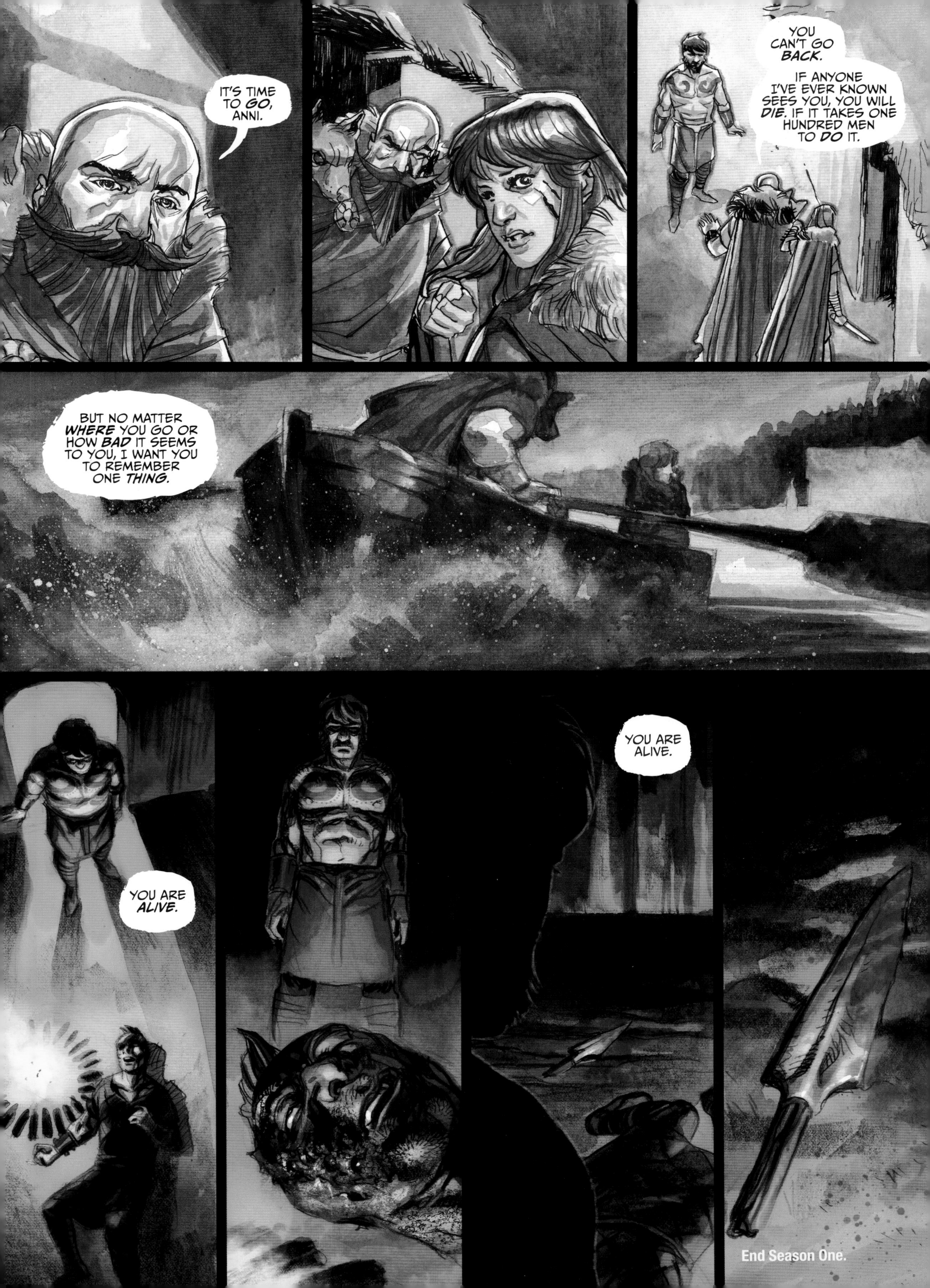
IT'S TIME TO GO, ANNI.
YOU CAN'T GO BACK.
IF ANYONE I'VE EVER KNOWN SEES YOU, YOU WILL DIE. IF IT TAKES ONE HUNDRED MEN TO DO IT.
BUT NO MATTER WHERE YOU GO OR HOW BAD IT SEEMS TO YOU, I WANT YOU TO REMEMBER ONE THING.
YOU ARE ALIVE.
YOU ARE ALIVE.
End Season One.

ORIGINAL SERIES COVERS

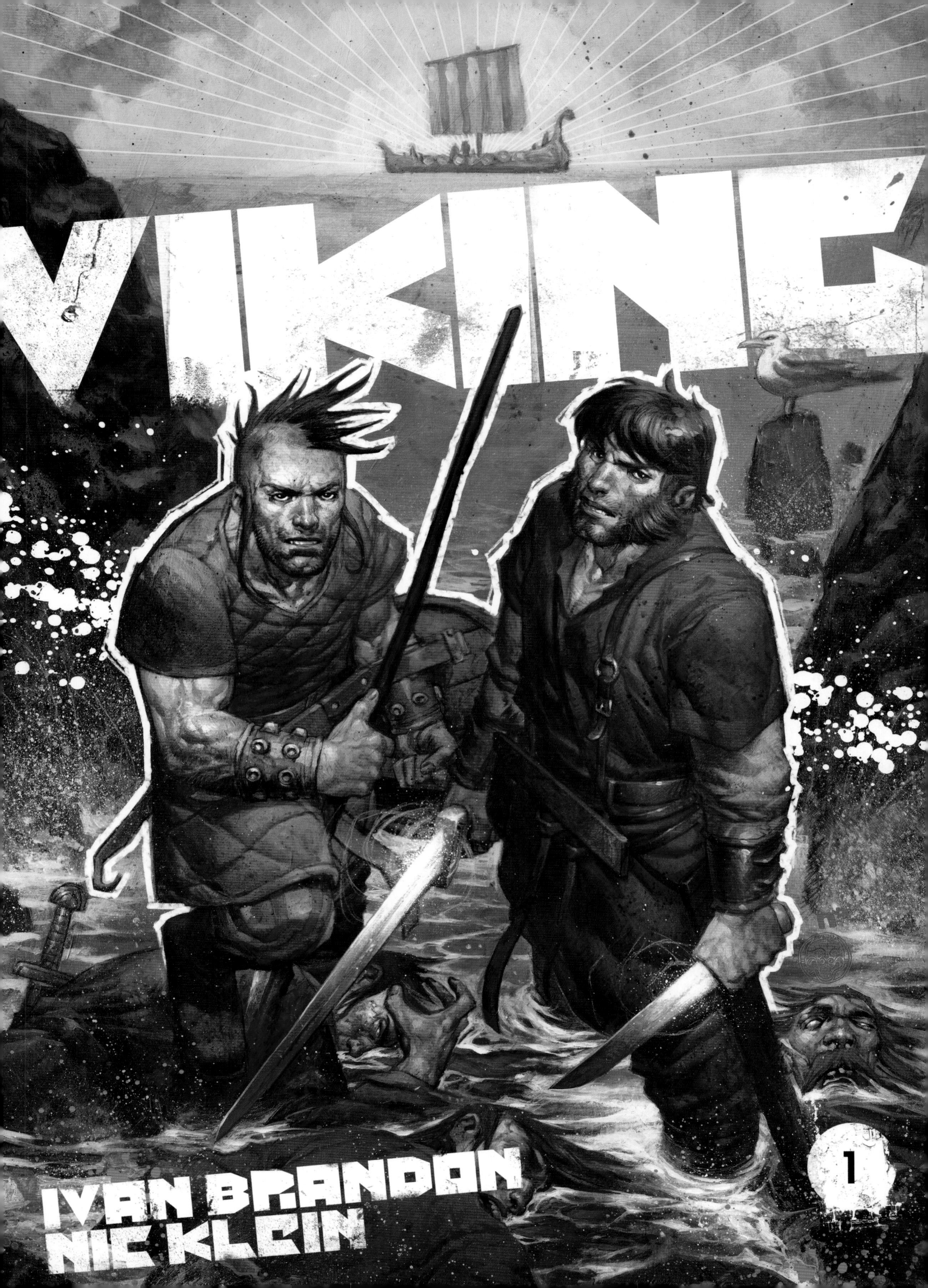

VIKING
IVAN BRANDON
NIC KLEIN
1

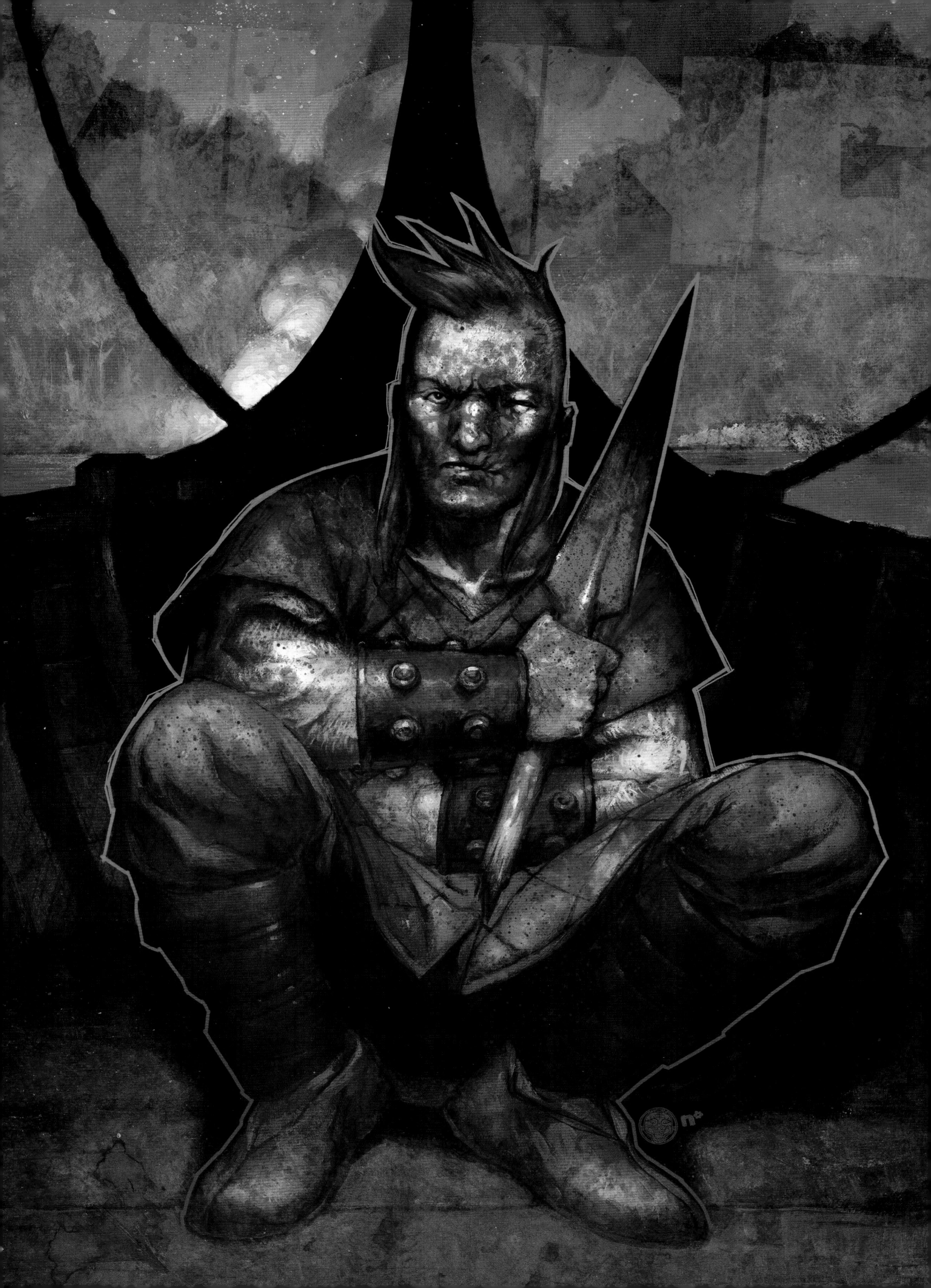

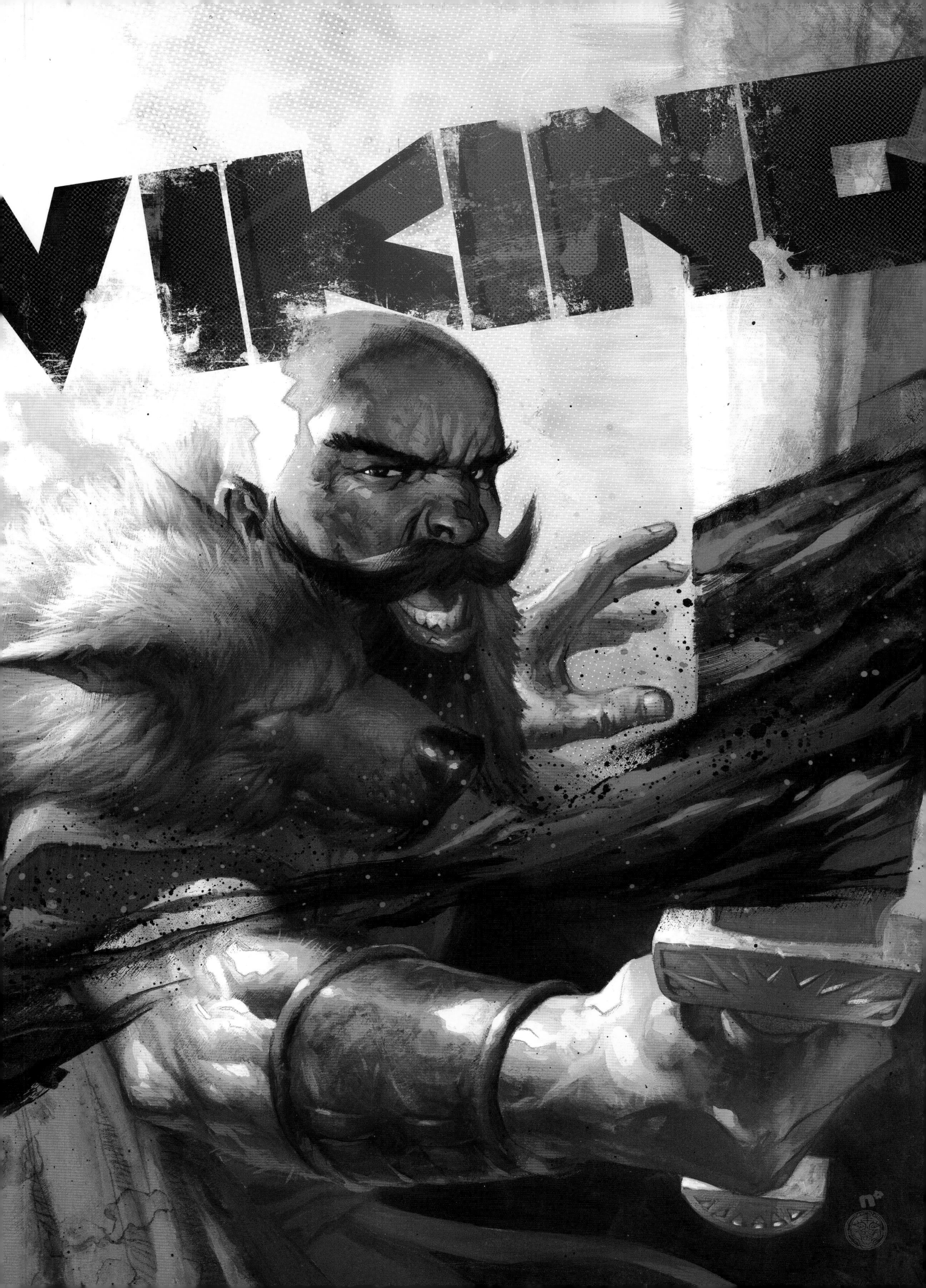

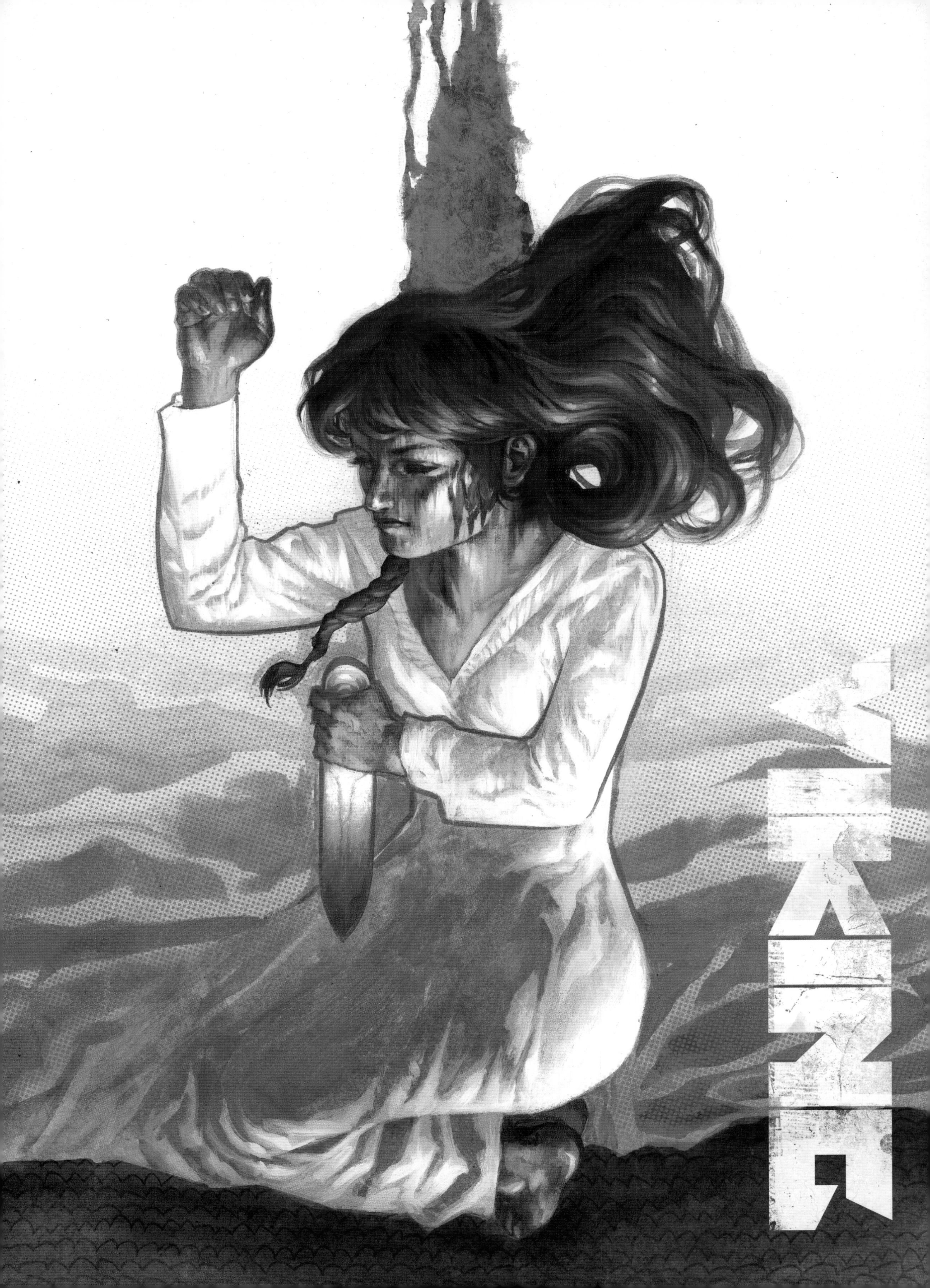
VIKING

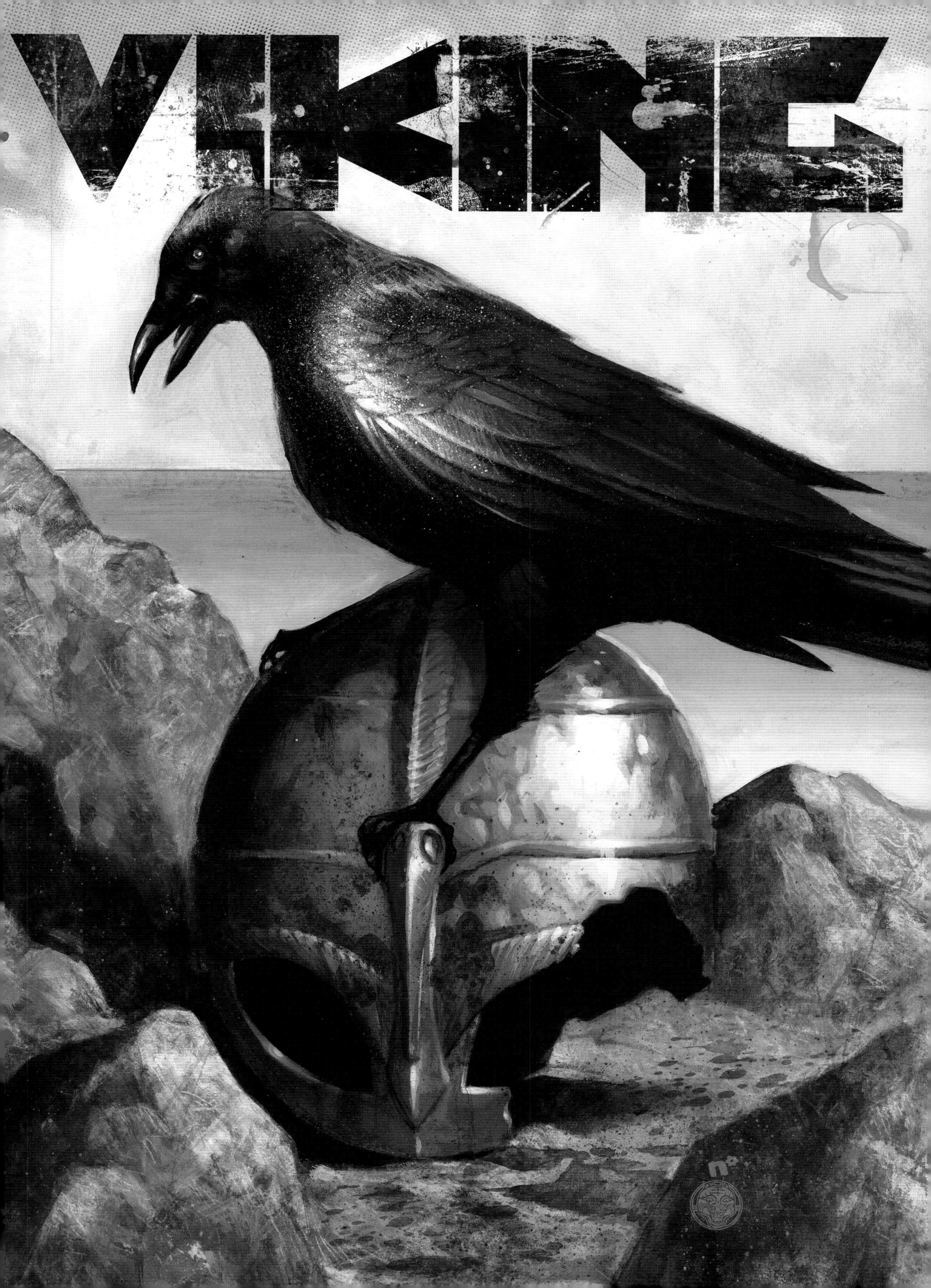
VIKING

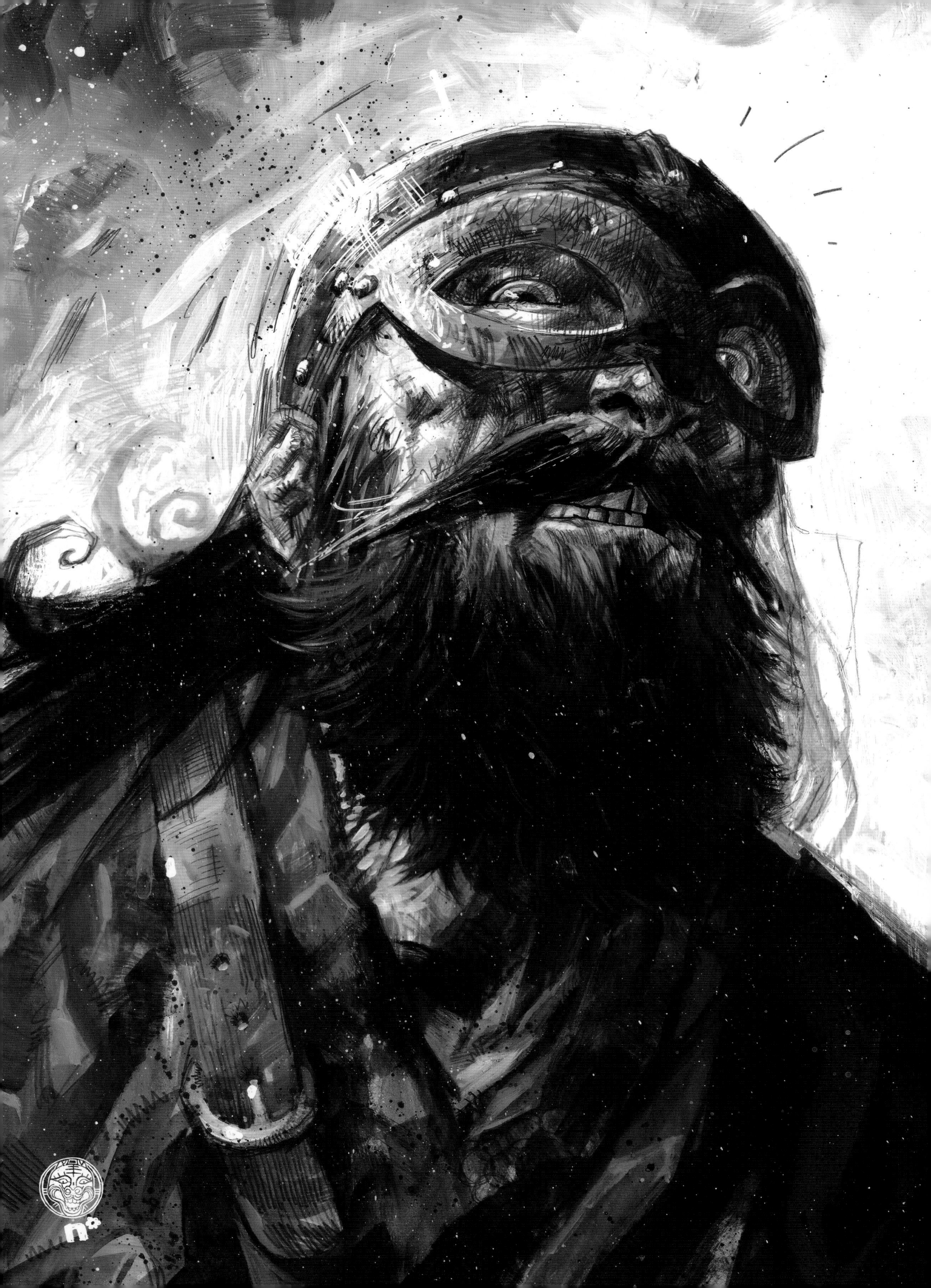

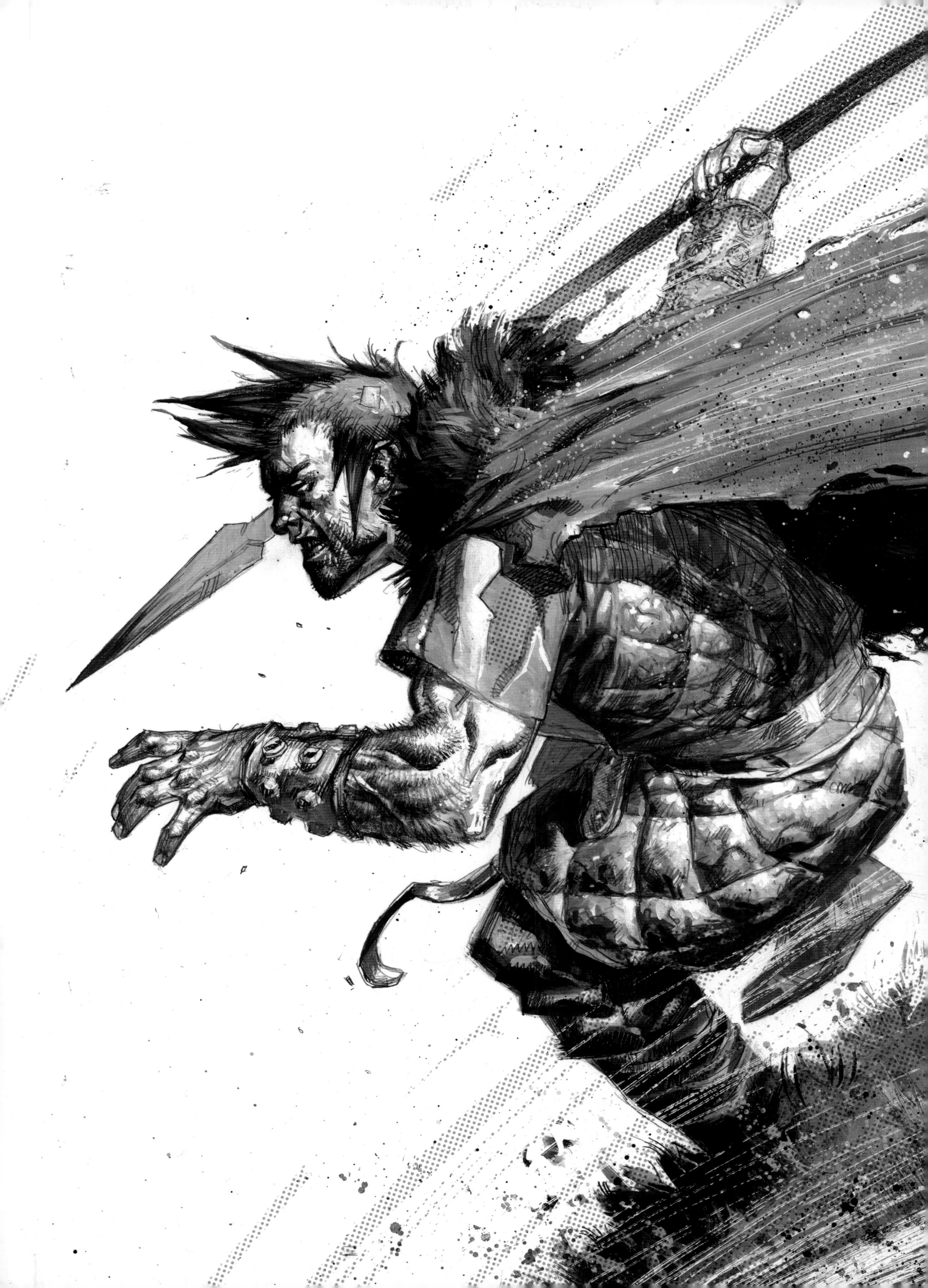

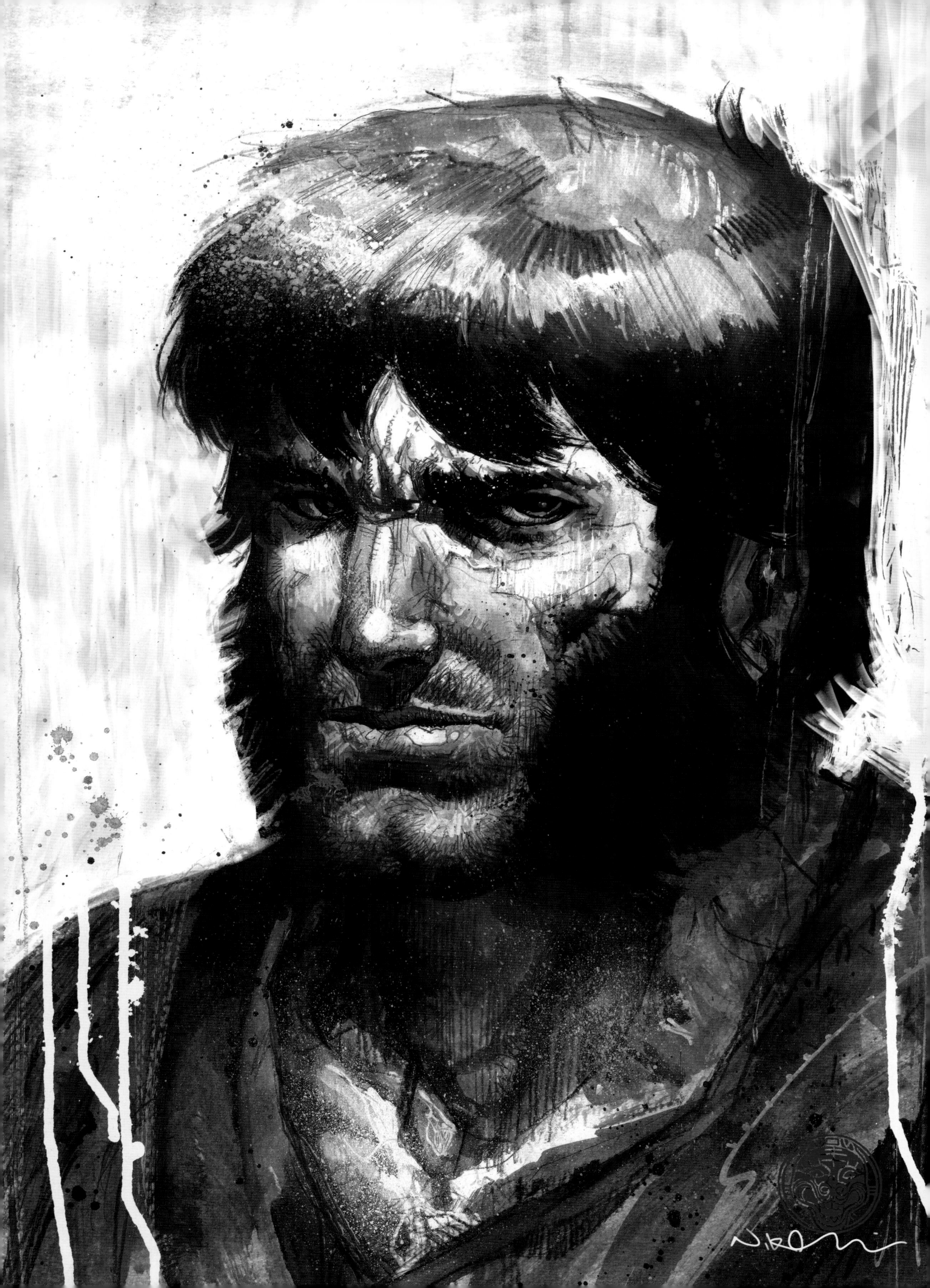

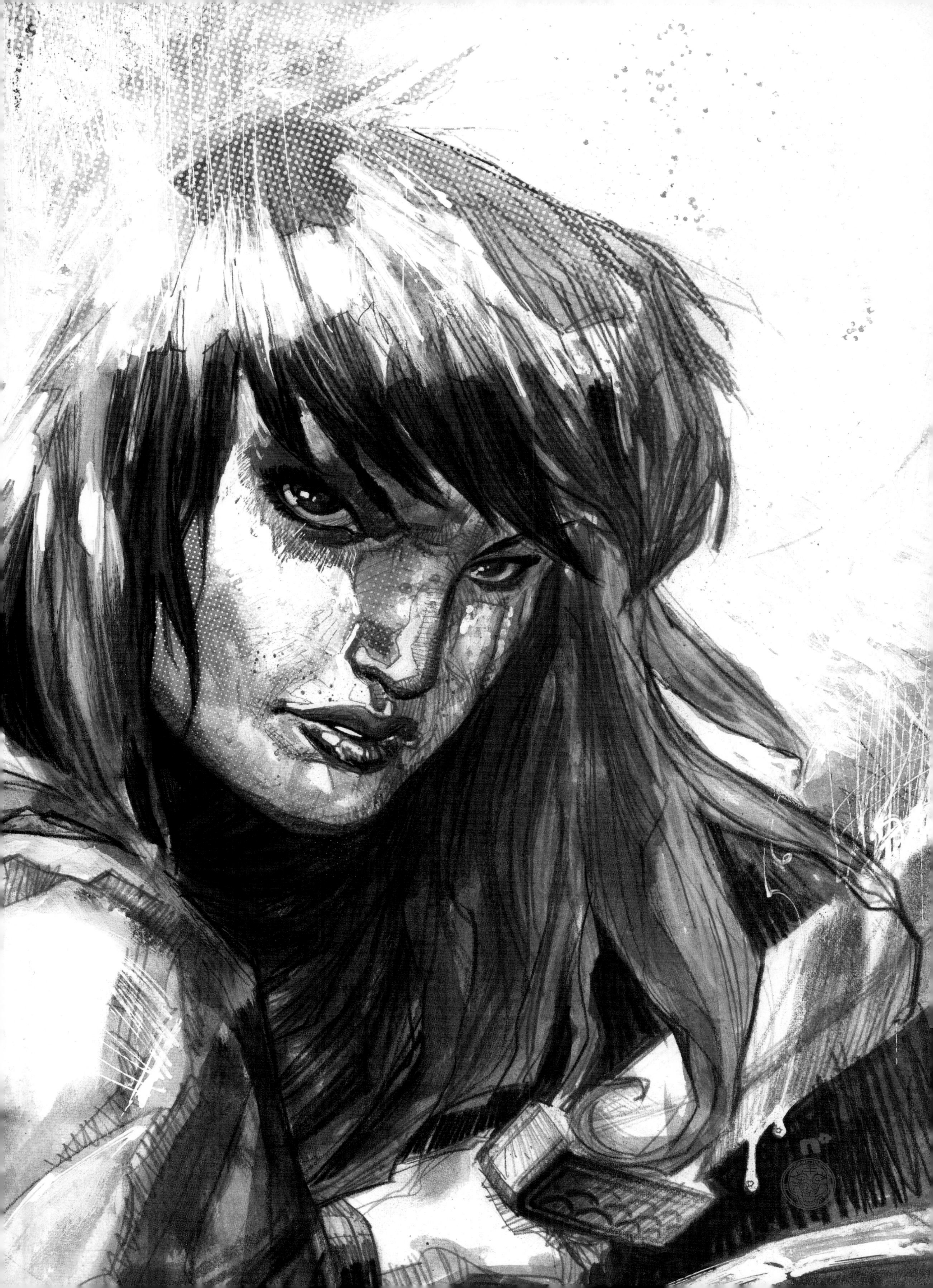

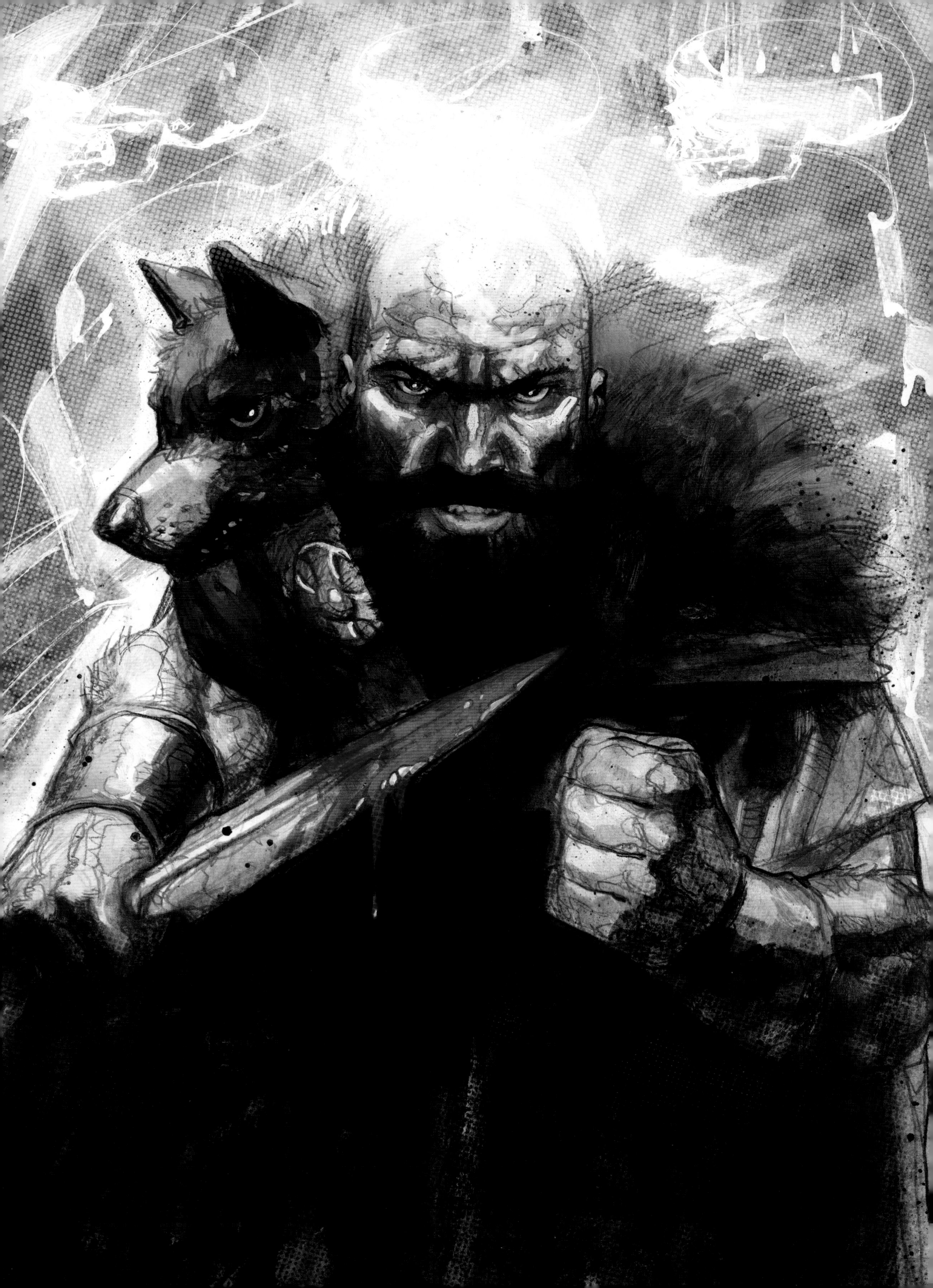

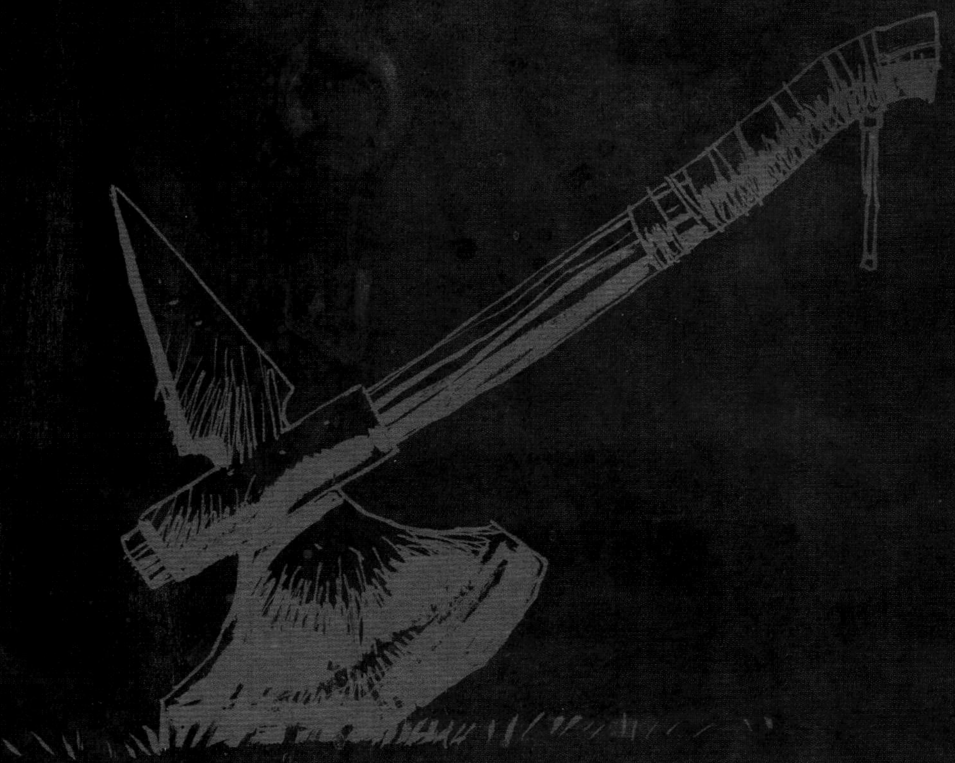

SKETCHES & MISCELLANEOUS

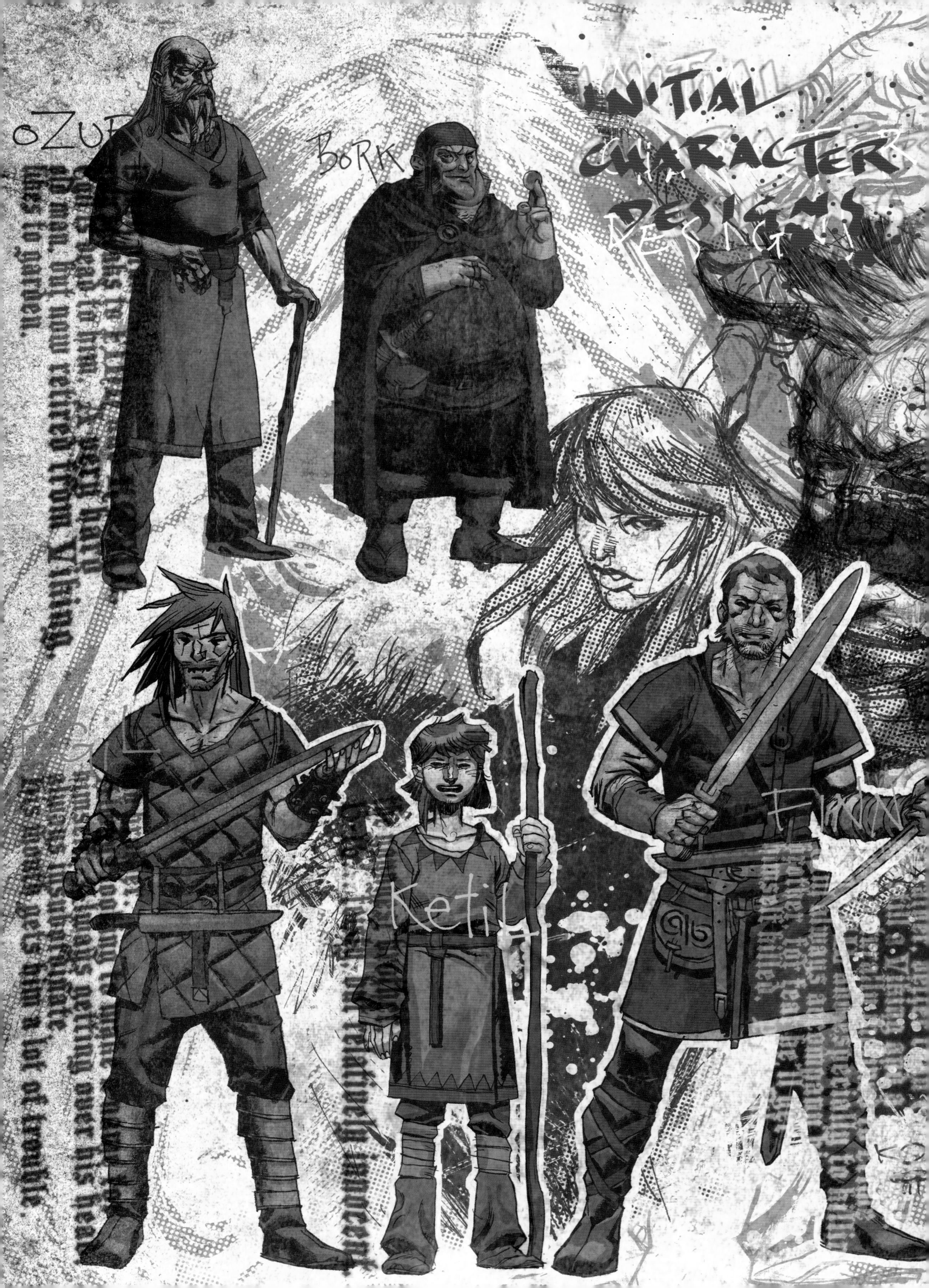

INITIAL CHARACTER DESIGNS
OZUR
BORK
Ketil
FINN

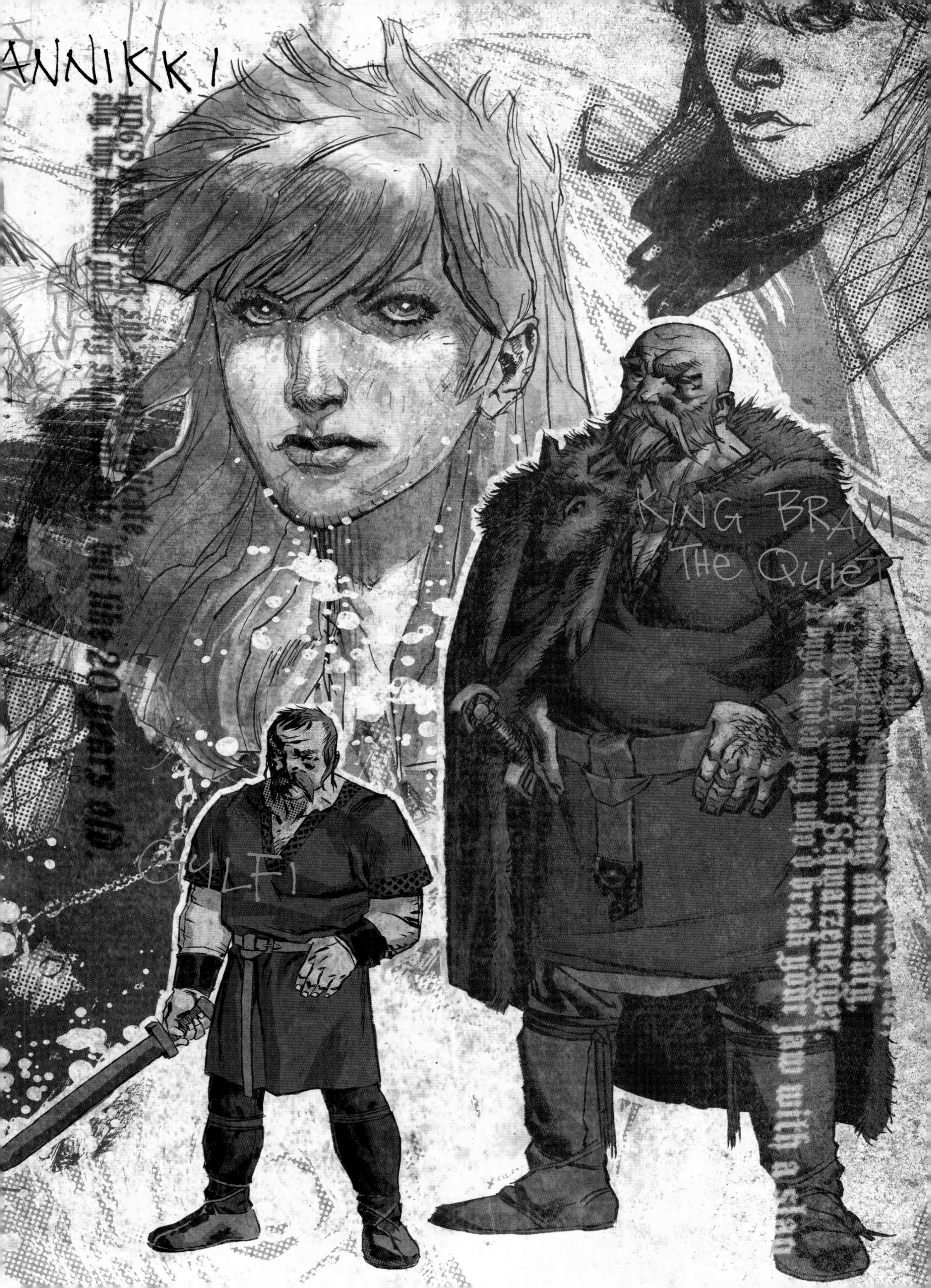
ANNIKKI
KING BRAM
THE QUIET
GULFI

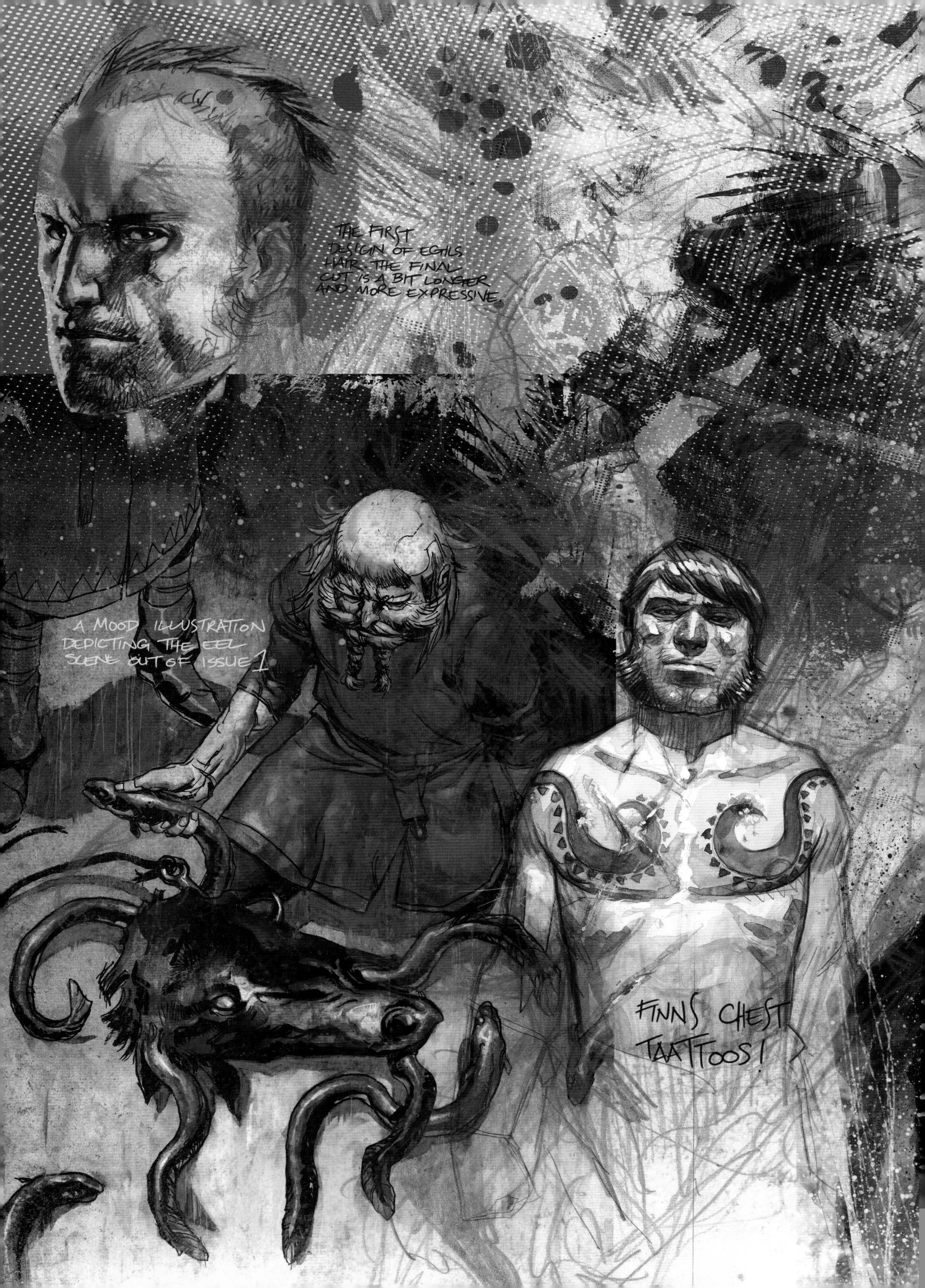
THE FIRST DESIGN OF EGILS HAIR. THE FINAL CUT IS A BIT LONGER AND MORE EXPRESSIVE.
A MOOD ILLUSTRATION DEDICTING THE EEL SCENE OUT OF ISSUE 1
FINNS CHEST TAATTOOS!

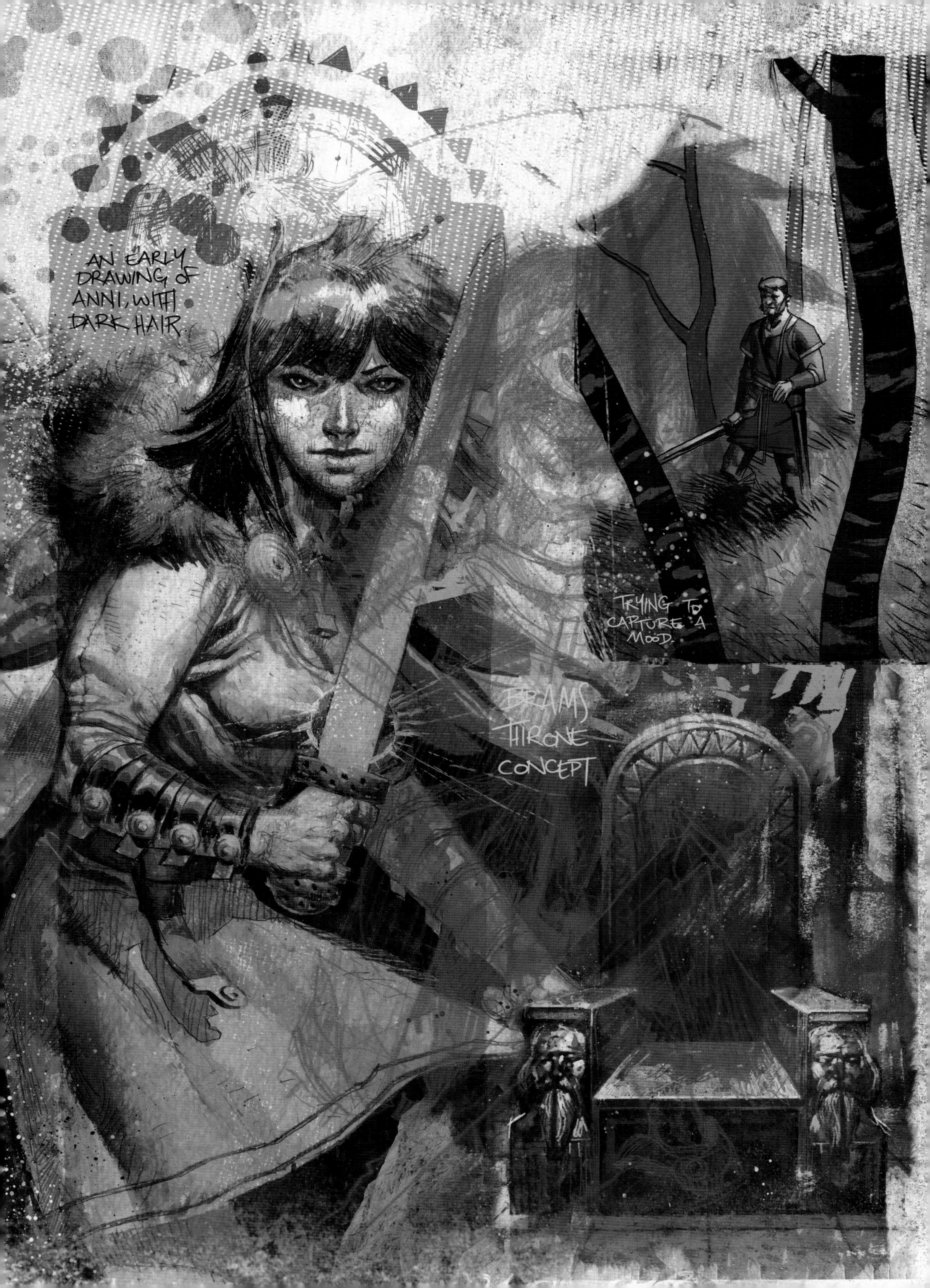
AN EARLY DRAWING OF ANNI, WITH DARK HAIR.
TRYING TO CAPTURE A MOOD.
BRAMS THRONE CONCEPT

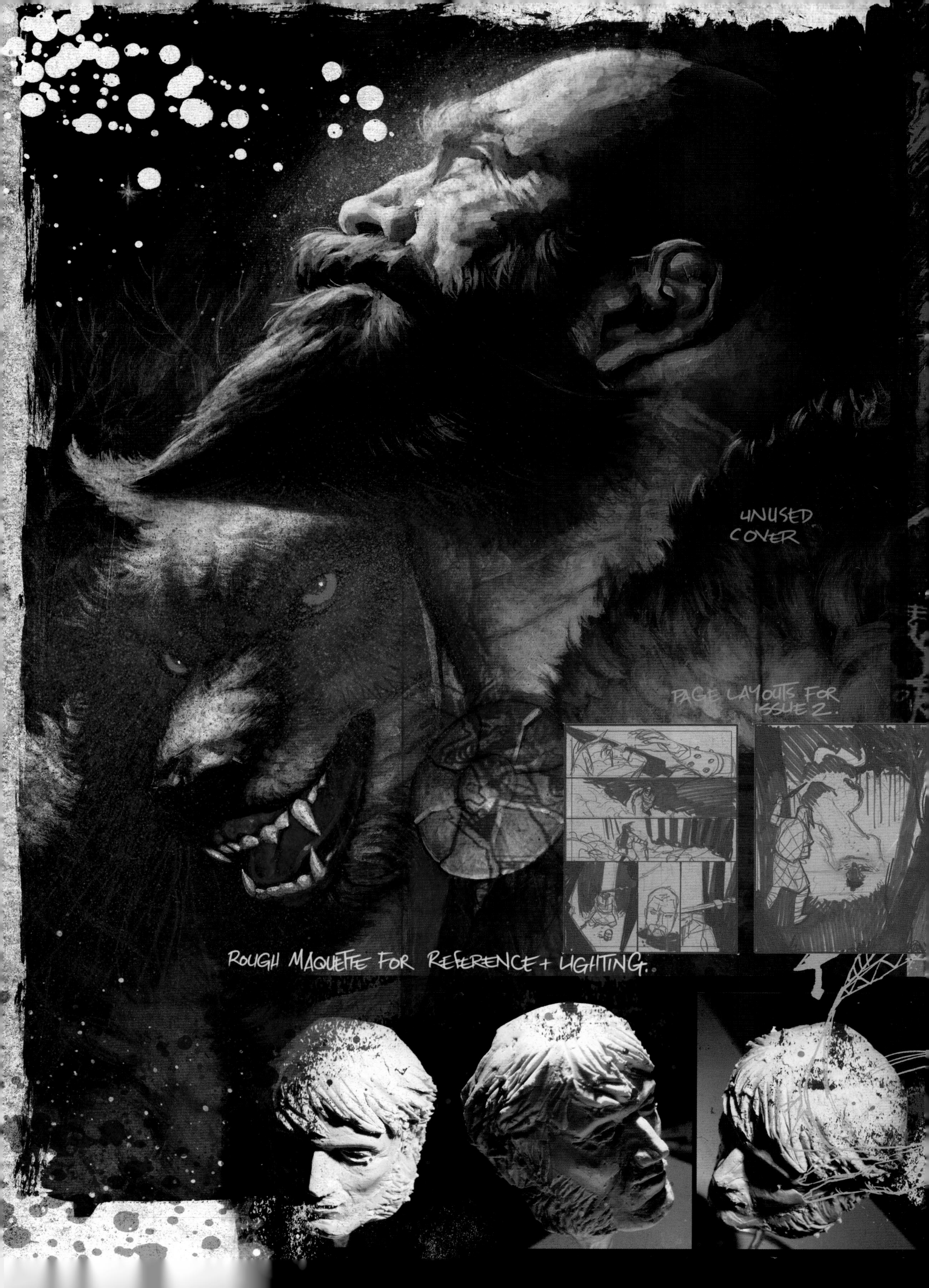
UNUSED COVER
PAGE LAYOUTS FOR ISSUE 2.
ROUGH MAQUETTE FOR REFERENCE + LIGHTING.

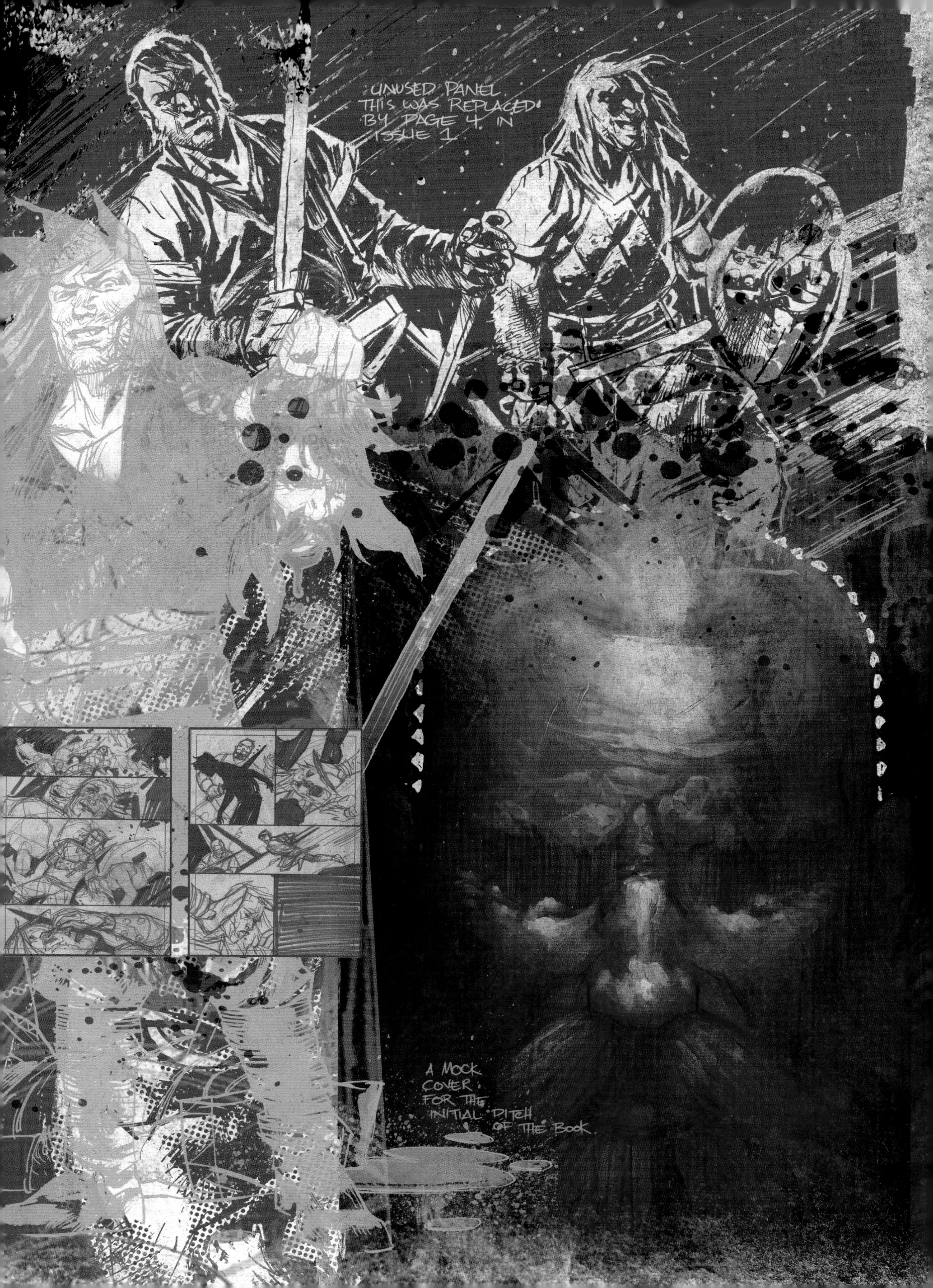
UNUSED PANEL THIS WAS REPLACED BY PAGE 4 IN ISSUE 1
A MOCK COVER FOR THE INITIAL PITCH OF THE BOOK.

GUEST PINUPS:

RAEL LYRA

SKOTTIE YOUNG

CHUCK BB
& NIC KLEIN

PHIL NOTO

RAFAEL ALBUQUERQUE

FRANK TERAN

JUAN DOE

DAVE CULLEN
& NIC KLEIN

JAMES HARREN

LEANDRO FERNÁNDEZ

KELSEY SHANNON

ANDY MACDONALD
& FABIAN SCHLAGA AKA 'MONK'

CHRIS SAMNEE

DAVID LAFUENTE

NATE SIMPSON

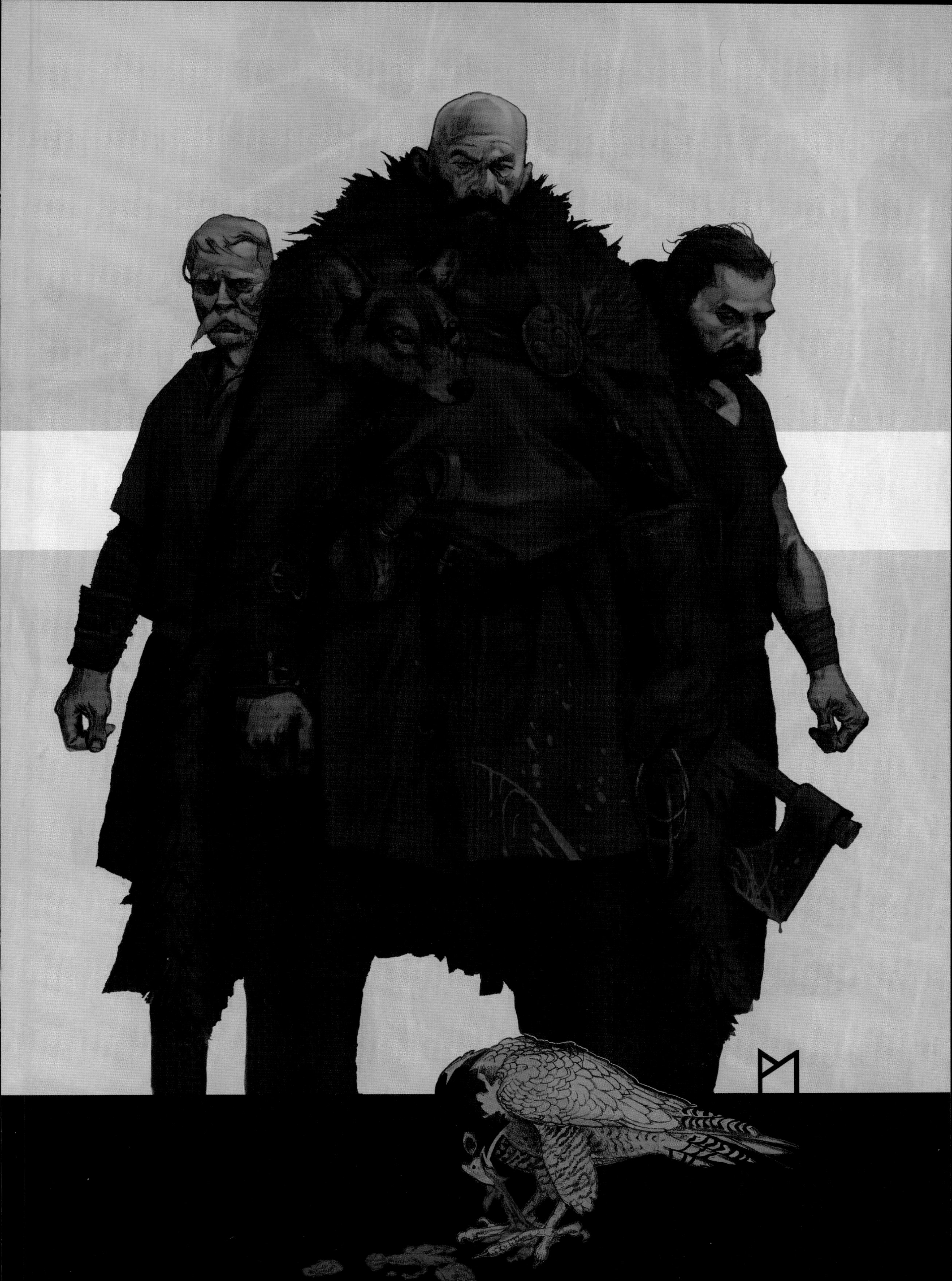

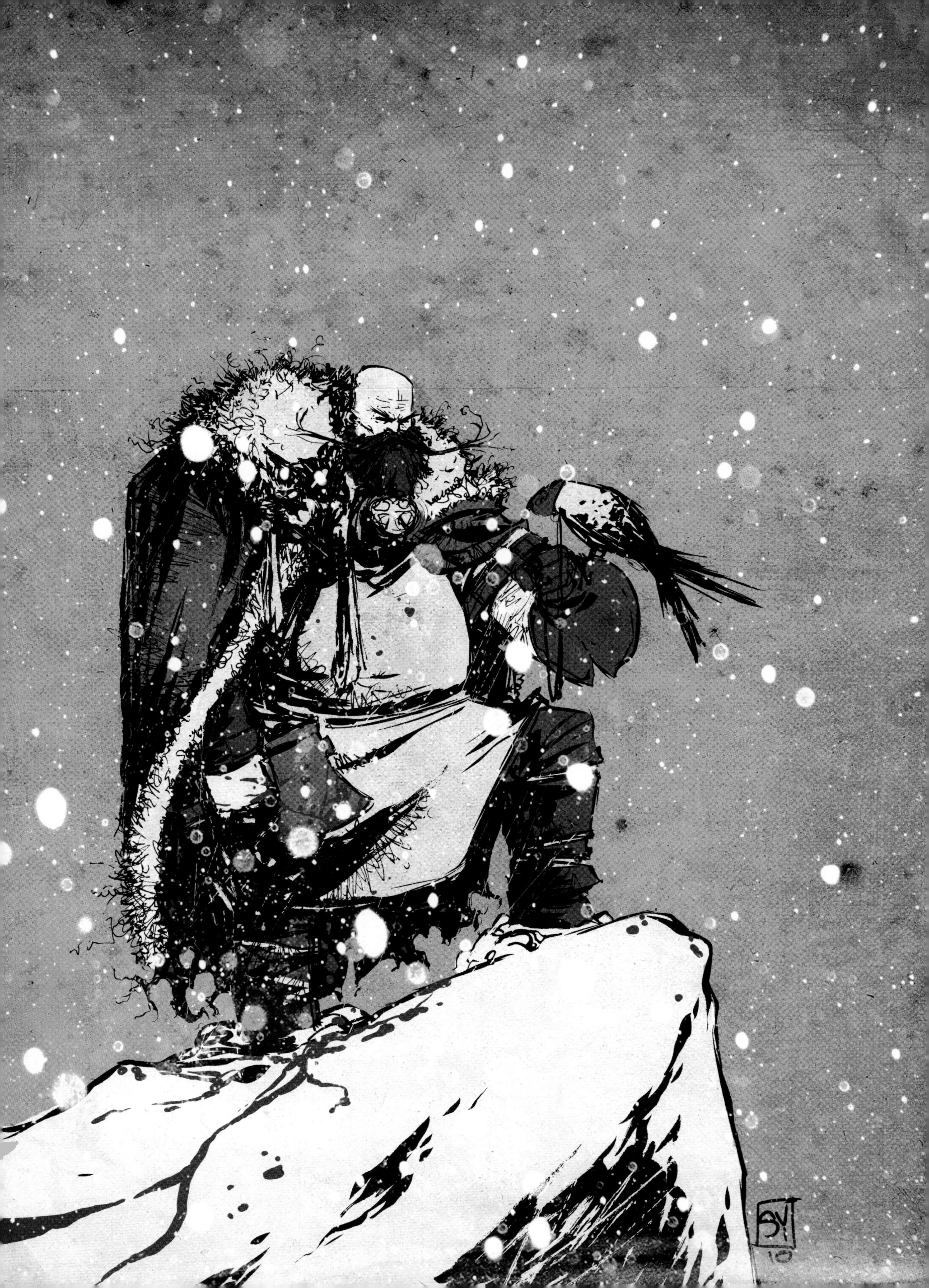

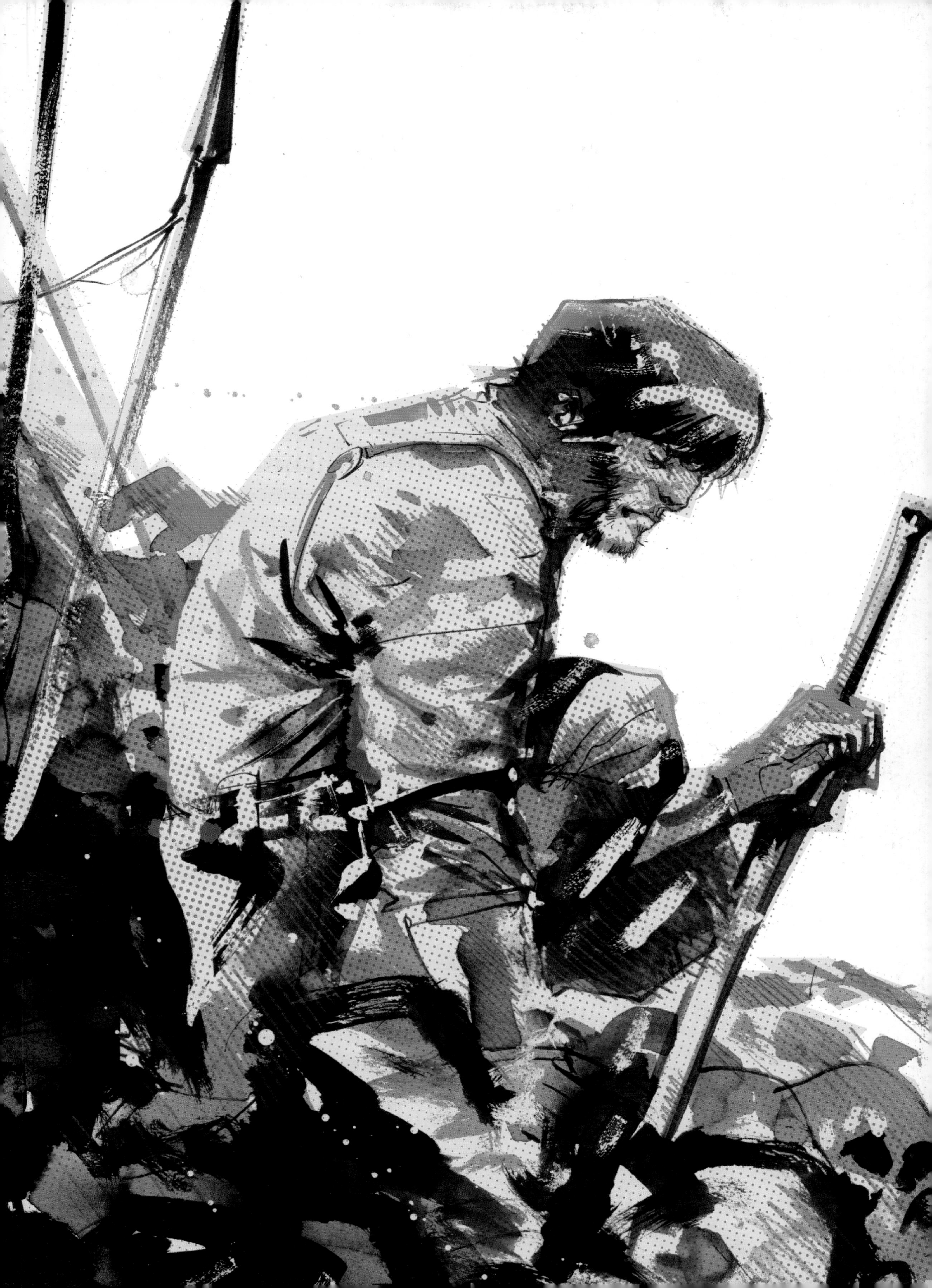

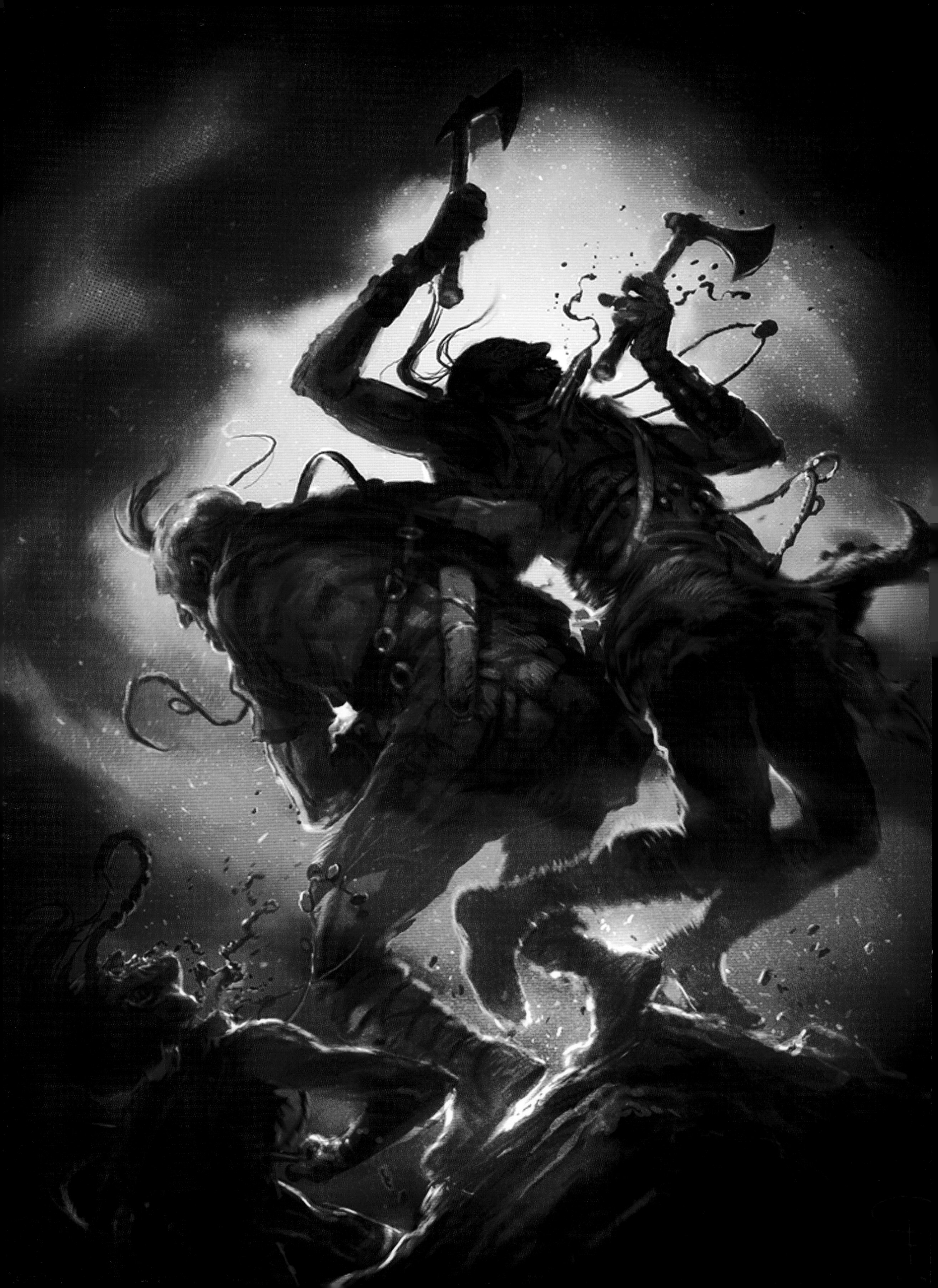

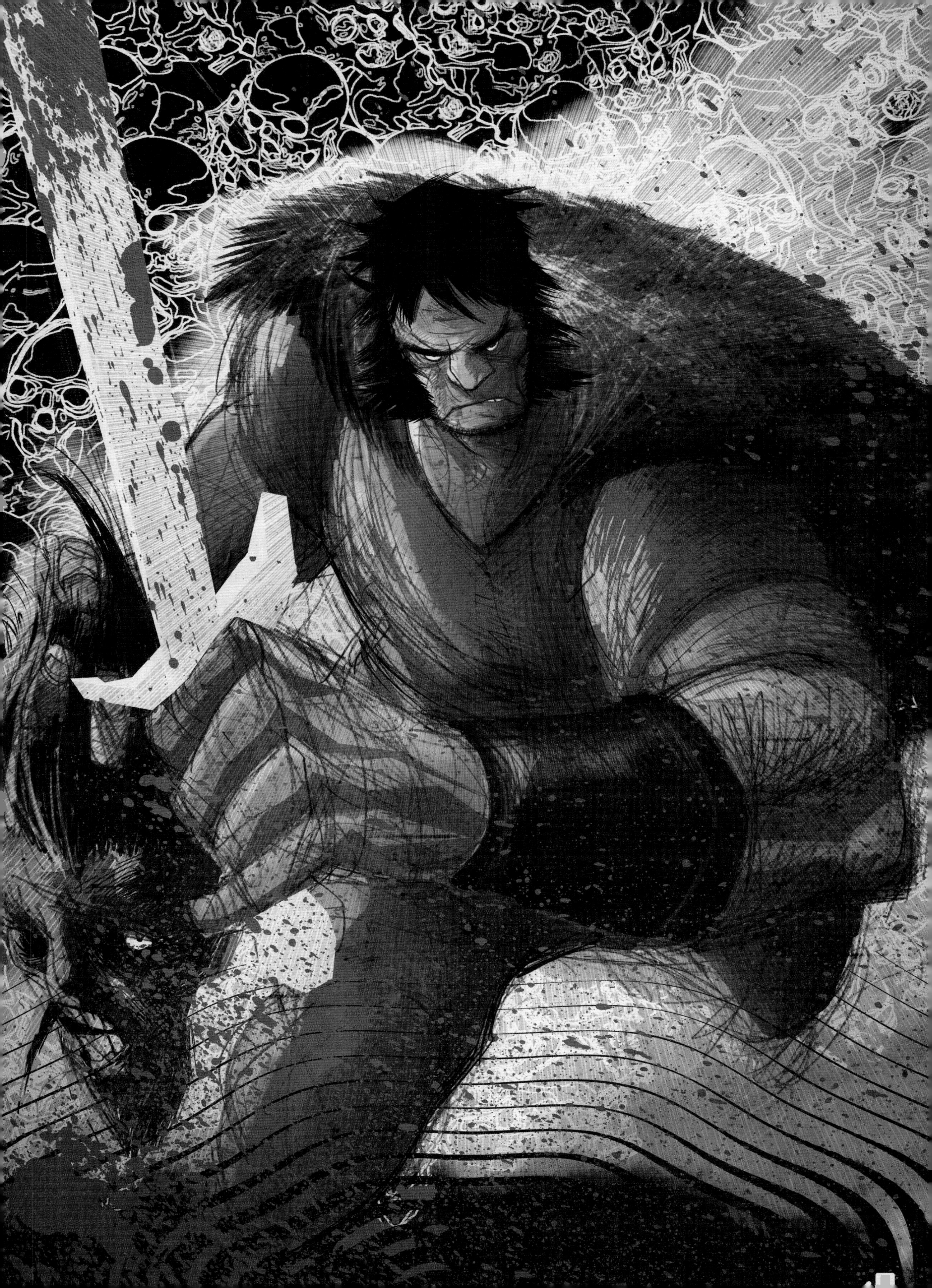

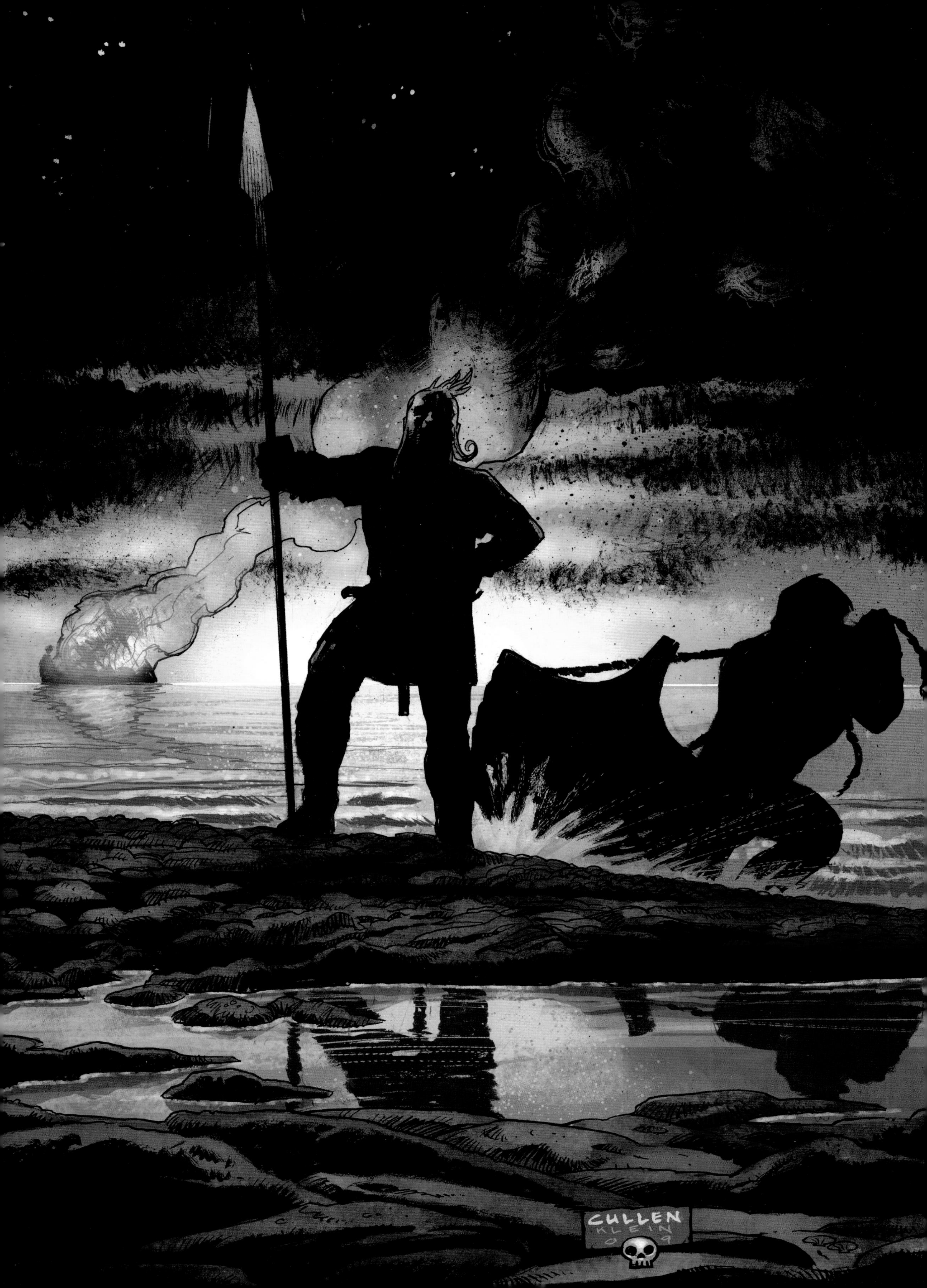
CULLEN
KLEIN
09

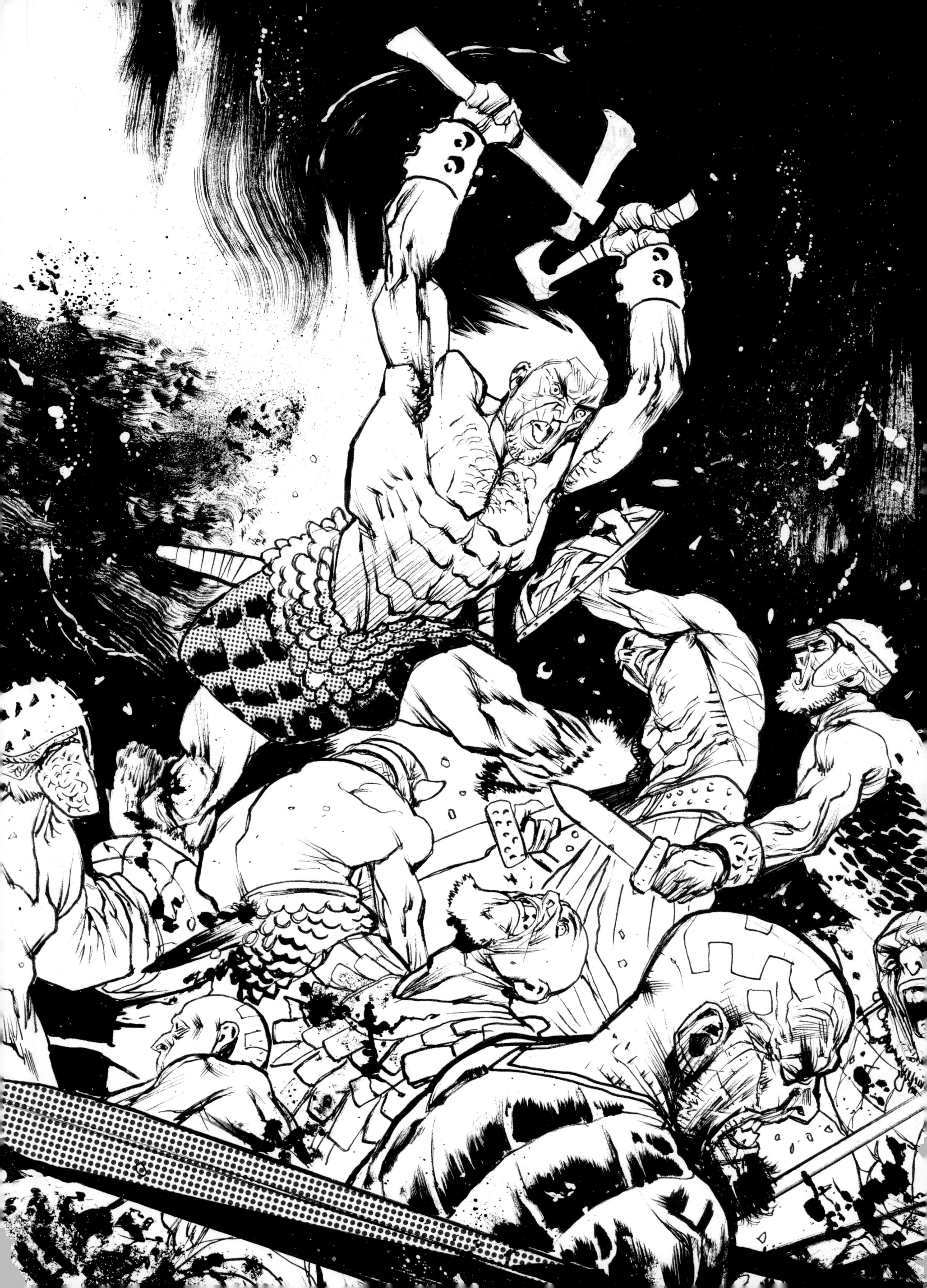

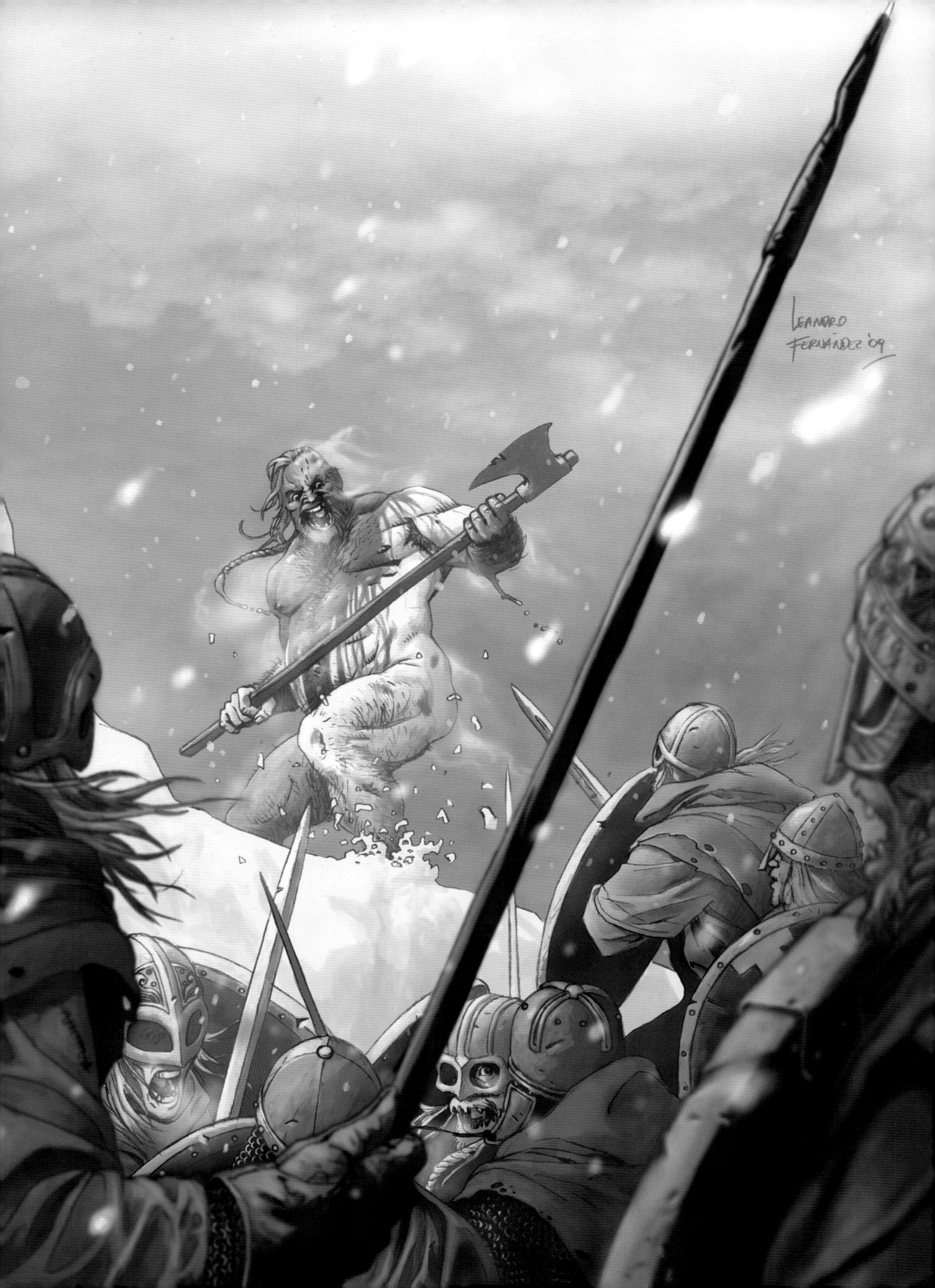
LEANDRO FERNANDEZ '09

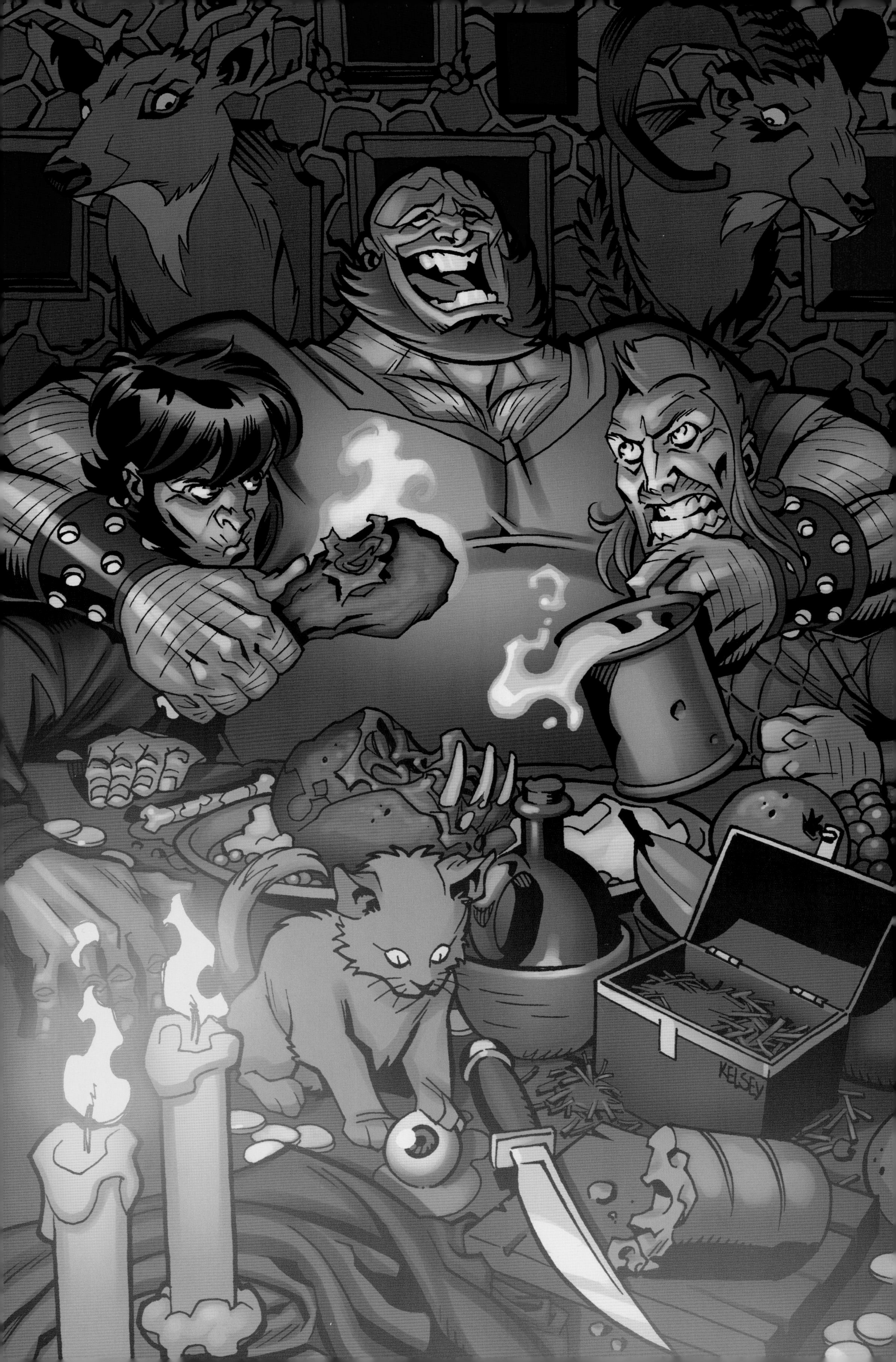
KELSEY

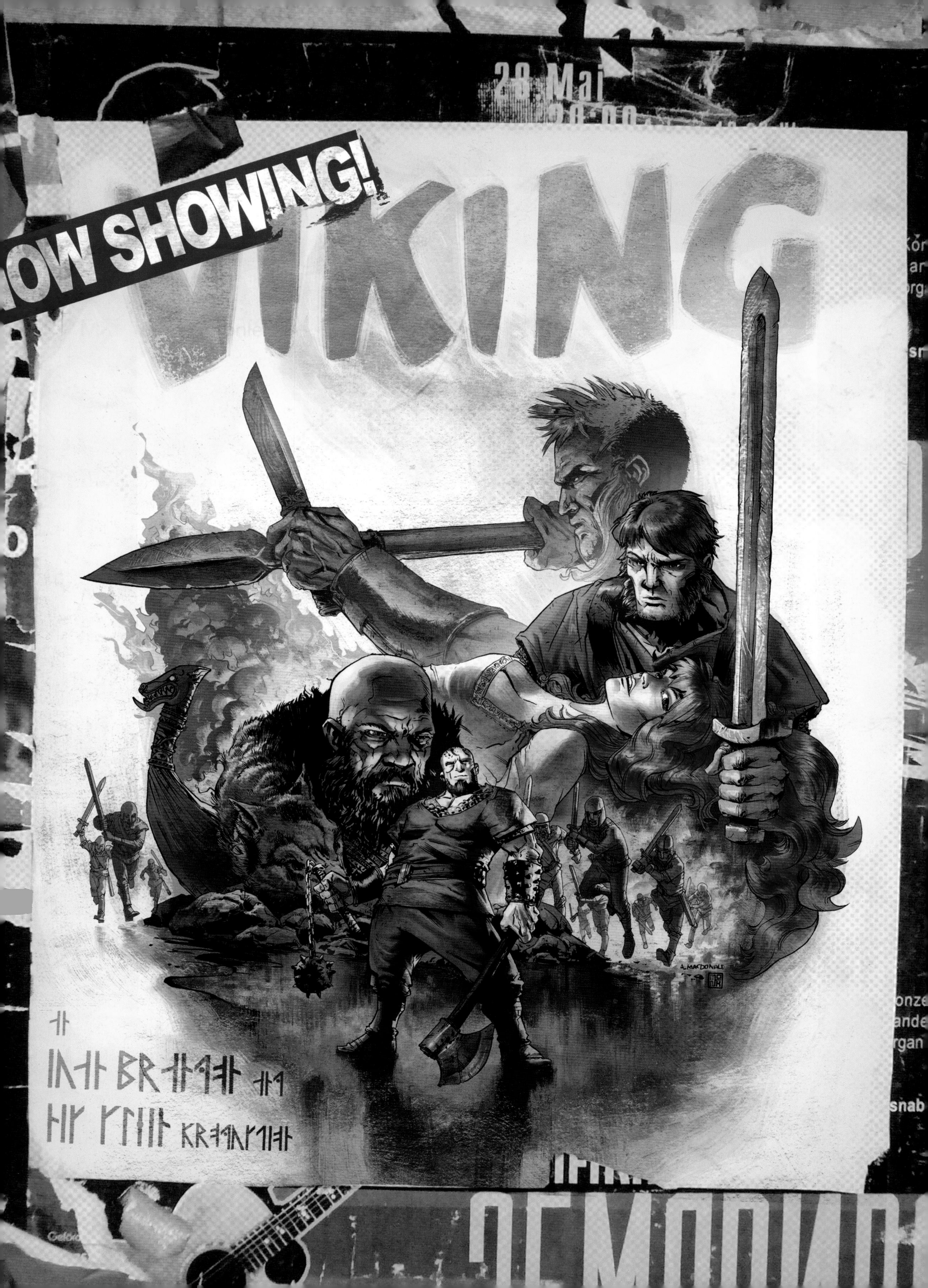
OW SHOWING!
VIKING
28 Mai
A. MACDONALD

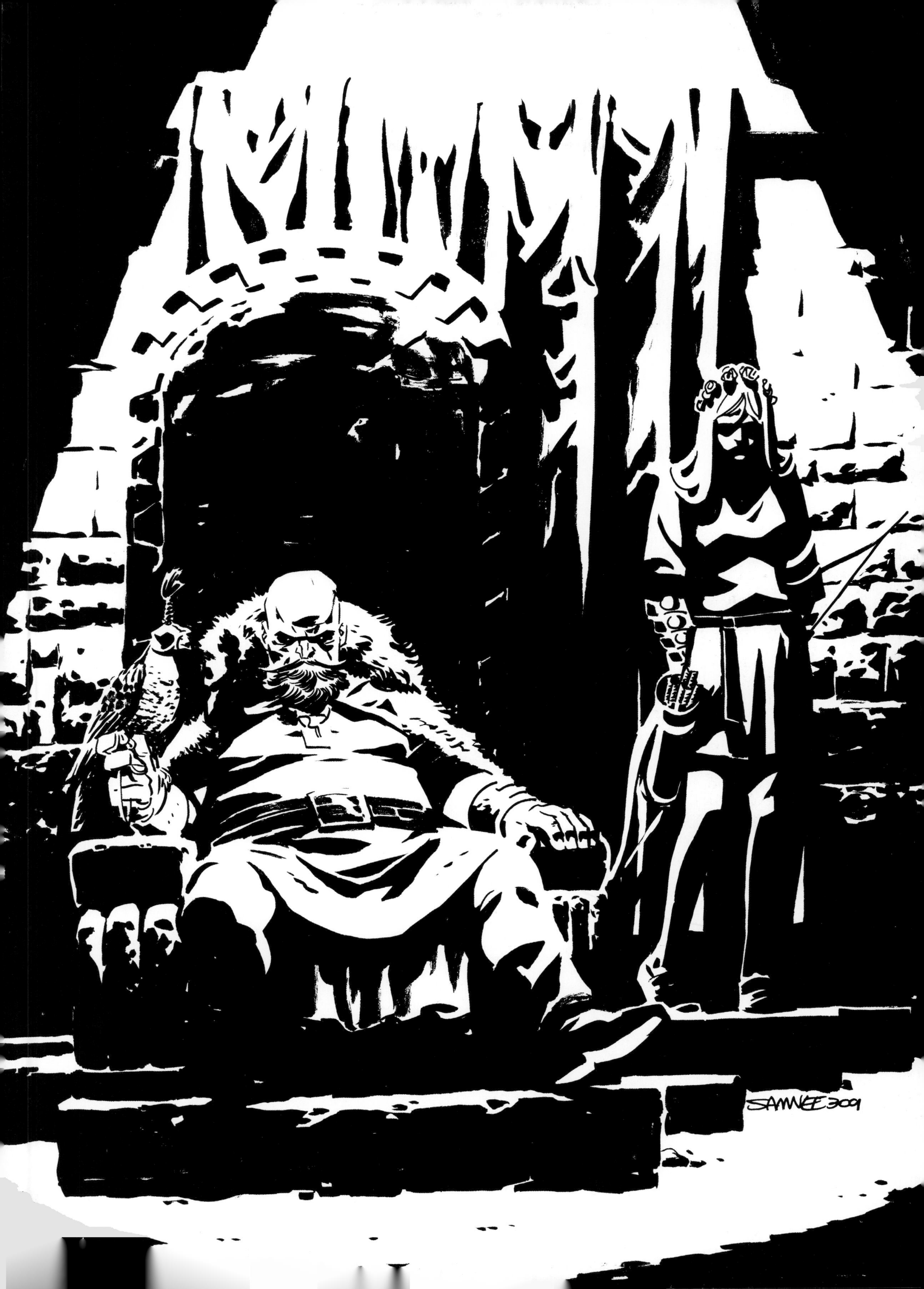
SAMNEE 2009

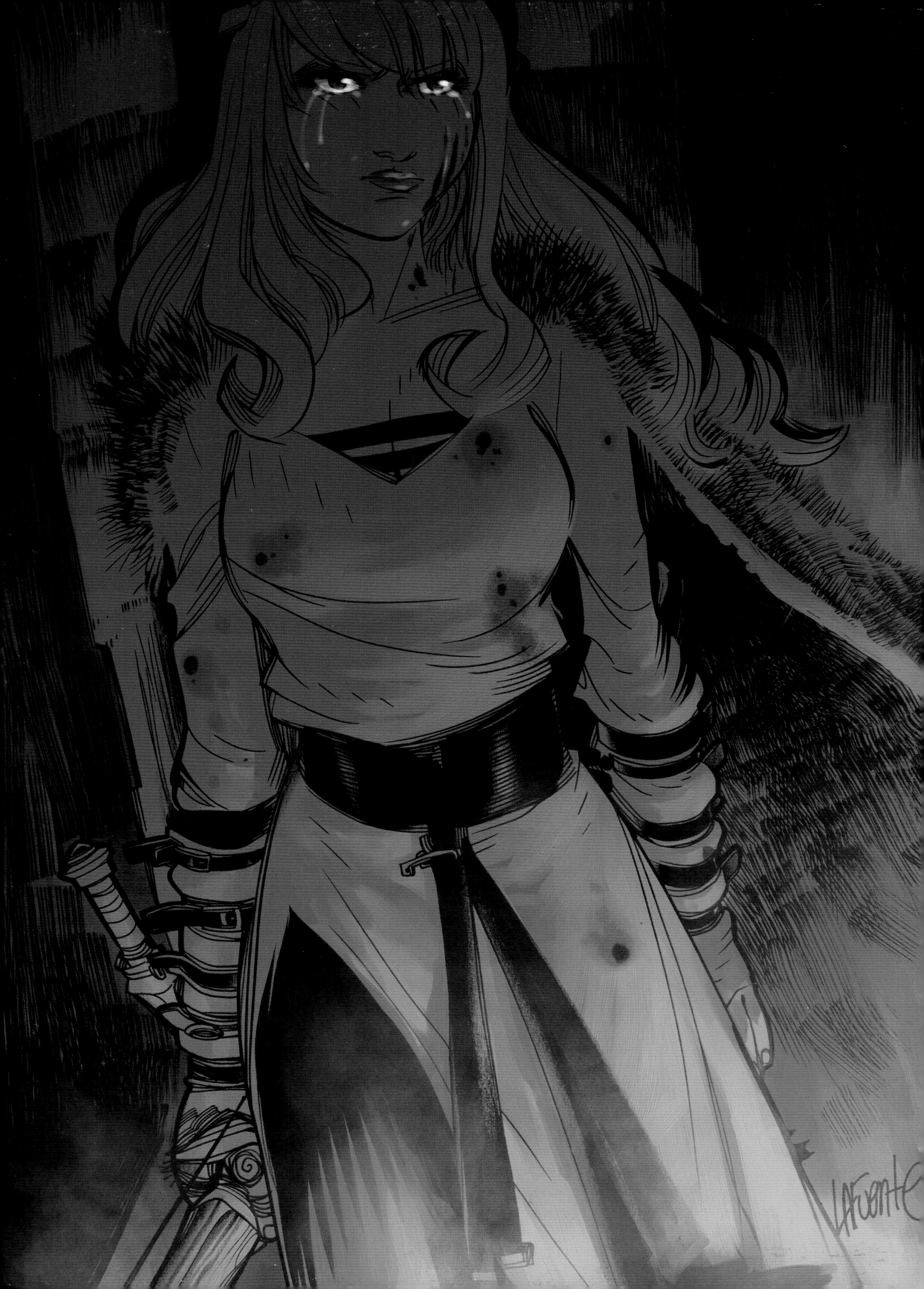
LAFUENTE

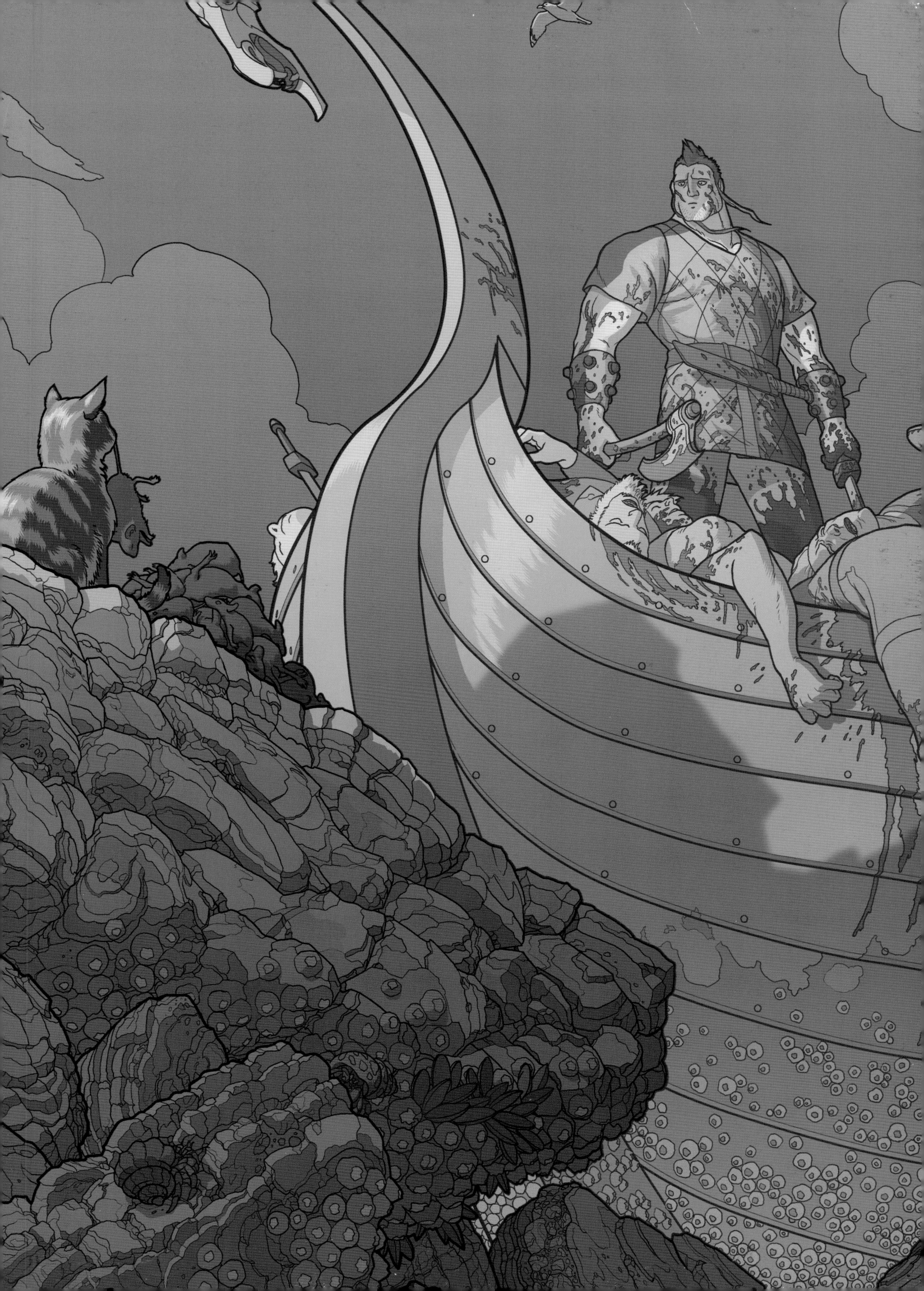

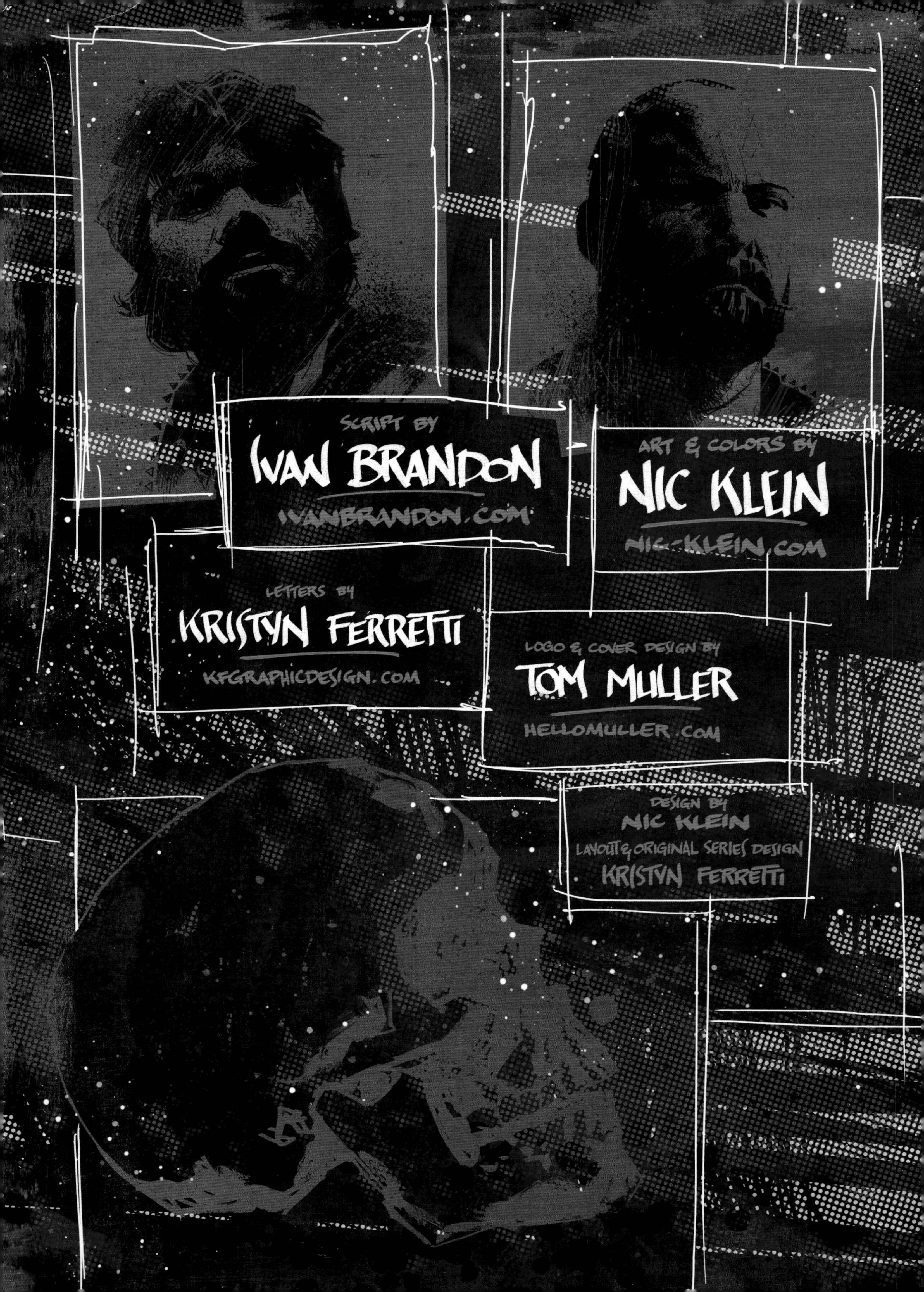
SCRIPT BY
IVAN BRANDON
IVANBRANDON.COM
ART & COLORS BY
NIC KLEIN
NIC-KLEIN.COM
LETTERS BY
KRISTYN FERRETTI
KFGRAPHICDESIGN.COM
LOGO & COVER DESIGN BY
TOM MULLER
HELLOMULLER.COM
DESIGN BY
NIC KLEIN
LAYOUT & ORIGINAL SERIES DESIGN
KRISTYN FERRETTI